595
199

D1275103

THIS IS
COMMUNIST CHINA

THIS IS
COMMUNIST CHINA

By the Staff of *Yomiuri Shimbun*, Tokyo
Edited by Robert Trumbull
Chief, Tokyo Bureau, *The New York Times*

DAVID McKAY COMPANY, INC.   New York

THIS IS COMMUNIST CHINA

Library of Congress Catalog Card Number: 68-29634

MANUFACTURED IN THE UNITED STATES OF AMERICA

VAN REES PRESS • NEW YORK

FOREWORD

The emergence of Communist China, one of the significant historical developments of the present century, has created shock waves that have been felt nowhere more sensitively than in Japan. If the Communists succeed in their efforts to create a monolithic new society in the world's most populous country, it may be Japan's destiny to contest with a powerful and united China for supremacy in the Asian region. In the past, the advantage of the Japanese over their similarly talented, equally industrious, and far more numerous Chinese neighbors has been a unity of national purpose and direction that a weak and fractured China has lacked. The spector of a vast, centrally motivated, and effectively governed homogeneous China as a rival power in East Asia is more disturbing to the Japanese than the intangible threat of a predatory ideology. Therefore, the prudent Japanese have been following events in the People's Republic of China with close attention. Lacking diplomatic representation—since Tokyo recognizes the Nationalist Chinese Government on Taiwan (Formosa)—and with close restrictions on the less formal contacts through trade and cultural exchanges, they have relied heavily for information on the reports of a small but highly qualified press corps in Peking.

Under an agreement between Japanese news-gathering organizations and their counterparts in China, the two countries began exchanging correspondents on a reciprocal basis in 1964. (The agreement took effect at about the time, by coincidence, that the Communist Chinese achieved their first explosion of a nuclear device.) The Japanese newsmen have had an advantage over other foreign correspondents in the Red Chinese capital of not only speaking and reading the language with fluency—which some of their European colleagues have also been able to do—but also of looking so much like Chinese themselves that they have been able to move more or less inconspicuously through the streets, among crowds, and wherever they have been permitted by the Communist authorities to go.

Since the appearance of the Japanese journalists on the China scene, their reports have been acclaimed by experts around the world as the most complete and penetrating of all the dispatches filed from that mysterious—and, to some nationalities, forbidden—land. Unfortunately, except when selected excerpts from these dispatches have been translated and transmitted abroad by correspondents in Tokyo, it has been only the specialists who have read them outside of Japan. Yet it is not without importance for the general reader in other countries to know what the Japanese are being told about Communist China in their own newspapers, for these are the accounts that condition the thinking on China by the Japanese nation. And it may be edifying and valuable for the informed reader to be able, for the first time, to appraise the quality of the Japanese reporting directly for himself.

Not content with simply maintaining a bureau in Peking, the widely-circulated Japanese daily *Yomiuri Shimbun*—*shimbun* is "newspaper" in Japanese—sent a team of journalistic and academic specialists on a three-month tour of Communist China in late 1966 and early 1967 for a report in depth on the principal aspects of the new social order taking shape in that country. The nine members of the

Yomiuri Task Force, as the paper called the group assigned to the project, possessed uncommon personal and professional qualifications for the job. Some had worked or studied in China, others were experts on China for Japanese schools and universities.

Their visit to the People's Republic corresponded with the peak of the Great Proletarian Cultural Revolution, at a time when the foreign newsmen regularly stationed in Peking were being prevented by unofficial pressure—there is no censorship as such of outgoing dispatches from Communist China—from reporting fully on the day-to-day developments in that upheaval as recounted in the ubiquitous wall posters put up in the capital city by the Red Guards. The Task Force also had special facilities provided for an unusual amount of travel. By their own account, they were permitted complete freedom—so far as they could tell—in interviewing whomever they wished.

Setting down their impressions for hand-delivery to the Tokyo home office, the *Yomiuri* reporters were able to write with unimpeded frankness. Their observations, as edited and supplemented here from the English translations furnished by *Yomiuri,* are offered not as an encyclopedia, guidebook, or Who's Who of Communist China, but as a recapitulation of what a particular group of Japanese specialists saw, heard, felt, and considered worth recording for their fellow countrymen. Some of the Chinese names, originally translated into Japanese and retranslated into a Roman spelling, may differ from the forms familiar to Western readers.

While it is hoped that the specialist will find material of interest in these observations, it must be pointed out that they were written originally for ordinary readers of a popular Japanese daily newspaper. (According to the Japan Audit Bureau of Circulation, the various editions of *Yomiuri* published simultaneously in five cities had a total average daily sale in January 1968 of 5,249,476 copies—the second largest in the country. The *Yomiuri* circulation in Tokyo alone was 3,192,431, the biggest in the capital city by a wide margin.)

Apart from whatever illumination these reports may provide on little-known developments in a largely closed society, it is important also to know that this material is what has been presented to millions of literate, politically aware Japanese as a firsthand account of conditions in contemporary China. Whether or not other China specialists agree with the findings of the *Yomiuri* group, it is significant that these writings presumably have influenced the thinking of a substantial segment of the Japanese population on a subject of vital interest.

The objectivity of the reports may be judged from the point of view of the individual reader. The official assessment in Communist China may be deduced from the fact that the publication of the series was followed shortly afterward by an order from the Communist Chinese Government closing the *Yomiuri* bureau in Peking. (The reason given officially was that the *Yomiuri* management had shown an "unfriendly attitude" toward the People's Republic of China by entertaining the Dalai Lama when the exiled leader of Chinese-occupied Tibet visited Tokyo in the autumn of 1967.)

Robert Trumbull

Tokyo, 1968.

The following contributed to the *Yomiuri* report on Communist China:

Churo Nishimura, 55, leader of the Task Force; had spent 12 years in Peking, Shanghai, Nanking, and other cities of China before World War II; was the *Yomiuri* correspondent in Peking from late 1964 to the end of 1965.

Takeo Takagi, 63, educated in Peking; was managing editor of *The North China Daily News,* Peking; editorial writer for *Yomiuri,* specializing in China problems.

Takuzo Kamai, 43, educated in Shanghai; former *Yomiuri* correspondent in Hong Kong, specializing in Communist Chinese affairs; now on *Yomiuri* staff in Tokyo.

Keizo Okubo, 45, educated in Shanghai; visited China twice since World War II; member of *Yomiuri* editorial staff specializing in international affairs and economics.

Mineo Nakajima, 30, instructor in Chinese history, Tokyo Foreign Language University.

Yoshiro Hoshino, professor of chemistry, Ritsumeikan University, Kyoto; visited China twice before making trip as member of Yomiuri Task Force.

Yasumasa Oshima, 49, professor of philosophy and ethics, Tokyo University of Education.

Tadashi Kawata, 41, professor of economics, University of Tokyo.

Yuji Muramatsu, 56, professor at Hitotsubashi University, Tokyo, specializing in Chinese economics.

Eisho Mitsuishi, 35, accompanied the Task Force as the *Yomiuri* staff photographer. *Kanae Mishina,* of the *Yomiuri* political reporting staff, toured Southeast Asia as a member of the Task Force on Communist China, to assess the reactions to Peking in neighboring countries. Kawata and Muramatsu traveled apart from the Task Force but contributed to the *Yomiuri* series.

CONTENTS

THIS IS
COMMUNIST CHINA

Chapter I

THE RED COUNTRY

PEOPLE, BANNERS, AND NOISE

It is a red country, red to the very core, reported the Japanese newsmen to their Tokyo readers when they returned from Communist China.

In the fields, farmers till the soil with a red flag planted beside them. The walls of homes are painted red, and on them are written teachings from Chairman Mao Tse-tung's Red Analects. Locomotives run on the railroads with red flags flying and with Mao's bust mounted in the front. Inside passenger planes, excerpts from the Analects are pinned on the cabin walls.

Streams of red paper bearing quotations from the works of Mao fly from automobile windshields, bicycle handlebars and the ears of wagon horses. Red flags, red paper, and red paint literally cover this vast land, where the hearts of 700 million people, clad in black "people's uniforms," are also literally and symbolically red.

The veteran correspondents found the Great Proletarian Cultural Revolution accompanied by an overwhelming assault upon the senses.

The country was flooded with the sounds of songs praising Mao Tse-tung and voices reciting quotations from Mao,

1

accompanied by an earsplitting din from gongs, drums, and cymbals.

They saw city streets jammed with mobs waving the red flag and youths wearing red armbands. Posters written in scarlet letters blanketed every wall and gate. Some walls had so many posters that the layers were about 10 centimeters [3.9 inches] thick.

The Task Force of the Tokyo newspaper *Yomiuri* had what its members called their baptism of the Cultural Revolution when they entered the frontier town of Shenchuan, across the border from Hong Kong.

They were greeted at the train by troupes of singers and dancers, sounding gongs and drums, who were identified as the Shenchuan station's own group for indoctrinating new arrivals in Mao's teachings.

A young woman started the performance by loudly reciting a phrase from Mao Tse-tung's quotations. This was followed by dances accompanied by the patriotic songs that the reporters were to hear over and over again, "The East Is Red," and "The Great Helmsman."

The girls were all clad in plain black or blue clothes, with some red material about the collar. The simplicity of the clothes made the red bands on their arms stand out conspicuously, and to the Japanese reporters their smiling faces were attractive.

All living things need the sun to grow, the thought of Mao Tse-tung is the sun, they sang in chorus. The flushed faces of the dancing girls shone with affectionate respect and trust for Chairman Mao, the visitors felt, and not a trace of gloom, representing the dark side of the Cultural Revolution, could be discerned from their faces.

The song-and-dance propaganda of Mao's teachings followed the newsmen all around China; in the trains, in airports, and—surprisingly—even in the plane bound for Peking, they heard and saw the songs and dances performed in

2

Mao's honor. However, underneath the songs and dances, the traveling team of Japanese newsmen and scholars found the country in 1966 and 1967 seething with change.

SUPPRESSING THE ANCIENT

Churo Nishimura, the 54-year-old head of the Yomiuri Task Force, had had many years of newspaper experience in China. Fluent in the language, he had spent 12 years in Manchuria, Peking, Shanghai, Nanking, and other cities before World War II. After the war he had been back three times, the last time for a one-year stay in Peking as the *Yomiuri* correspondent, the first Japanese newspaperman regularly assigned to the Communist Chinese capital.

Returning with the Task Force in late December of 1966, Nishimura was appalled—like many other Japanese—by the excesses of the movement that had been unleashed by Mao to counteract what he regarded as a dangerous tendency in the population to deviate from classic Communism. "China under the Great Proletarian Cultural Revolution is in a state of turmoil," Nishimura declared flatly.

One of the academic members of the *Yomiuri* team, 30-year-old Mineo Nakajima of the Chinese department of the Tokyo Foreign Language University, was shocked at the cultural havoc being wrought by the Maoist partisans.

All cultural legacies of the old society are regarded as unmitigated evils in today's China, he lamented. In the current Cultural Revolution, he found the Chinese trying to rewrite their very ancient history in a thoroughgoing manner.

The condemnation, made fashionable by the Cultural Revolution, of the "Four Olds"—old thought, old culture, old manners, and old customs—had made it impossible for the Chinese of today even to see many of the once highly

3

prized cultural assets of their country, the young scholar found.

When he visited the thirteen mausoleums of the Ming Dynasty on the outskirts of Peking, he was bewildered to see slogans of the Cultural Revolution written boldly, in red paint, on the walls of the palace. What puzzled him even more was the fact that the palace was shown only to foreigners. Remnants of the past such as this palace, which bear testimony to the power and glory of feudal dynasties, would serve as "accidental teachers" if they were shown to the people, he thought.

But when Nakajima put this idea to a woman guide, she replied, "Old culture represented by places like this does more harm than good."

Visiting a famous museum in Kwangchow [Canton], Nakajima found it locked. A poster outside bore an explanation, in the name of the Kwangchow Museum Red Guard, saying:

"The items exhibited here have created many problems because the museum has been influenced by the bourgeois reactionary line of thought for a long time."

To avoid further contamination of the public by the old values represented in the ancient culture of China, the museum had been closed.

DECADE OF UPHEAVAL

A different kind of discovery was in store for Takeo Takagi, whose acquaintance with Chinese affairs had been long and intimate. Educated at the French School in Peking, he became a newspaperman in prewar China. During World War II he was managing editor of *The North China Daily News* in Peking. After his repatriation to Japan following the end of the war, he became a specialist on China for *Yomiuri*. On his last previous visit, in 1955, the Communist regime

4

under Chairman Mao Tse-tung had been in full control of the country for only six years. Yet by 1955, the year of the dramatic appearance of Premier Chou En-lai at the conference of Asian and African states in Bandung, Indonesia, the prestige of the Peking Government in the Communist bloc and the "Third World" of the uncommitted countries was at a historic peak.

Although the war in Korea had ended inconclusively, the performance of Communist Chinese troops against the American forces had aroused the admiration of former colonial peoples everywhere, causing even many anti-Communists in the East to feel a thrill of pride in an Asian country's successful defiance of the mightiest power on earth. The fervid nationalists in former colonial lands, still resentful and suspicious of the West, saw the Communist Chinese as their champion against renascent imperialism.

The determination in Peking to "liberate" Taiwan [Formosa] from the American-supported rule of President Chiang Kai-shek and the Nationalist Chinese was supported by the neutrals as well as by the Communist powers. There was widespread sentiment everywhere—including the United States—for the admission of the People's Republic of China to the United Nations. And the Soviet Union, then the principal adversary of the United States in the ideological struggle that had split the principal elder powers into two camps, was Communist China's staunchest ally.

In 1955 Takagi sensed that Chairman Mao Tse-tung and other veteran revolutionists were basking in a mood of well-being, while such stirring slogans as "Long Live World Peace" and "We Will Never Fail to Liberate Taiwan" adorned cities and towns. The slogan "Follow the Example of Our Soviet Big Brother" appeared without fail at factories, to emphasize the granite-like Sino-Russian unity and national construction.

Yet the people, the ordinary Chinese, appeared uneasy.

While their leaders spoke in glowing terms of the "Great China," the people avoided meeting or talking to foreigners.

The ordinary Chinese seemed to Takagi, in 1955, to be people herded into a Red country, vast and empty, poor and cold.

But when Takagi returned eleven years later, with his *Yomiuri* colleagues, the situation was entirely reversed.

There no longer existed among the Chinese leaders that feeling of well-being of eleven years ago. They were now dramatically split into the mainstream faction led by Mao Tse-tung, and the anti-mainstream or "authority" faction led by Chief of State Liu Shao-chi, and relationships had grown so strained and complicated that comrades of yesterday had become enemies of today.

In the midst of these upheavals, Takagi was profoundly impressed by the powerful energy of the Chinese people. He told his Japanese readers that rising living standards, and a rising political awareness, geared to "Mao's thoughts," were clearly evident in the free and confident manner in which the people talked to him, so different from their reticence on his earlier visit. Above all, he was struck by the vigorous construction and development going on everywhere despite such adverse circumstances as natural disasters, the Sino-Soviet ideological dispute, and isolation from the rest of the world.

He speculated that the Mao-Liu confrontation seemed to be leading to a bloody showdown, but confessed that the bottom of the politics in "People's China" is so fathomlessly deep that it is hard to predict what will gush up from below.

Chapter II

THE RED SUN IN THEIR HEARTS

MAO WORSHIP

The Japanese journalists perceived immediately that to understand what was going on in Communist China it was essential to study the mystique of Mao-worship. Having themselves been liberated from Emperor-worship scarcely two decades earlier, the Japanese were amazed at the mass veneration poured upon the plump, septuagenarian Chairman of the Chinese Communist Party. Whereas the Emperor of Japan had once been considered a descendant of the Sun Goddess, the teachings of Mao Tse-tung constituted a second sun in the heavens over China—a Red Sun, that never sets, noted Takeo Takagi, the veteran reporter. From early in the morning he listened to the rays from the Red Sun jog the souls of the people, flowing over the country through loudspeakers blaring away the melody of "Tung Fang Hung" [The East Is Red].

"The East is Red. The Sun rises over China. Mao Tse-tung appeared and brought happiness to the people. Hurrah, hurrah, Mao is the savior of the people." So runs the refrain that constant repetition burned into the brains of the visitors from Japan. In Red China, all types of music

played and songs sung throughout the country seemed to contain verses that praised Mao as the immortal sun.

"The ship that sails the vast seas relies on its helmsman. The growth of all living things depends on the sun. . . . The thought of Mao Tse-tung is none other than the immortal sun." When this song was sung in Chinese, the reporter saw many people shedding tears. He wondered how foreigners could comprehend this sun worship of Mao Tse-tung, this fanatic Mao-worship which burns in the hearts of the Chinese people.

Takagi began by interviewing as many Chinese as he was able to meet.

In Shanghai, a Mrs. Chang Yu-mei, 50, of Kan Chuan Hsin Tsun, told him:

"It is because of Chairman Mao that I can receive my monthly pension of 35 yuan and live so happily. Before the liberation, I used to work at a textile factory. In those days I was often beaten by my superiors and was forced to work day and night. I was not even given time to eat lunch. I had three children, but all died of malnutrition. My eldest, a 17-year-old daughter born after the liberation, is now in middle school."

This 50-year-old woman had bought herself a volume of Mao's Analects, pasted the teachings on the walls, and read them every day. She said that was the least she could do for Mao.

Takagi talked with the chief technician of a Shanghai factory that makes the popular Hero brand fountain pen that has recently gained wide popularity even in Japan because of its cheap price and smooth writing quality.

He asked how the factory produces such a good-quality pen at such cheap prices. The answer that bounced back was this:

"Our factory has a long history, since 1931. It went bankrupt four times in the past because of the dumping practices

8

of the imperialists. But after the liberation we followed Mao's teachings of self-regeneration and concentration of strength. The result was that we succeeded in bringing about a technical revolution in our factory."

At a fertilizer factory in Taiyuan, Takagi found a technician, wearing a leather jacket, who apparently was the plant manager. He had sharp, piercing eyes and looked very intelligent.

"This factory is the product of the Great Leap Forward in 1958," he said proudly. "It is the triumph of the thoughts of Chairman Mao."

"How did the factory become such a success?" asked the reporter.

The man replied that by studying the thoughts of Mao the people were able to grasp advanced ideas—and this, he said, became the source of endless energy.

A VISIT TO MAO'S BIRTHPLACE

Listening to this chorus of adulation for their leader, Takagi became determined to probe into the undercurrents of Mao's thoughts and to investigate the birthplace of the "red sun" that so passionately stirred the Chinese people, united them, and put them in an intoxicated trance of ecstatic happiness.

Emulating the Chinese, he turned to their new Bible, the Analects of Mao, for guidance and read:

"Anyone who wishes to correctly understand a matter must first of all come in direct contact with that matter. That is, he must live in the environment surrounding that matter. Otherwise, he can hardly expect to find the answer."

Encouraged by these words, he boarded the twin-engine airplane of the Chinese People's Airlines and left for Changsha and Mao Tse-tung's birthplace, with the air stewardess's song of "Tung Fang Hung" ringing in his ears.

9

From the airport at Changsha it was about sixty miles by a road surfaced with clay—appropriately red—to Shaoshanchung, the peasant village in Hunan Province where Mao was born on December 26, 1893. Takagi's automobile, made in Shanghai, threaded through hordes of marching Red Guards, the youth army of Mao's Great Proletarian Cultural Revolution. Constantly waving red flags and brandishing red-bound books of quotations from Mao's works, they were making the pilgrimage to their hero's birthplace from many parts of China. To Takagi, the public road resembled a red river—a red stream flowing endlessly toward the valley where Mao Tse-tung was born—and the plain between the mountains around Siushan was transformed into a sea of people.

Talking to Red Guards in their own language, Takagi learned something of the mystique of their pilgrimage. For example, all made at least the last part of the journey from Changsha to Shaoshanchung on foot, although the walk took two and a half days. The long trek, he was told, was made not only to train themselves physically, but also so that the youths would truly understand the thoughts of Mao by experiencing the hardships suffered by their senior revolutionists in the 10,000-kilometer Long March.

While the hike to Shaoshanchung could hardly compare with the grueling 6,200-mile walk at whose end the remnants of Mao's revolutionary army had holed up in the caves of Yenan many years before, the experience did acquaint millions of Maoist youth with many survivors of the earlier revolution.

Occasionally they would find an old man who took part in the Hunanese peasant movement staged by Mao more than forty years ago. The Red Guards would gather around him with notebooks in hand and listen intently to his story. On the way to Siushan they would stop overnight at People's Communes and listen to the farmers, who would tell

10

them of past hardships and of the difficulties they encountered during the period of the Great Leap Forward that preceded the Cultural Revolution. From these listening sessions, the Red Guards would learn the "experience of revolution."

The overnight stops by the Red Guards caused no special problem to the communes, Takagi learned. In fact, the farmers actually welcomed them, because the youths helped in the farm work. Moreover, the Red Guards were news-carriers who related interesting stories of other provinces to the farmers.

After spending the night at a commune, the Red Guards customarily cleaned their quarters and assisted the farmers with morning chores before resuming the trek, and this amity between the Red Guards and the farmers symbolized to Takagi the strength of this Cultural Revolution.

The walking Red Guards provided a sort of Maoist fashion show. Each group had a style of its own, some wearing boards bearing quotations from Mao's Analects strapped to their shoulder packs. Invariably, all of them were equipped with red flags and red leggings.

The pilgrim groups included many girls, who usually led the singing of songs in praise of Mao.

Takagi was informed that the Red Guards converged on Shaoshanchung at the rate of 50,000 a day and stood in line an average of five hours to get a glimpse inside the cottage where Mao was born. It was truly a staggering sight to see 50,000 people congregate daily at this small village, whose permanent population is only 2,800, he reported, and after the 50,000 Red Guard youths finish observing Mao's home, he said, they are so deeply moved that they again start singing songs praising the chairman. Gongs are sounded everywhere in the village. The youths shout *"Mao chuhsi wan sui"* [Long live Chairman Mao], and it becomes a festival of the revolution. The smiling villagers, of whom about 2,000 have

11

Mao as their surname, say that "in our village, every day is New Year's. We have guests and festivals every day."

Takagi thought that this gaiety found every day in Shaoshanchung was out of keeping with the austerity of the Maoist revolution, since Mao's Analects say, "Revolution does not mean inviting guests and having feasts."

The house where Mao was born looks no different from others that one sees everywhere in rural China, Takagi found when he reached this national shrine of the Cultural Revolution.

Nationalist troops that occupied the town in 1924 demolished the house to vent their pent-up anger against the Communists. After the troops left, people started almost from scratch and rebuilt the house, including its outer walls of clay. All pieces of furniture belonging to Mao and his family had survived the Nationalist occupation, thanks to the efforts of villagers who kept them hidden at the risk of their own lives.

The rooms are arranged in the typical style of a Chinese farmhouse, according to Takagi's description—the main hall with the kitchen at the back and the left wing consisting of the dining room in front and two bedrooms, one occupied by the parents and one by Mao, in the rear. Mao's room has an attic where Communist Party cells used to hold secret meetings.

Takagi watched the Red Guards and noticed that their faces were red with apparent excitement. They were entranced, he felt, at having been able to realize their long-cherished dream of immersing themselves in the religious atmosphere of Mao's home. They uttered not a sound and quietly listened to the guide's explanation. They studiously took notes, their breathing heavy. To the Japanese reporter, their facial expressions were more solemn than that of a priestess who enters the sacred halls of a shrine.

They took about twice as long as he to inspect the house,

12

examining all rooms—the storeroom, the grain shed, and even the cattle stables. Takagi heard heavy sighs when the guide showed them an iron comb and explained how Mao, when he was seven or eight years old, used to groom the cows with it.

To the Red Guards, the sons of Mao the Red Sun, this old establishment is a shrine of revolution. It is also an academy for studying the teachings of Mao. It is here that the "inheritors of the revolution," as the Red Guards are called, are expected to find spiritual sustenance to continue their revolutionary work. Here, they heard how six of Mao's close relatives sacrificed their lives for the sake of the revolution. This selfless act of giving one's life to the people, the Red Guards believed, was the true expression of Red spirit and loyalty. As they listened to the story of the Mao family, they looked at the photos of the Maos on the wall, with tears welling up in their eyes.

Mao's former home is situated in a valley sandwiched between two mountains. In front of the house are acres of rice fields and ponds. After inspecting Mao's home, the youths went to wash their faces in a pond where Mao, when he was seven or eight years old, reportedly swam. They then went into a paddy field and each scooped up a fistful of soil. As Takagi watched, each of them molded the dirt into a small heart shape, engraved on it the words "Long live Chairman Mao," and then placed it carefully in their pockets as if it were the most valuable thing on earth.

Takagi recalled a song popular in Shaoshanchung when Mao was an infant:

"Over the heads of the peasants are three swords—debts, taxes, and high interest. And before the eyes of the peasants are three roads—to run away, to be killed, or to be sent to jail."

Of course, said Takagi, life at the home of Mao's parents —well-to-do middle-class farmers—was not as miserable as

13

that depicted by the song, but the majority of the farmers in the village were not so wealthy.

Mao began working at the age of six, but it is believed that in those days he performed such menial tasks as housework or caring for the cattle. At the age of 16, Mao became a full working hand on the farm. And through the labors he experienced in childhood, he came to understand the needs of the farmers, his followers say, and thus he acquired the character fundamentally required of a Chinese politician. And in his youth he experienced the social convulsion that marked the closing days of the Ching Dynasty.

Takagi studied the history and character of the Hunan people for a clue to Mao's personality. The natives of Hunan province are impulsive, he said. They also have the trait of doggedly pursuing their aims. The people of Mao's home village were especially noted for being clever and agile, with a leaning toward the mystic that Takagi associated with the Chinese type of spiritualism which is evident in Mao's thoughts.

On the other side of a mountain and about 60 kilometers [24 miles] north of Shaoshanchung there is the castle town of Ninghsiang. At the same time that Mao was doing farm chores, Liu Shao-chi (the out-of-favor head of state), who was born in Ninghsiang, was probably a grubby boy of about four or five years of age. Needless to say, in those days there was no communication between Mao and Liu, who are now engaged in a battle for survival. But there seems to be some kind of significance in the fact that both Mao and Liu spent their youth in the same district.

LEARNING TO BE A LEADER

As a schoolboy in Shaoshanchung, Mao was said to have been mistreated by an ill-tempered father at home and abused by an impatient teacher in the classroom. Eventually, when he was about the same age as the happy Red Guards who now shed tears of emotion when they visit his former home, he left Siushan and entered a school in nearby Siang Hsiang County. Here again he was persecuted, this time by ill-natured classmates, Takagi related. The people of Siang Hsiang County traditionally thought of themselves as superior to their neighbors. Mao, being from Hsiangtan County, was duly qualified to be despised, and he was treated even worse because of his shabby clothes. The fact that he was shunned by his classmates, who were of the landowning class, is supposed to have had considerable influence in molding his character, according to analyses by some Chinese.

A favorite story is told about Mao's difficulties in getting admitted to the Tungshan middle school. He was a tall boy for his age, close to six feet. He had no difficulty reading historical novels, and had memorized most of the Chinese classics, but otherwise his scholastic achievements were next to nil. When the tall boy entered his office, the principal looked curiously at him and asked, "Your name?" "Mao Tse-tung," the boy answered. And then ensued the following dialogue between Mao and the principal:

Principal: Mao Tse-tung, where is your home?

Mao: I used to live in Siushan.

Principal: You are too old.

Mao: No, teacher, I am fifteen years old.

Principal: No, I say that you are about seventeen or eighteen.

Mao: It isn't so, teacher, I have just turned fifteen.

Principal: So.... Have you graduated from primary school in this town?

Mao: I studied two years under instructor Wang. I can read any kind of novel.

Principal: Have you gone through the primary-school readers?

15

Mao: No, I have not read them.

Principal: Can you read the textbooks for second-graders?

Mao: I can read most of them, but there are some words that I do not understand.

Principal: Have you studied arithmetic?

Mao: No, teacher.

Principal: How about history and geography?

Mao: I have not studied them.

Principal: Write me two lines from the classics.

Mao immediately took up a brush and started writing. The characters were poorly written despite the fact that he had long, shapely fingers.

"That won't do. Your writing is poor. I cannot allow you to enter our school. After all, we do not have any primary curricula here," the principal said.

"Please, let me enter the school," Mao said.

"It will not do you any good, because you do not have scholastic ability," the principal retorted.

"Please, teacher, at least admit me into the school as a temporary student, and then let me take some exams to test my ability," Mao pleaded.

"I cannot do that. It is only a waste of time."

"Please let me attend school here. I promise I will study very hard," said Mao.

Listening admiringly to Mao's enthusiastic plea at the principal's office was a teacher named Hu. He was impressed. So he told the principal that though Mao had not gone through the normal primary-school curricula, he would probably become a good student if given some extra studies.

It was only when the teacher, Hu, volunteered to give Mao extra tutoring that the principal relented and allowed the boy to enter the middle school, Takagi related.

In 1911, Mao boarded a small steamer on the Siang River and traveled from Siang Hsiang to Changsha, carrying books and clothes on a shoulder pole. There, he enrolled himself in one middle school after another.

Meanwhile, the revolution of Sun Yat-sen against the Manchus had begun. During these hectic days, Takagi said, Mao gave up his studies and joined the revolutionary army. He served for about six months as a common soldier, but little else is known about how he spent his time in the army.

Takagi believes that Mao dreamed of becoming the supreme leader of China while still in his teens, and cites conversations attributed to Mao—when he was only 18 years old.

According to the Mao legend, in 1912 he had a reunion with three comrades of the revolutionary army, Tan Wupen, Liu Hang, and Peng Shih-liang. The four friends climbed Mount Yo Li, where Mao in later years composed a poem, *"Oh, this great land in the dusk. . . . Who are to be the masters that will rise and fall in this land?"*

In a tearoom at Tien Hsin Ko, on the mountain top, Takagi related, the following conversation was said to have taken place among the young revolutionists:

"Our country has now become a republic," said Tan Wupen. "Anyone can become the President of China, even you or I."

"That is right," said Peng Shih-liang. "And if I become President, I will appoint you the Prime Minister."

Then the young Mao said quietly, "Without joking, let us seriously consider how a person can become a President. One must study, and after finishing college one must study abroad."

"It is not necessary to be educated in order to take authority," said Tan. "Did Emperor Shih Huang, of the Chin Dynasty, or Emperor Wu Ti, of Han, study? Genghis Khan was merely a Mongolian warrior."

"Then what must one do to take power?" Mao asked.

17

"A politician must have the will to fight," Tan replied. "A politician must be aggressive and must treat people without any emotion. He must crush anyone who opposes him. Everyone wants to become a President. Therefore, in order to prevail over opponents, one must be prepared to sacrifice all things. Even assassination will become necessary at times."

"Can a single politician alone defeat his enemy?" asked Mao.

"That is the important part," said Tan. "A person alone can accomplish little. One must gather comrades with common ideas and common goals, and use their power to crush the enemy. Of course, if there are any traitors among the comrades, or if anyone tries to usurp your power, then—*swish!*—with one swing of the sword! In this manner, one must strengthen his power."

Tan's words are supposed to have had a great influence on Mao, Takagi remarked, but at that time he was pursuing his education.

Mao entered a public (government-supported) teachers' college where the instruction was based on experiments, and learning on concrete facts, not abstract theories. A great deal of emphasis was placed on instilling the merits of the Chinese people and the importance of Chinese tradition and geography into the minds of the students. With few exceptions, the teachers' college system did not allow advancement to higher educational institutions. Therefore, many students became frustrated, which ultimately led to intensely rebellious feelings against existing conditions. And Mao spent five years in such an environment.

As a sophomore, Mao wrote the following poem in his notebook:

"Youths are full of high spirits. Indolence is the source of all evils. Now is the time to stand up and fight courageously."

18

In the following year Mao became associated with the printing and distribution of a pamphlet denouncing "imperialist" designs on China, including "treacherous Japanese plots."

"Oh, the shamed people!" Mao wrote in the pamphlet. "With what should we avenge ourselves? The responsibility rests with us students."

Mao used his summer vacations on penniless trips to the towns and villages in Hunan Province, where he stayed at a number of farmhouses and made a detailed survey of the state of the villages. It was these trips that became the seed and later the bud of Mao's thoughts, according to Takagi. It was then that Mao started mapping out his concrete plans for social reform, an idea that had been burning in his mind for years.

Traveling by plane and car, Takagi followed in Mao's footsteps in the search for deeper understanding of the motivations behind the revolutionary leader's later policies. Describing the trip, Takagi noted that it was a rural area with abundant water from the Siangchiang River and Tungting-hu Lake, and with fertile plains, living up to its old name of the "district of fish and rice." But when Mao visited the area, peasants of Hunan Province did not always enjoy the affluent life befitting residents of a place thus named. Mao's ideology, therefore, is based on the actual life of the peasants in Hunan Province at that time.

With this experience as a starting point for his ideas, Mao then advocated night-school education for peasants in order to link theory with practice, and in 1917, while still a student himself, he placed an advertisement to solicit students for his new Laborers Night School:

"Workers, come and listen to me. What is the thing that you find most inconvenient? Do you remember this saying: I hear but cannot write, I write but cannot read, there are numbers but I cannot count. This is it.

19

"You laborers must work and therefore cannot learn the abacus. But now we have found a good method. The No. 1 Teachers' College is opening a night school."

The advertisement was written in Pai-hua, a colloquial language that was seldom used in writing in those days. Many common expressions were used so that everyone could understand it. Mao most probably acquired this simple literary style through his contacts with the soil-tilling farmers. The reason why even primary-school children can memorize quotations from Mao's works is that Communist ideology is converted into simple colloquial expressions. Mao seems to have a magic touch in the use of Pai-hua, Takagi observed.

After instructing the peasant-workers in revolutionary goals, the next step would be to arm them, and finally to urge them to rise up.

The book *Quotations from Chairman Mao Tse-tung* says:

"It was the class struggles of the peasants, the peasant uprisings and peasant wars, that constituted the real motive force of historical development in Chinese feudal society."

This saying was and still is the single giant hard core of Mao Tse-tung's ideology, Takagi said, and he noted that among objects of Mao-worship are numerous weapons for peasants. Most of them red-tasseled spears with steel tips, rifles, machine guns, trench mortars and handmade mines and grenades, and with them are plans and textbooks for military training written and edited by Mao Tse-tung himself. The materials were on display at the former site of a peasant training institute in Kwangchow and the Museum of Revolution in Yenan, as well as at Shaoshanchung.

WALKING IN MAO'S FOOTSTEPS

As the tour of places associated with Mao's early life continued, Takagi's impatience with the continual propaganda

20

onslaught became greater. One day his dispatch to *Yomiuri* began this way:

"Tomorrow I shall visit the place where Mao Tse-tung reportedly spent his early married life with Yang Kai-hui, the daughter of his benefactor, Yang Chang-chi.

"This way of expressing an intention to visit the residence, however, is normally used only by such people as we, who walk the path of bourgeois democracy. Any follower of Mao would say: 'I am going on a study tour to the former site of the Chinese Communist Party Hunan district committee headquarters, the sacred site of the revolution.'

"The difference of expression used in referring to a visit to the same place illustrates the big gap in the way of thinking between Japanese democrats and the Chinese people, who are constantly showered with the radiation from the unsinkable Red Sun. It is this gap which we must keep in mind when we study Communist China.

"On the night before the visit, I lay down on a comfortable bed in the guest home operated by the Changsha branch office of the International Tourist Bureau. But I found it difficult to sleep.

"From outside the window, I heard the constant bellowing of a loudspeaker which repeated over and over the words, 'Mao Tse-tung's thoughts, Mao Tse-tung's thoughts.' It seemed a woman announcer was reading a speech by Lin Piao or some other party official.

"The shrieking of the broadcast lasted for several minutes, and finally came to an end. Relieved, I closed my eyes to get some sleep—but to no avail. The loudspeaker this time started broadcasting the chorus of the favorite Red Guard song, 'Tung Fang Hung [The East Is Red].' And then followed another song, 'The Helmsman.' After the music, the loudspeaker resumed where it had started—the speech on Mao Tse-tung's thoughts. Thus I was kept awake until about

21

three o'clock in the morning by the noise of what seemed to be an interminable broadcast.

"Thanks to the broadcast, even I—born tone-deaf—learned all the 'Tung Fang Hung' and the complete lyrics of 'The Helmsman.'

"And as I finally dozed into a restless sleep I abruptly fell into a nightmare.... I recall that there was a constant buzzing in my ears while I dreamed. I concluded that the source of this strange noise entered my dream from the opening verse of Mao's poem, *In this small world, the bluebottle shouts, buzz buzz....*' Once more I felt the constant pounding in my head. The loudspeaker was blasting away again, this time a song derived from the Liberation Army's military code of ethics. When I looked at my watch, it was past 5 a.m."

Totally exhausted by the nightmare and the sleepless night, Takagi got up, staggered to his feet, and left for Ching Shui Tang where, in 1920, Mao became a Marxist, an instructor in Chinese literature, and principal of the primary school affiliated with his teachers' college.

It was there, or specifically in House No. 22, Ching Hui Tang, Changsha city, where, a year later, he married Yang Kai-hui and spent eighteen months of his newly-married life. The place in the old days was located in beautiful surroundings on the city's outskirts. The area was quiet and had a beautiful lake—an ideal setting for a newlywed couple. But now Changsha city has expanded to this area, bringing with it squalid homes and factories clustered close together.

But long before he arrived at his destination, Takagi knew the exact location of Mao's former residence; for here also was a queue several hundred meters long. Red Guards from various districts had formed up along the streets to visit Mao's home. It finally dawned on him that the endless broadcast, which had deprived him of sleep, had been a service by city authorities for the Red Guard youths who had stood

vigil in the night, and he could only conclude t
did not bother the proud neighbors of Mao's
dence.

He walked along an alley lined with Red Gua
sides and turned a corner to find the front entr
historic site. Even inside the gate, there were scores of Red
Guards lining the path toward the residence that became the
party's Hunan headquarters.

When the Japanese reporter was noticed, the young people began to applaud heartily. This was not unexpected, for
it is considered etiquette in Communist China to applaud
a guest. Takagi reciprocated and applauded them as he
walked toward the house. The youths kept on applauding,
smiled, and approvingly pointed to his left arm, where he
had a red armband of the Red Guards given to him the day
before in Siushan by a girl delegate of the Siushan Primary
School's sixth-grade pupils. The fact that he wore it apparently delighted the Red Guards, and when he waved that
arm in greeting, the youths responded with shouts of "Long
live Chairman Mao!"

In the garden of Mao's former home there were many
beautiful trees and flowers, but it was difficult to get a good
view because it was so filled with Red Guards, and as he
walked into the garden, Takagi thought he saw several Mongolian girls and blue-eyed young people from Sinkiang-
Uighur Province among them.

After threading through the lines of youths, he reached
the entrance located on the right side of the building, and
the room that he stepped into had a dirt floor.

On the right side of the dirt-floored room was Mao's living
room, which contained a big table, a chair, and a lamp—all
reportedly used by Mao. On the left of Mao's room was the
dining room, and on the right his wife's bedroom. A large
rosewood bed, covered with a pink bedspread, occupied
close to half of the entire floor space.

he lattices supported by the bed posts had beautiful
paintings of birds and flowers on silk cloth. The bed had
probably been given to Yang Kai-hui by her father as a wedding present, Takagi surmised. Though befitting a new
bride, the elaborate bed seemed out of place in the home
of a Communist leader who had an intense desire for a violent revolution. Mao had carried out his underground work
in this house. There was a bed in the guestroom where Mao's
comrades often slept, and Takagi was told that Liu Shao-chi
spent several days in this house as Mao's guest. Who then, he
speculated, could have predicted that this top guest would
become Mao's "enemy"?

TWO ROADS TO THE TOP

Delving into the early relations between Mao and Liu,
Takagi discounted a belief that they had both studied at the
same teachers' college in Changsha. By 1920, while Mao was
organizing socialist youth groups and Communist Party cells
in Hunan, Liu Shao-chi was taking lessons in Russian from
the wife of a representative of the Communist International
at a foreign-language school in Shanghai, he found. Liu later
went to the Soviet Union end entered the Eastern Labor College. He returned to China the following spring and became
the secretary of the Chinese Communist Party Central Organization.

Mao in those years was actively engaged in underground
work, establishing night schools for peasant-laborers and
universities for the working class. The revolutionary goal of
Mao and Liu was the same, but the starting point of these
two differed markedly. Mao mainly worked with peasants,
and thought that China's geographical features and climate
must be considered in any plans for revolution. Liu, on the
other hand, went to the Soviet Union, studied Russian, and

launched his revolution from within the proletarian organizations in the industrial cities.

The two met on September 5, 1922, at a convention celebrating the founding of the Cement Workers Union in Changsha. Liu was among twenty guests who were invited to the convention. And most likely he stayed at the Communist Party Hunan branch's "underground" headquarters —overtly the residence of a primary-school principal named Mao Tse-tung.

The difference in character between Mao and Liu was apparent even in those days, Takagi learned. Liu Shao-chi was the one with new knowledge of labor activities, which he had acquired directly from the Comintern in Moscow. Mao, who had never been abroad, stayed in the countryside of Hunan Province and worked out a Chinese type of revolution.

"Mao concentrated on farmers and Liu on industrial workers," Takagi wrote. "This pattern seems to have stuck with the two men from the birth of the Chinese Communist Party to this day, when the two men are engaged in bitter polemics and what may be their final battle."

Despite the vivid contrast in the revolutionary histories of these two men, Mao and Liu had spent fifty-odd years experiencing together the sweet and the bitter of their common struggle. These two had frequently risked their lives for the cause. And yet, Mao and Liu had ultimately come to the point of a tragic and grim confrontation. Takagi could not help wondering whether this was because of their difference in personality, or whether it was plain destiny.

THE BELOVED LEADER

It is not possible for an American or a Japanese to visualize the power that Mao Tse-tung wields over the 700 million Chinese, and the veneration to which he is subjected by his countrymen, commented Churo Nishimura, the *Yomiuri* group chief as he too assessed the phenomenon of Mao-worship. He felt that if there ever were an American statesman who combined the virtues, wisdom, and talents of George Washington, Thomas Jefferson, and Abraham Lincoln, he could not hope to gain as much popularity and exert as much influence as Mao Tse-tung.

He recalled a scene, still vivid in his memory, that he witnessed in Peking on October 1, 1965, the fifteenth anniversary of the founding of the People's Republic of China. Standing on a wooden platform about two hundred meters away from the high red walls called the Tien An Men [Gate of Heavenly Peace], he looked through binoculars to see what was happening on and around the walls.

Chairman Mao stood on a platform on the gate for about three hours, chatting with Chief of State Liu Shao-chi and Prince Norodom Sihanouk of Cambodia and his wife, who were visiting Peking at the time. When a long parade ended, hundreds of thousands of spectators, each carrying a placard or a portrait of Mao, surged toward a stone rail facing a moat in front of the gate. They apparently wanted to see the Chairman close at hand.

Cries of "Long live Chairman Mao!" rang out among the crowd, soon turning into a chorus: *"Mao chuhsi wan sui!"* Nishimura was surprised to find that most of the young men and women jamming the space next to the stone railing were shedding tears, and he realized that the whole thing was not just an act, but that the Chinese people genuinely love and admire Mao.

There were about thirty high-ranking officers and officials in uniform standing on the platform beside the Chairman. When Mao started to walk away, these officers, led by the Foreign Minister, Field Marshal Chen Yi, formed up in two lines and saluted him. Mao glanced at them, but did not return the salute. Before leaving the platform, he stopped and waved again to the crowd jamming the plaza. The scene was enough to indicate to Nishimura that Mao was superior— much superior—to Chen Yi and other field marshals.

In the eyes of the people Mao is the leader of the revolution whose great accomplishments can never be dismissed. He fought and won wars against the Japanese forces and the Nationalist Government. He strove with success to elevate the living standards of the Chinese people. China is still far from being an affluent society, Nishimura noted, but people are now fed, clothed, and housed sufficiently, and they thank Chairman Mao for enabling them to emerge from the abject poverty that had afflicted them.

Mao's personality also figures largely in the people's attitude toward him, Nishimura learned. Unlike many other dictators, Mao is a warm-hearted man, a type found frequently among farmers. He may be described as "a man of *nin* [benevolence]," a virtue that is highly prized in Confucianism. The feeling that the Chinese people have for Mao is a mixture of respect and affection quite different from the Soviet people's reaction toward Stalin.

Nishimura spoke from his own experience, "The Soviet people were merely 'awed' by their dictator. They did not love him and did not even respect him. I should know," Nishimura added, "for I was detained in Soviet prisoner-of-war camps for two years after the war and I had many opportunities to observe the Soviet people's attitude toward Stalin."

According to Nishimura's observation in Communist China, Mao projected a strong image of kinship with the common man. Since his childhood, the Japanese reporter wrote, Mao has been known for his inclination to love people. He presumably inherited this trait from his mother, who was a devout follower of Buddhism.

Nishimura quoted provincial newspapers that described Mao's conduct on unofficial trips to rural areas. On such excursions, the dictator wore an informal shirt, straw hat, and rubber shoes.

"He approaches a group of farmers lined up on a road to greet him," the description continued. "Spotting an old man crouching on the ground to pay him respect, Mao walks up to him and squats down also, so that he can talk face to face with the man. Mao asks the man's age, and listens carefully as the old farmer describes crop conditions and states his opinions on how to improve the crops."

"There is not a trace of authoritarianism in the way Mao speaks to the aged farmer. Nor is there any indication that the Chairman is putting on an act to win the farmer's heart. Here, it seems, is a man who loves agriculture and loves old people, and that is all there is to it," said Nishimura.

On one of Nishimura's many trips, he went to Shanghai, Nanking, Soochow, and Hangchow without being accompanied by a guide, and talked to scores of Chinese citizens. Without a single exception, these people spoke happily of their good living conditions and told him that they were grateful to Chairman Mao for making it possible for them to lead a comfortable life.

Mao's deification, Nishimura discovered, is easily justified by some Chinese. They say, "In the old days before the Liberation, we sought the help of gods and the Buddha. But the gods and the Buddha did not do anything for us. It is Chairman Mao who saved us and gave us the good life we are enjoying now. It is quite natural for us to respect Chairman Mao more than gods and the Buddha."

And now they also teach their children to love and respect Chairman Mao. While visiting a mausoleum in Nanking, Nishimura met a man, his wife, their small boy, and the child's grandfather. The couple, Mr. and Mrs. Chang Chih-chin, were primary-school teachers. They accepted his offer to take a photograph of their baby and send it to their home in Shanghai.

After he took the picture, Mrs. Chang asked the child, "Who is the person you like best?" The boy quickly replied, "*Mao chuhsi* [Chairman Mao]." Asked whom he liked best after Chairman Mao, the youngster said, "*Kungkung* [Grandpa]."

The grandfather told the reporter about the bad old pre-Liberation days when he had barely managed to eke out a living.

"I was a farmer but I just could not make my living by tilling the soil, because the landowner took seventy percent of the crops I raised," he said. "So I went to Shanghai and worked as a coolie. I worked fourteen hours a day and received the daily wage of twenty-five sen [200 Japanese yen— 54 cents—by Nishimura's calculation].

"I did not have a house to live in, so I slept under a bridge or under the eaves of a building at night. Compared with those days, I live like a king now. I am glad that I lived a long time, otherwise I could not have seen the good days we are having now. The good days came because Chairman Mao did so much to bring about a new age."

As he finished his story, the grandfather clasped his hands and muttered, "May the old man live long!"

This is the reason why even the leaders of the faction in authority, Nishimura concluded, alluding to the group in nominal power under the leadership of Liu Shao-chi, cannot openly launch an anti-Mao movement. Any attempt to overthrow the Chairman would end in failure.

Chapter III

ANATOMY OF THE GREAT
PROLETARIAN CULTURAL
REVOLUTION

YESTERDAY'S HERO

"Who is our enemy and who is our friend? . . . This is the most important problem in the revolution." These words found in the Analects of Chairman Mao Tse-tung were originally published in March 1926 in Mao's first theoretical writing, *The Analysis of Classes in Chinese Society*. The Japanese reporters found that this was during the purges of the Great Proletarian Cultural Revolution, once again an important problem.

Old China hands like Nishimura often were deeply affected by the abuse visited upon prominent persons whom they had known and respected in Peking and other cities. He related one such case of which he had personal knowledge. Setting the scene, he described a large street in Peking called Tai Chi Change, which in the old China was the part of town where many embassies, including those of Japan and Britain, were located. At about the middle of the street there is the Communist Party Peking Municipal Committee building, where the recently purged Peking mayor, Peng

Chen, once reigned. In front of this building is a small structure called the International Club.

Surrounded by an iron fence, the stylish but old Western
building has a large flower garden, a tennis court, and a
pool. The members of the club are mainly foreigners living
in Peking. Occasionally, cocktail parties and dances are held
there.

On an April day in 1965, a short, stocky man about 55 or
56 years of age, with close-cropped hair and wearing a civilian uniform made of expensive woolen material, sat on a
sofa in the second-floor hall of the club. He was surrounded
by nine Peking-based Japanese correspondents and a press
official of the Chinese Foreign Ministry.

"Revisionism is something we cannot tolerate under the
same sun with us," he said.

This man, who talked eloquently about the "new culture"
and criticized revisionism for four and a half hours, was the
party's vice chief of propaganda, Chou Yang. Chou in those
days had far-reaching authority as the virtual leader of the
new art and culture movement promoted by Mao Tse-tung.
But in July last year, only fourteen months after the interview in the club, the prince of China's cultural world and
the fighter against revisionism was himself branded as, of
all things, a "revisionist." His tragic fate was to be forced
to wear a dunce cap and be dragged about the streets. Nishimura noted that not only the cultural world but the whole
of China was greatly shocked by this incident. And, combined with the purge of the Mayor of Peking, Peng Chen, a
month earlier, the humiliation of Chou Yang served notice
that the Cultural Revolution was not merely a movement to
create a new culture, but a revolution that reflected a fierce
political struggle within the Communist Party.

The *Yomiuri* observers thought that the confrontation between the Mao-Lin[1] "mainstream faction" and the Liu-Teng[2] "authority faction" was more than a bloody clash for power. When Mao's wife, Chiang Ching, the heroine of the mainstream faction, defined the fight as a "class struggle between the proletariat and the bourgeoisie," she was reflecting the fact that the two opposing camps are in fact engaged in a grave ideological dispute over domestic and foreign policy matters that had its origins in economic and international crises of the past twenty years.

Mineo Nakajima, the youngest member of the Yomiuri Task Force, made an intensive study of the historical factors behind the Cultural Revolution. A graduate of the Chinese Department of the Tokyo Foreign Language University, at the age of 30 years he was a teacher of modern Chinese history at the same institution, and the following analysis is based primarily on his reports to *Yomiuri*.

After the end of the Korean War in 1953, China finally launched a full-scale national development program. The Government mapped out three Five-Year Plans for what it called the transformation of the country. The announced goal of this 15-year transition period was to build socialism on a long-range and gradual basis. In foreign policy, advancing gradually was translated into the "five principles of peace."

But the situation changed markedly and rapidly after July 1955, when Mao published a report entitled, "On Problems Concerned with Agriculture Cooperation," in which he called for immediate collectivization of farms. Only a year later, Mao, in one step, had accomplished his aim of

[1] Lin Piao—Defense Minister, now considered Mao's chief supporter.

[2] Teng Hsiao-ping, Secretary General of the Communist Party. Considered along with Liu Shao-chi, Chief of State, leader of the authority faction.

socialist transformation of the country by organizing high-level agricultural cooperatives on a nationwide basis.

However, the rapid reform caused various tensions and gave birth to what were called "contradictions" in the country.

About the same time, a series of violent incidents rocked the world socialist bloc, such as the criticism of Stalin, the riot in Poland, and the uprising in Hungary, leading to even further confusion within the ranks of Chinese Communists.

In order to alleviate these so-called contradictions, Mao launched a kind of liberalization campaign with the slogan, "Let a hundred flowers bloom and let a hundred schools of thought contend." Together with the Party rectification policy and the drive to promote long-term coexistence with the various democratic parties, this developed into a nationwide mass movement during the first half of 1957. However, the "hundred flowers" movement boomeranged in a totally unexpected manner—criticism of the Communist Party and Mao's authority. Mao interpreted this reaction as a reflection on his own policy, concocted by the enemy of the classes. He immediately set in motion an anti-rightist movement, which he called a class struggle. These events occurred in the latter half of 1957.

In 1958, Mao put forward a program called the "Three Aspects of the Red Flag"—the Great Leap Forward, People's Communes, and the General Line of Socialist Reconstruction. This was the most vivid expression of Mao's concept of socialism and has become the banner of the Cultural Revolution. But in 1959 the Great Leap Forward was on the verge of collapse, and Mao's whole program had become the target of severe opposition. The communes were in serious trouble, and famine was widespread. In addition, the Sino-Soviet rift had developed into almost an open confrontation.

Although Mao had crushed some of his critics by autumn of 1959, he was compelled gradually to tolerate economic

33

adjustment policies that had, in effect, been drawn up by his opponents. Still, Mao refused to recognize the Great Leap Forward policy as a mistake. He thought that the adjustment policy which Liu's group was vigorously promoting would result in restoring the bourgeoisie to the position of authority. His answer was a renewed campaign for a fierce class struggle.

The conflict between Mao and the Liu-Teng faction did not come to the point of an open split during the economic adjustment period in 1960, for in that year the power clique or authority faction was, along with Mao, energetically criticizing modern (Soviet) revisionism. It is believed that the two groups definitely broke in 1965, the year before Communist China was to embark on the third Five-Year Plan. At the Communist Party Central Committee conference in September–October 1965 the mainstream faction and the opponents of Mao's policies divided into two opposing camps. Mao, in his own version of the breach that emerged from that conference of 1965, said, "I felt the need to criticize the revisionists within the Central Committee."

The issues on which the two camps clashed can be boiled down to two points—domestic problems and foreign policy matters.

On domestic policy, the dispute revolved around the question of how to promote the third Five-Year Plan. The Liu-Teng group demanded that the economic adjustment policy be continued, but this was opposed point-blank by Mao, who was convinced that the Great Leap Forward method was the only way to construct his vision of socialism.

The point of dispute on foreign policy matters was centered on how to deal with the Soviet Communist Party in conjunction with the escalation of the Vietnam war. The fundamental problem was whether or not the Chinese Communist Party should organize an international united front with the Soviets and work with them on this basis. On this

34

issue, Mao adhered adamantly to his hard-line policy against the Soviet Communist Party, and against the U.S.A.

At this point the Liu-Teng supporters, who until then had agreed with Mao in his attacks on modern revisionism, probably thought that they were no longer able to go along with his assertion that the United States and the Soviet Union were enemies on the same level. The Liu-Teng faction holds that there is nothing wrong in forming a world-wide united front, including the Soviet Union, against the United States. This argument contends that the Soviet Union is a socialist country, even though revisionist. They point out that the Chinese Communist Party, during the war against Japan, had even cooperated with the "reactionary Nationalists" of Chiang Kai-shek. Therefore, they ask, why shouldn't the Party work with the Soviet Union when Communist China is fighting for its life against the great enemy —the United States?

REVOLUTION IN THE MAKING

The inner conflicts of the Chinese Communist Party were toward, at this time, a climax unknown to the ordinary citizen in Peking, Nishimura observed. While looking out of a window of the Hsin Chiao Hotel in Peking's Chin Min Hsiang district, in January 1965, he recalled, he saw that the night sky and the big buildings near the Tien An Men Square were brightly illuminated. As he listened, he heard the sounds of gongs and drums, the singing of choral groups, and fireworks. Wondering what the commotion was all about, he hurried to the square in an automobile and found a huge crowd watching a group of young boys and girls, dressed in the costumes of minority groups, dancing frenetically to band music.

When he questioned one of the people watching the dancing, he was told that they were celebrating the election of Peng Chen, the mayor of Peking, to the post of vice chairman of the Standing Committee of the National People's Congress, and the reelection of President Liu Shao-chi and Chairman Chu Tei. The results of voting had just been announced by the Third National People's Congress, which had been in session since late 1964. Yet it is these three, Nishimura commented, honored by the people with dancing, fireworks, and illuminations, who have almost been pushed out of their posts of leadership in present-day China. If the Chinese were baffled by these events, the foreigners were even more so.

But in reviewing the past ten years of Chinese history, the chief of the *Yomiuri* team found indications that the Cultural Revolution had, in effect, started as early as 1960.

One of the pointers that many observers failed to notice at the time, he said, was the new movement for discipline and purification instituted in the People's Liberation Army when Lin Piao took over as Defense Minister from Peng Teh-huai, who had been purged as a revisionist.

Lin Piao saw that the morale of the soldiers who hailed from farm villages was low because of the confusion in the People's Communes, the Japanese correspondent recalled. Many soldiers seemed to be acting arrogantly because of their victory in the Korean War, and the faction demanding more modern weapons was growing increasingly stronger.

Lin Piao decided that the troops must return to the spirit of the founding days of the Red Army, when Mao established the doctrine of intimate contact between soldiers and population. The main object of this movement, Nishimura noted, was to instill into the soldiers the spirit of sacrificing the ego for the sake of the public by putting politics foremost and arming themselves with the thoughts of Mao. The movement was completed in June 1965 with the abolition of military ranks in the army, a step that was to encourage strength through comradely unity, as in the Yenan days.

Thus Mao, who had said that government is born at the point of a gun, consolidated the Liberation Army under his own mantle as the initial step to prepare himself for the expected fierce struggle against his critics.

Mao's next step was to reorganize the farm villages. This was achieved through a movement to restore the People's Communes, which had been almost taken over by former landlords after the three consecutive years of natural disasters and famine. This program, called the "Socialist Education Movement," was designed to purify the thoughts, politics, organization, and financial aspect of the People's Communes.

"Thought purification" was the most important of the four aims, Nishimura found. He spoke to many members of People's Communes, who invariably said:

"Of the four purifications, the most important is purifying one's thoughts. If we manage to purify our thoughts, the other three can be purified automatically. Our minds and the communes have been thoroughly cleansed by Mao's thoughts." The movement launched in 1963 was a bitter struggle, according to Nishimura. In the People's Communes the poor farmers formed associations, reinforced by outstanding retired soldiers from the Liberation Army and party cadres from various cities, to promote the "four purifications" vigorously.

Mao's self-assumed task, as seen by Nishimura, was to remove the resurgent influence of landlords and wealthy farmers in the country's villages, where the impulse toward conservatism remained strong. He was applying the same principles of guerrilla warfare that had always guided his military policy: first occupy the villages, and thus encircle the cities. This would allow them to surround and crush the urban strongholds of the power clique and revisionists. In other words, he used the "four purifications movement" as a valuable stepping stone for the main goals of the Cultural

37

Revolution. If Mao had launched a struggle against the "power clique" without control over the army and the farm villages, the Liberation Army would probably have split in two and most of the farmers would have sided with the landlords, making civil war inevitable.

Parallel with the "four purifications movement," Nishimura said, Mao also advanced the Cultural Revolution in the propaganda and cultural fields.

Mao places particular emphasis on propaganda activities, the reporter noted. On August 8, 1966, he presented the Party Central Committee wtih the "16 Articles on Cultural Revolution," instructing Party members to undertake a vigorous propaganda program in the ideological field. Later, criticism was turned against the group that had entrenched itself in the Party propaganda section of the Peking Municipal Committee.

Ultimately, the movement burgeoned into a political struggle that caused the downfall of Chow Yang that Nishimura described earlier, and then developed into a system of kangaroo courts aimed at humiliating members of the authority faction—a picture that Nishimura found too sordid to be brushed aside as merely "an incident of the Cultural Revolution."

One of the secrets of Mao's war strategy, Nishimura concluded, is to "avoid a showdown with the enemy until you have overwhelmingly superior forces." Through patience and careful groundwork, Mao took control of the Liberation Army, the farm villages, and the Party propaganda machine. Thus, with the backing of "overwhelmingly superior forces" and with the Red Guards acting as the spearhead, Mao drew his foes into the ultimate showdown.

WHAT IS THE "AUTHORITY FACTION"?

Takuzo Kamai was one Japanese journalist who refused to accept a cliché without knowing the definition. On his extensive travels in Red China, he kept asking one question: "What *is* the 'authority faction'?"

During a bus tour on the morning of New Year's Day, he tried to get an answer from a man who had been serving at the Peking branch of a travel company for six years since his graduation from a first-class university.

The man answered, "People who follow the bourgeois line, thereby obstructing the revolution."

But this did not explain anything to Kamai, so he asked, "Why is Liu Shao-chi regarded as a member of the authority faction?"

The answer was: "We are not concerned about Liu as a person. We are concerned about his thoughts."

Kamai then asked, "What is your personal viewpoint?"

"At present," the Chinese answered, "the masses are criticizing the authority faction. The debate is still going on. Everything will be cleared up by the debate."

"Will Liu be relieved of his posts as head of the state and Communist Party leader?" Kamai asked.

"That is another thing to be decided by the masses. What we know for sure is that they—the authority faction—tried to suppress the revolutionary masses."

But the *Yomiuri* correspondent felt that he had still to get an answer to his basic question, "What is the authority faction?"

So he sought the answer from people working at a textile plant where wall newspapers were plastered all over the place by Red Guards. The first person he spoke to was a woman, about 50 years old, who served as chief of the administrative office.

He said to her, "I see many wall newspapers around here. Are the criticisms directed against the plant superintendent?"

She answered, "Yes. There used to be more before. All the people in managerial posts are being criticized, all section chiefs and department directors." She added wryly, "Well,

39

I would say that I am doing well. I am criticized only a little."

Then Kamai talked to a laborer, about 40 years old, who was eating a bowl of noodles with chopped chicken during a lunch recess at the workers' living quarters.

"People in managerial posts belong to the authority faction, without exception," he said. "We are determined to criticize, fight, and overthrow the bourgeois authority faction."

A Hong Kong expert on Communist Chinese affairs told the reporter, "The current revolution is aimed at examining all leaders. This is indicated by Mao's statement that 'people in authority should wash the dirt from their faces before they start working again.' But the fact is that you can always trump up a charge against someone, whether or not he has actually committed some offense."

It became evident to Kamai that the Cultural Revolution would lead to the purging of principal officials throughout Red China. A warning was issued in the spring of 1966 that the whole affair was a revolution in fact as well as in name. That warning was true, Kamai said. The Cultural Revolution was designed not only to "reshape and revitalize the revolutionary consciousness of the people," but also to destroy the existing system completely and to establish a new one.

All persons who held more or less important posts in the districts Kamai visited were being denounced as members of the "authority faction." It seemed to him that nearly every city in China was filled with such people. But there were a few exceptions, such as Changchow and Loyang. In these cities, appeals made through loudspeakers mounted on cars parading the streets did not carry much force or intensity.

Tourist agency employes and young hotel workers in Loyang told him, "There is nothing to criticize here. Comrade Liu Chien-hsun, first secretary of Hupei Province, who moved to the central government last October, was a fine person and so is Wen Min-sheng, who has been promoted from second secretary to first secretary."

They apparently told the truth, Kamai found later. News from China after he returned to Japan said that Chairman Mao had said that Liu Chien-hsun of Hupei Province is the only local leader who supported the revolutionary faction in wall newspapers.

It seemed to Kamai that practically anyone holding a position of authority could be included in the authority faction.

Premier Chou divided members of the authority faction into five categories: those who have turned against the Communist Party, those who "follow the path of capitalism," the "diehards" who adhere to the "reactionary line," those who have acknowledged errors but continue to make ideological mistakes, and those who "have made separate, temporary errors."

Kamai concluded that the authority faction can be defined by deducing the common denominator of the people belonging to these five different categories. The authority faction is, he found, the bureaucratic machinery of the Communist Party itself.

The much-criticized followers of the Liu-Teng line are all elite members of the Party. With a few exceptions, those who held high posts in Government and Party organizations on the national and local levels have been virtually banished from their offices. This means that the authority faction forms more than 95 percent of people in the leader classes, while the main Mao-Lin faction constitutes more than 95 percent of the 20,000,000 Communist Party members and the entire mainland Chinese population of 700,000,000.

Takagi found that the cleavage of the Cultural Revolution followed distinct intellectual and class lines.

Tracing the social level of the people described as pro-Mao, he discovered that few of them have ever received a regular school education and that many, coming from destitute peasant families of the lower class, had been farmhands and laborers. Also, some joined the Red Army at the age of 15 or 16 years, when they were still students, and got their later education under Mao. For these, the army was truly their "university," as slogans of the Cultural Revolution claim. These men have never been taught any other ideology than Mao's thoughts. They have not digested Marxism directly, said Takagi; they learned Communist theory through the lens of Mao (this lens has a filter called the "Chinese race"), and once this lens is removed, Marxism-Leninism disappears from their minds.

On the other hand, Takagi found that the majority of persons associated with Liu are intellectuals from the middle or lower-middle class. Numerous leaders in this group are graduates of famous universities, and some studied in Japan. They are usually intellectuals, men of letters or leaders of student movements. They did not become Marxist through the lens of Mao's thoughts; rather, many of them had mastered Marxism by themselves in their school days. Most of them had engaged in underground activities in areas of northern China, where they organized workers and young people and thereby contributed to the growth of the Chinese Communist Party.

It was in North China in 1928 that Liu Shao-chi started building the foundation of the Chinese Communist Party. Pro-Liu elements have existed in areas extending from Hopei to Shansi for forty years. In 1930 he became secretary of the Manchurian Committee, and in 1933 he led a spinning-mill strike in Tientsin. He joined the Long March in 1934, but left it halfway and returned to Manchuria for underground activities. In 1936 he established the Chinese Communist Party's Northern Bureau and thus created the anti-Japanese front in North China. In 1941 he became a political commissar of the new Fourth Army.

He often returned to the Yenan stronghold in the intervening years, but his arena of activity was mostly in Japanese-controlled zones. The people who, under his leadership, fought and shared their fate with him in those days now form the nucleus of the pro-Liu faction. During the war with Japan, in particular, they were engaged in difficult and dangerous underground activities and struggles. They feel that, unlike their comrades who were simply shouting for resistance against the Japanese and calling for the revolution from far away in Yenan, they were exposed every day and every hour to the danger of being killed, Takagi learned.

The social level of those backing Liu is linked with the image of literary men, who are the traditional Chinese intellectuals; they contend that even those from the bourgeoisie can be united with workers, farmers, and soldiers if they "remake" themselves. In contrast, the Mao main-current faction is particular about the family background of Party members and is likely to look askance at the activities of anyone from intellectual antecedents.

Liu's weakest point is the army, according to Takagi. Mao, founder of the People's Liberation Army, has lived with the troops as a revolutionist for much of the past half-century. But Liu was linked with the army for only two years during his fifty years as a revolutionist—between September 1939 and early 1942, when he served as a political commissar with the Fourth Army. Consequently, not a single portrait of him was displayed by troops of the People's Liberation Army after his appointment as head of state.

However, though he is not very popular with the army,

43

Liu has behind him a substantial number of city workers as well as party leaders throughout the country who have given half of their lifetimes to the organization of the Communist movement in China. Many of these believe that Mao's radical errors, made since the 1958 Great Leap Forward campaign, were corrected by Liu's moderate policies and that today's China was built up in this way.

Nevertheless, Liu and his supporters are being attacked by the Maoist faction as revisionist elements "walking the path of capitalism."

Although the news media often describe the Liu faction as "anti-Maoist," these people are not necessarily opposing every aspect of Mao's thoughts, Takagi found. In fact, many have voiced their support of Mao's principles. In other words, as their opponents have put it, they are "waving the Red Flag and opposing it at the same time." This is why it is difficult to discern the true affiliations of any group, and why there is so much confusion in China.

The people in authority fully recognize Mao's individual achievements in building Communist China. They are critical, however, of the fanatical individual worship of Mao as practiced by the Red Guards. They also acknowledge the absolute need of Mao's teachings in studying the Chinese revolution. However, they think that it would be close to "superstition" to continue worshiping "Maoism" in the same manner that Communists follow Marxism-Leninism.

They recognize the fact that Maoism is a development of Marxism-Leninism, but with the reservation that the most important and fundamental works of Mao were written in the 1940s, such as his thesis on guerrilla warfare. They believe that Mao's works written in the 1950s are being used by the Party merely to justify its policies.

The people in authority pour scorn on Mao's followers who loudly warn that there is an impending danger of the revival of capitalism in the process of building socialism.

They recognize the need for the technocrats, the scientists, and the technological experts in the building of a modern socialist country, and do not arbitrarily brand such technicians as "elements walking the path of capitalism."

This type of thinking naturally conflicts with the recent reform in the education system and other policies of Mao. Liu's supporters are not entirely opposed to giving labor priority over education, such as the present program of mixing—half and half—classroom studies with industrial and farm work. But the process of mixing, they contend, should be gradual. They maintain that emphasis should not be placed too heavily on labor education to the exclusion of scholastic education.

Judging by these views, the Communist Party authority-faction members are undoubtedly "revisionists" from the viewpoint of Maoism. But Takagi doubted that these men can be categorized in the same class as the Soviet Communist Party members whom the Chinese call "Khrushchev revisionists."

Mao and Liu agree on one point—that in the international Communist movement, the most dangerous thing is modern revisionism. But to Liu, modern doctrinarianism is equally dangerous. Because of this belief, he has tried to apply the brakes to the fanatical worshiping of Mao's thoughts.

On Sino-Soviet relations, the supporters of Mao hold that the Khrushchev-type revisionists are counterrevolutionaries, and that therefore the relationship between the two countries must take the form of enemy versus enemy. The backers of Liu are more flexible in their way of thinking. They consider that the Soviet revisionists and the Soviet Communist Party are separate entities.

In the earlier days, there was not much of a gap between the political beliefs of Mao and Liu, and the differences could be papered over by compromises. However, during the past few years the rift between the two lines has widened.

According to one analysis Takagi heard, Mao has frequently rejected Liu's "walk slow" policies and has followed the radical path of adventurism, leading to one failure after another. As a result, Communist China suffered several setbacks internally in carrying out its socialist revolution and constructing a socialistic country. Following each reverse, Mao was able to weather the crisis through the efforts of Liu's supporters.

Hence, Takagi decided the Liu group might have agreed that "Mao Tse-tung is a great helmsman," in the words of the popular Communist Chinese song, but that he had a bad habit of suddenly steering toward the left. In Takagi's view, the dispute between Mao and the Eastern European countries, especially the Soviet Union, over leadership in the Communist world finally made the rupture in China complete. Liu and his principal supporters, who were high-ranking members of the Chinese Communist Party, gained more power each time Mao made a mistake. Following the break between Peking and Moscow, Liu's "revisionists" threatened Mao's throne—and it was at this point that the Great Proletarian Cultural Revolution went into action.

DEFINING THE ENEMY

Yomiuri's young historian, Mineo Nakajima, found it hard to classify all the anti-Maoists by ideology. He was struck by the fact that a number of people in the despised authority faction had, in fact, supported Mao's announced goals of the Cultural Revolution based on the "three red banners of the general line of socialist reconstruction, the Great Leap Forward, and the people's communes."

Many of the men who are now being denounced as "people in authority" were advocates of the Great Leap

Forward in bygone years, Nakajima pointed out. Li Ching-chuan, first secretary of the Southwest Bureau, was one of the three leaders of the movement, together with Tan Chen-lin, a member of the Communist Party Political Bureau and vice president of the State Council, and the late Ke Cheng-shih, who was a member of the Communist Party Political Bureau, first secretary of the East China Bureau, vice president of the State Council, and mayor of Shanghai. When Peng Teh-huai and other critics of the Great Leap Forward within the party charged that the People's Commune had been created prematurely, Li wrote a thesis saying that "the People's Commune is a natural outgrowth of the social development of the country." He praised Mao's views of socialism and denounced the critics of the Great Leap—and now he in turn is a target of the Cultural Revolution.

Chiang Wei-ching, of the Kiangsu Provincial Committee, had frequently called on the public to connect the Mao-thought with productive activities after he appealed for agricultural collectivization at the eighth national conference of Communist Party delegates in 1956. Tsao Ti-chiu and Chen Pi-hsien of Shanghai had worked under the late Ke Ching-shih as members of the Great Leap Forward faction. In 1960 Chen attracted public attention by writing a thesis entitled "One Hog for Each Ninety-nine Square Meters of Field on Shanghai Farms" in *Red Flag*, the organ of the Chinese Communist Party.

These facts indicated to Nakajima that men who are now being subjected to kangaroo courts as authority-faction members did not oppose Mao and object to his idea of the Great Leap Forward from the outset. This applied to Liu Shao-chi and Teng Hsiao-ping, too. Another example is Tao Chu, former chief of the Communist Party Propaganda Department, who had supplied a theoretical basis for criticisms in his article published in 1960 under the title, "An Essay on the Problem of the Law of the Transition Period," based on

Mao's view of socialism. All these men rose markedly in their political positions because of distinguished service in carrying out the Great Leap Forward policy. Therefore, Nakajima could not pinpoint the reason for the formation of an opposition authority faction by examining the theoretical views of the persons concerned.

Nor could Nakajima find the reason in the personal ties of individual politicians. Tao Chu, for example, was closely associated with Lin Piao in the beginning.

In Nakajima's opinion, the Chinese Communist Party is a secluded organization whose power structure is based on a patriarchal system. And this power structure is the reason behind the recurring political upheavals, which cannot entirely be explained by bringing up conflicting theoretical views or disagreements among politicians on policy matters.

The fate of Tao Chu was seen in a different light by another reporter, Kamai. He heard from some people that Tao Chu, former chief of the Propaganda Department—called by wall posters an executor of the Liu-Teng line in opposition to Chairman Mao—was a member of what is called the "reactionary self-preservation faction." According to these informants, Tao was a position-seeker as well as a brilliant civil servant. He had displayed great skill as an administrator in carrying out the land reform during the early years of the People's Republic and in promoting the People's Communes more recently. Always, he accurately guessed the will and wishes of his superior and put them into practice. Full of hope, Tao went to Peking, the arena of the country's political activities, and faithfully carried out the orders of President Liu Shao-chi and Secretary-General Teng Hsiao-ping. But this act of loyalty proved to be his undoing, and Tao was charged with having "aided the authority faction."

Viewed from this angle, Kamai suggested, Li Hsueh-feng, who replaced Peng Chen as the first secretary of the Peking Municipal Committee, would be the most notable example

48

of the "self-preservation faction." However, members of the Mao-Lin main-current group view Li in a slightly different light. They probably believe that he is a genuine bedfellow of the "authority faction," and that he was the man chosen by the Liu-Teng leaders to fill the post vacated by the dismissal of Peng Chen.

The tragedy of the so-called "self-preservation faction"— those who had elected to play it safe by sitting on the fence —was seen by Kamai in relation to Japanese standards of behavior and loyalty. In Wuhan, he saw a rally where a number of "bad ones" were subjected to the hisses and boos of spectators. Most of the victims were middle-aged men of imposing features who looked at the crowds contemptuously—men who fitted perfectly the image of "people in authority." But there were also several young women standing with bowed heads and wearing triangular hats forced on them by their captors. The hats bore labels in Chinese characters saying, "The self-preservation group following the reactionary line." These young women were employed as clerks in the administrative sections of universities, or worked as members of the Cultural Revolution organizing group. Apparently they had been charged with having blindly followed the orders of the authority-faction members —mostly university presidents, deans, and Party secretaries.

By Japanese standards, Kamai observed, they had faithfully followed the orders of their superiors and had performed their duties well. But in China, where importance is attached to the thought of people and the outcome of their actions, these women were accused of having assisted the authority faction, or of having feigned ignorance.

IN THE CITIES AND PROVINCES

As they traveled across China, the *Yomiuri* team found that the Cultural Revolution had spread across the whole of

49

that vast land, but that its success varied from area to area.

Mineo Nakajima reported that people in the central Government were not the only persons being attacked. In all major cities he visited, local leaders of the authority faction were also being severely criticized. In Peking, large posters criticized Li Ching Chuan, first secretary of the Southwest Bureau, and Liu Lan-Tao, his counterpart in the Northwest Bureau. Their organizations have farflung networks of branch offices in local provinces. In Nanking, Chiang Wei-ching, first secretary of the Chinese Communist Party Kiangsu Provincial Committee, was being attacked. Posters denouncing him were displayed conspicuously outside the gate of the Nanking People's Hall on the day he gave an address as a representative of his committee at the Sun centennial celebration in the same hall.

As he took the rostrum, Nakajima was surprised to see that he was wearing a uniform, since he is a Communist Party official and not a military man. It looked to the Japanese teacher as though Chiang was trying to impress upon the audience that he also has a position and power as a member of the Kiangsu Military District Political Committee, which belongs to the Liberation Army's Nanking Command.

But the Maoists didn't always have the upper hand. The rendezvous of Red Guards in Shanghai is the old Bund, the embanked thoroughfare along the Whangpoo River, which is lined by imposing buildings housing the Shanghai Municipal Committee headquarters and the Shanghai Federation of Trade Unions. One night Nakajima joined a throng of Red Guards and went to the "strongholds of the authority faction," which are not usually visited by "foreign guests" The Red Guards were writing slogans and pasting posters all over the outer walls of the front hall and the façade of the Municipal Committee building. But this was only one side of the picture. A soldier armed with a bayonet was standing guard at the closed door. It appeared that he had sufficient authority and dignity to keep the Red Guards from approaching the entrance. Despite all the hullabaloo by the Red Guards, Nakajima felt that the authority faction still remains strong. This was also true in the provinces, where Nakajima thought that authority-faction members presumably turned against the Mao-Lin main-current leadership because of problems occurring in their respective districts, such as the question of minority races. These local personages enjoy the support of a large body of citizens who daily perform their tasks as office workers and plant employes and who feel that "politics" alone will not enable them to run their organizations and machinery smoothly.

Actually, the historian found that the authority faction is a force made up of various groups in different districts, which are all criticizing and resisting the Maoists but are not necessarily connected directly with each other.

But this widespread authority faction had succeeded in consolidating its power in various parts of the country by running the Communist Party Central Committee Regional Bureaus on its own initiative, and each regional bureau was a citadel of the anti-Maoists.

The Chinese mainland has been divided into six districts ruled by their respective bureaus since their reorganization in 1961. It has become abundantly clear that local regional offices were impregnable strongholds of the authority group, and according to Nakajima's analysis, the bureaus derive their strength from three elements:

First, these bureaus are not only local subdivisions, but are also the main organizations representing the Party's Central Committee, as specified in Article 29 of the Party Constitution. The second factor is that in most cases, the leader—first secretary—of a regional bureau controls military affairs as well as political activities through serving concurrently as an army commander or as a member of the army's political committee. This system is related in a large degree to Communist China's military conscription law, which makes it a principle for each district to have its own army. Last, local sectionalism peculiar to Chinese society is still evident, and the Chinese people are apt to be drawn to leaders of their respective districts.

All these factors have allowed local leaders to isolate themselves from the central Government and to form their own independent kingdoms, while the central Government in Peking is in the throes of internecine struggle.

The Northeast Bureau, which rules the Liaoning, Kirin, and Heilungkiang Provinces, is a stronghold of the authority faction led by Sung Jen-chung, first secretary of the bureau, and Li Fan-wu, first secretary of the Heilungkiang Provincial Committee. This group operates out of Harbin.

However, Nakajima also heard that Sung Jen-chung had made a self-criticism and cooperated with pro-Mao revolutionary rebels in seizing power. Fan Fu-sheng, first secretary of the Heilungkiang Provincial Committee, also joined the revolutionary rebels. But even without them, the authority faction still has much power in Shenyang, the capital of Liaoning Province and a center of heavy industry.

In Luta city, Mayor Hsu Hsi and Hu Ming, deputy first secretary of the Municipal Committee, have offered strong resistance to the authority faction. On the other hand, army troops were mobilized to quell a riot instigated by the authority faction in Changshun, the provincial capital of Kirin.

The authority faction was firmly entrenched in the East China Bureau, whose territory embraces Shanghai, a stronghold of the faction, and Shantung, Kiangsu, Anhwei, Chekiang, Kiangsi, and Fukien Provinces. How deeply the problem is rooted here is indicated by the fact that the post of bureau first secretary has remained vacant since the death of Ke Cheng-shih. However, the pro-Mao groups are pressing hard against the entrenched opponents. Chen Pi-hsien, secretary of the East China Bureau and a member of the Shanghai Municipal Committee, and Tsao Ti-chiu, mayor of Shanghai, have been dragged about the streets by Red Guards. Other men who are being severely criticized as being in the authority faction include Li Pao-hua, third secretary of the East China Bureau and first secretary of the Anhwei Provincial Committee; Tan Chi-lung, secretary of the East China Bureau and first secretary of the Shantung Provincial Committee; Chiang Wei-ching, first secretary of the Kiangsu Provincial Committee, and Yeh Fei, first secretary of the Fukien Provincial Committee.

Although in the North China Bureau all authority-faction leaders seem to have lost their power, Nakajima thought that their counterparts in East China were far from being finished. In Tainan, the capital of Shantung Province, Tan Chi-lung, first secretary of the Provincial Committee, and Pai Ju-ping, governor of Shantung, are resisting the pro-Mao faction. In Tsingtao, clashes have occurred not only between the authority faction and the Mao-Lin main-current group, but also between opposing groups within the pro-Mao ranks.

Chao Kai, the mayor, and Li Pao-hua still hold sway in Hofei, the capital of Anhwei Province. In Foochow, the capital of Fukien Province, Mayor Lin Po is putting up resistance against the Mao faction.

The Central-South Bureau, the stronghold of Tao Chu, has such authority-faction leaders as Wang Jen-chung, first secretary of the bureau; Chang Ping-hua, secretary of the bureau; Chang Ti-hsueh, first secretary of Hunan Province; and Chao Tzu-yang, first secretary of the Kwangtung Provincial Committee. A violent anti-Mao riot was reported in Nanchang, Kiangsi Province. Clashes have occurred even in the Kwangsi Chuang Autonomous Region, which had been least plagued by such problems.

The situation is most complicated in the territories ruled by the North China, Northwest China, and Southwest China Bureaus, Nakajima reported. These areas embrace Inner

Mongolia, Sinkiang, and Tibet, the frontier districts inhabited by minority races, and trouble has occurred frequently since 1958, when the Chinese Communist Party adopted the policy of eliminating the racialism of minority groups. The worst of these incidents were the 1959 Tibetan revolt and the defection of tens of thousands of Chinese from Sinkiang to the Soviet Union in 1962.

The complexity of China's race problem is indicated by the fact that all members of the State Council's Nationalities Affairs Committee—Chairman Ulanfu, Vice Chairmen Wang Feng, Liu Chun, and Tan Tung—have been exposed and criticized by the Mao-Lin main-current faction.

The authority faction in the North China Bureau was led by Li Hsueh-feng, first secretary of the bureau; Ulanfu, second secretary of the bureau and first secretary of the Inner Mongolian Autonomous Region Committee; and Lin Tieh, third secretary of the bureau and first secretary of the Hopei Provincial Committee.

It was no easy task for the Mao group to wrest power from the authority faction in Taiyuan, capital of Shansi Province. Ever since Ulanfu—"Father of Inner Mongolia"—was subjected to criticism, local army troops led by Liu Chang have been resisting the Maoists in Huhehot and other communities of Inner Mongolia. Liu is commander of army troops in Huhehot, the capital.

The Mao-Lin group has been unable to launch attacks on the authority faction in the Northwest Bureau, which rules Shensi Province, Kansu Province, the Ninghsia Hui Autonomous Region, Tsinghai Province, and the Sinkiang Uighur Autonomous Region. There is a theory that the Mao-Lin faction has refrained from taking action in this bureau in order to avoid spreading disorder to the territories under its jurisdiction. The Mao-Lin group has many powerful enemies in the bureau leadership, including Liu Lan-ta, first secretary of the bureau; Wang En-mao, first secretary of the

Sinkiang Uighur Autonomous Region Committee; Wang Feng, first secretary of the Kansu Provincial Committee, and Chang T-chih, secretary of the bureau and commander of army troops in Lanchow. It is generally believed that in Sinkiang, Wang En-mao and Tao Chih-yueh, vice commander of the Sinkiang Military Area, are pitting themselves against the Mao faction and that they have the anti-Han racial feeling of the Uighur tribe in their favor.

It is said that anti-Maoists in the Southwest Bureau, which rules Szechwan Province, Kweichow Province, Yunnan Province, and the Tibet Autonomous Region, are led by Li Ching-chuan, first secretary; Li Ta-chang, secretary; and Liao Chih-kao, secretary of the bureau and first secretary of Szechwan Province. It has been revealed that authority-faction leaders in Szechwan Province were involved in a plot to effect an anti-Maoist coup d'état. There were also reports that rebellions had occurred in Kweichow and Yunnan. Yen Hung-yen, first secretary of the Yunnan Provincial Committee, was said to have committed suicide.

The greatest problem for the Mao-Lin group has been the authority faction in the Tibet Autonomous Region. The Panchen Lama—installed in power to replace the Dalai Lama, who fled to India when the Communist Chinese invested Tibet—has been severely criticized as a reactionary. Chang Kuo-hua, first secretary of the Tibet Autonomous Regional Committee, still remains in his post and is prominent as a leader of the authority faction in the area.

The indications are, Nakajima concluded, that the struggle for power resulting from the Cultural Revolution will go on for a considerable period of time in the provinces and frontier districts.

Chapter IV

REVOLUTION BY POSTER

NEWS ON THE WALL

Churo Nishimura remarked, after his return to Japan, that correspondents residing in Peking are viewing the Cultural Revolution "through the peephole of wall newspapers."

With access to the makers of news and policy virtually nonexistent, the wall newspaper or poster—the terms were used interchangeably in the press—was the principal source of information (or misinformation) available to outsiders on the progress of the Cultural Revolution. *Hsinhua,* called in English the New China News Agency, and such newspapers as *Jenmin Jih Pao*—People's Daily—maintained silence on the events that were rocking China and arousing the curiosity of the entire world. For many months, the international press depended for China news on the reports of Japanese correspondents to their organizations in Tokyo. The correspondents, in turn, were totally dependent for "hard news"—if that is what it was—on what was appearing from day to day in the wall posters.

The members of the Yomiuri Task Force, not being required to file day-to-day news developments, took an interest in how the Japanese reporters regularly assigned to Peking were doing their jobs. They made a practice of touring the city twice a day to read the wall posters. To avoid attracting attention, they wore Chinese clothes and shoes and jotted down their gleanings more or less surreptitiously with ball-point pens that sometimes froze in the cold weather. Their facility in reading Chinese gave them an advantage over the other foreign correspondents, many of whom had lost their Chinese assistants because of pressure by the Red Guards.

The *Yomiuri* travelers became equally fascinated by the famous wall posters. Takagi, for one, found them an endless fascination, giving the scene a life and color lacking in the Chinese press. "Day after day," he reported, "loudspeakers in the streets bellow 'Mao Tse-tung's thoughts.' When I switch on the television set, the screen only shows the world of smiling Mao attending a Red Guard rally in Peking's Tien An Men Square. I am completely isolated from any news in the true sense. *People's Daily* has lost its charm and vitality and has turned into a spiritless paper, a sort of civilian version of the *Liberation Army Daily*, printing news about a day old. And yet I am not lonely. I feel that I do not even want to bother myself reading a paper in China, because there is plenty of news out in the streets. One of the first things that come into view is the wall poster. The news in the wall poster is fresh and full of vitality compared with the spiritless and formularized presentation in the mass media.

The wall posters often say, "Let us bomb and kill the first secretary of the so-and-so province committee," or "So-and-so division chief of the party committee in such-and-such city is a degraded rightist." Some of the malicious posters are like the Japanese magazines that unashamedly exploit the scandals and private affairs of certain individuals. If one were to spend all day reading these posters, one would certainly not be bored. Whether the reports are true or false, one gets the feeling of looking at China in the naked state— the true "people's China," where the society has had its sur-

57

face skin peeled off, exposing the inside to the bright sun. It also seemed that the oppressed people were using the posters as a vent to release their frustrations.

Thanks to the wall posters, the reporters were able to obtain a close, speedy, wide, and vivid view of the recent movements in China. They felt that never before had news been so freely and openly offered since the "liberation," although released unofficially. The news of criticism and dismissals of men in high positions was inevitably reported first in the wall posters. It was the wall posters that reported the criticism and purge of the former mayor of Peking, Peng Chen; the self-criticism of President Liu Shao-chi; and the surprising downfall of Tao Chu, the propaganda chief who had been actively engaged in the Cultural Revolution.

"These wall posters do a thorough job of degrading and ridiculing those under attack," Kamai observed, describing how personal names were distorted into insulting shapes on some placards. For example, the name of Tao Chu was written with characters that are pronounced with the same sound—Tao Chu—but mean "swine."

It was also the wall posters that reported the details of the Party Central Committee meeting, although the news was about two or three months late. If it had not been for the wall posters put up by the Peking Red Guards, who maintain a direct link with the Party and the Mao-Lin Piao line, the details of the committee meetings would have been veiled in semipermanent secrecy.

DOWNFALL OF THE PRESS

Prior to the Cultural Revolution, the Japanese reported, *People's Daily*—in name and body—was the "textbook for the 700 million Chinese." The newspaper was virtually a guide to living. It would be an exaggeration to say that it was impossible to live in China unless one read *People's Daily*, but

the paper's daily editorials were used as instruction material for the workers' study classes in various organizations,
including factories and People's Communes. But the light
emitted by the "red lighthouse," as *People's Daily* was called,
was not that of the Red Sun—Mao's thoughts. Thus, whatever
People's Daily now reports is criticized or received skepti-
cally by readers. The paper is now in disgrace, without an
editorial of its own.

Takagi explained that the wall posters had displaced the
established organs as the public's chief source of news because almost all important posts in the mass communications
media—broadcasting, news services, and newspapers—were
occupied by men whom the Mao faction had denounced as
revisionists. Among these, Takagi mentioned an editor who
had been accused of combining two different photographs
to make it appear that Liu Shao-chi had stood next to Mao
at a function in Tien An Men Square.

Kamai came to the same conclusion. He reported that the
newspaper was frequently forced to issue a revised edition
after some of its items were pronounced "unsatisfactory" by
critics. Wu Leng-hsi, editor-in-chief of the paper, was
branded as a reactionary and relieved of his post because
People's Daily was connected directly with the Communist
Party's Propaganda Department, a citadel of the authority
faction. By the same token, some local newspapers were attacked by the pro-Mao faction as being under the control of
the first secretaries of the Communist Party's Provincial
Committees, which were considered strongholds of the authority faction.

According to Takagi, Mao's men judged that the established mass media could no longer serve the party. The
media would still remain as the party's official organs, but
they could not serve the purposes of Mao's faction because
the main power structure of these agencies was composed
of men supporting the ideology of Liu Shao-chi and Teng

Hsiao-ping. This is one of the reasons why wall posters put up by Red Guards are so widely used.

The standard media were eventually restored to their former function and place after Maoists had been put in control. Kamai described the contents of a typical issue of *People's Daily*, that of March 19, 1967. He said that the first page was devoted entirely to a letter sent by the Communist Party Central Committee to the revolutionary workers at factories and mines throughout the country, with a summary of the letter being printed in red ink on the upper half of the page and the full text in black ink on the lower half.

On page 2 was an editorial entitled "To Pay Respect to the Heroic Vietnamese People Engaged in a War"; there was an item, with a photograph, about the secretary-general of the New Zealand Communist Party leaving for his country after visiting Communist China; and there were articles about revolutionary and productive activities of the "production corps of workers" at a machine factory in Mukden and a plant in Nanking that makes machines used in sowing rice.

Page 3 carried the text of a wall poster displayed by revolutionary rebels at a boiler plant in Harbin, with an editor's note on the subject.

Pages 4 and 5 were devoted to stories on the international situation, and page 6 carried photographs showing how workers succeeded in carrying out the revolution and increasing production.

Chinese newspapers have no news pages, women's columns, or entertainment pages, and Kamai added that they do not carry advertisements. To his Japanese readers, Kamai reported that there are, of course, no "Help Wanted" in Chinese newspapers, and he noted that a Chinese woman who had visited Japan said that such a feature could not help people solve their problems.

The New China News Agency is closely associated with

People's Daily, and some reporters serve concurrently at both organizations. *People's Daily* has an editorial staff of 300, all university graduates, in addition to 300 reporters stationed at its local branch offices. The average salary is 103 yuan [$41.20] a month for reporters, and 55 yuan for workers in the printing shop.

The majority of Chinese reporters are university graduates with a bourgeois background, Kamai learned. During the Cultural Revolution, some of them have been attacked and purged for following a bourgeois line of thought. Kamai thought that some people from the families of peasants and laborers would become reporters and take over at newspaper offices in the future.

WEN TOU—THE LITERARY STRUGGLE

Takagi pointed out that the wall posters—*ta tzu pao* in Chinese—did not originate with the Red Guards, but have long been a feature of the Communist revolution. Since the birth of the Party, he said, the Chinese Communists have been effectively using wall posters as a revolutionary weapon. In his youth, Mao used them to solicit students for his Laborers' Night School. Posters are not necessarily put up by the Red Guard only. Any policy decision made by the Communist Party Central Committee is put up on the walls by the Party, and Government instructions are posted by the State Council.

One can say that the semipermanent posters bearing quotations from Mao and painted or engraved on plaques in the streets, hotel rooms, and airport lobbies are also a type of *ta tzu pao.* The only difference between ordinary wall posters and those containing Mao's sayings is that no one is allowed to criticize the latter. The public must absorb Mao's teachings into the heart and soul, like a radioactive substance, and digest them. Accordingly, the Mao posters do not conform with the popular concept of ordinary wall posters, but the fact that they appeal directly to the public shows that they have the same type of function.

On a walk in Kwangchow one day, Nishimura observed that among the multitude of slogans plastered on the walls along Peking Street—formerly Yung Han Avenue in pre-Communist days—the most numerous were "Long live Chairman Mao!" and "Long live the Chinese Communist Party!"

On each 5-meter section of walls there was an average of fifteen posters, he related in a dispatch to *Yomiuri*. Invariably, these two slogans were among the fifteen. The next most numerous slogans were "Let us walk together with the Communist Party!" and "Let us listen to Chairman Mao!" Two slogans appeared in pairs: "Long live Mao's thoughts, which lead us to victory!" and "Chairman Mao is the red sun of our hearts!"

Other slogans that frequently appeared on the walls were: "Unite our hearts to serve the people," "Industry and agriculture, arms and culture go together," "Let us all learn from the Liberation Army," "Consolidate the dictatorship of the proletariat," "Let us read Chairman Mao's books," "Let us materialize the thoughts of Mao," and "Raise high the great red flag of Mao's thoughts and carry out the proletarian revolution to the very end."

Other slogans had a broader outlook, such as "Keep the thoughts of your homeland in your heart and direct your eyes to the world."

Judging by the nature of these slogans, Nishimura concluded that the overt purpose of the Cultural Revolution was "Give your life to the people and serve the Communist Party loyally while studying the thoughts of Mao Tse-tung!"

These slogans frankly state what the Party wants from

its people in the Cultural Revolution, aside from the struggle for power in the political hierarchy.

Takagi explained how the wall posters served an important function in the Maoist revolution. He explained that there is a Chinese term, *wen tou*, which means "literary struggle." Compared with *wu tou*—armed struggle—*wen tou* uses persuasion as its weapon. Therefore the wall posters are the backbone and main weapon of Mao's "mass line," which relies strongly on mass mobilization. The *Yomiuri* reporter quoted Mao: "The fact that there are varying opinions among the masses is fundamentally a normal phenomenon. We not only cannot avoid the clash of opinions, but such disputes are necessary and beneficial. Through moral debates, the masses will come to grasp the truth, rectify their errors, and gradually come to adopt a unified view. . . . There is the possibility that on some occasions the minority will have the truth in their hands. Because of this, even if the minority opinion is in the wrong, we must allow them to explain their views and also allow them to reserve their own opinions."

When he saw the deluge of wall posters on the streets, Takagi noticed that there were an extraordinary number of what Mao calls varying opinions. This type of phenomenon —differences of opinion—could hardly be expected in China's normal mass media, which serve as the Communist Party's organ. Indeed, the walls of Chinese streets seemed to be alive with varying disputes and many ideas.

Takagi found that the wall posters were not confined to criticisms of anti-Party activities and bourgeois elements. Wall posters have criticized Premier Chou and even Mao. He mulled over this problem and came to the following conclusions: There are 90 members of the Communist Party Central Executive Committee. Among these members, more than 70 had at one time or another been criticized by wall posters. Does this mean that the remaining 20 members are "pure" followers of Mao Tse-tung? Not necessarily so, he thought. It is easy to become the target of criticism if one actively engages in Party work. Those who escaped criticism probably have done nothing and probably are incapable of doing anything, or, he speculated, they could be opportunists.

BELIEF AND DISBELIEF

A Chinese whom Takagi met on the street, who appeared to be a skeptic, told him that there are many influential politicians who are one time or another attacked by the posters. But in many cases, wall posters criticizing these people were later replaced by posters supporting them. And after that, criticisms against these politicians gradually disappeared from the posters. Therefore, it cannot be concluded that any person attacked by wall posters would automatically be purged. As long as "disputes of varying opinions" are recognized in China, and as long as this principle remains the very backbone of wall posters, it is not impossible to express opinions opposing the reports made by the posters. Moreover, excluding decisions made by the Party Central Committee, it is common practice in China to criticize reports of posters, counter-criticize, and then explain the reasons why the reports created such a controversy.

This made sense to Takagi because he believed that in any society, be it free or socialist, the iron rule of news reporting is based on the absolute necessity for recipients to have faith in the sources releasing the news. This is more true in socialist countries, where all reporting is controlled by the Government. Unless the people have absolute faith in mass media, in this case wall posters, the Government cannot be expected to carry out political and social programs smoothly.

Not everyone Takagi met casually seemed to take the wall posters so seriously. One day when he was engrossed in one of the wall posters, a kindly-looking man came up to him and offered some advice: "Don't believe it! It is all rumor."

"It is?" asked the reporter.

"Yes. It's got to be a rumor. Tomorrow there will probably be another poster criticizing this," he said.

"But I still think it is interesting," answered Takagi.

"It might be interesting for foreigners, but these reports are either groundless or exaggerated. If one of the Red Guards cuts his finger in a minor clash, they will report the fracas the next day as a bloody tragedy," the man said.

The correspondent wondered who this middle-aged man, dressed in civilian clothing, could be, and wondered if he might perhaps be a schoolteacher "walking the path of capitalism," angry because he could be criticized any day by his students.

Takagi pointed out that the wall posters had various purposes, which sometimes could be distinguished by the color of the paper on which they were written. Red and pink paper were used for a type of poster called *hai pao,* meaning "to inform widely," containing instructions and notices issued by the Communist Party and its organs. Another kind for which red paper was used was called *hsi pao* —"good news." Takagi saw accounts of Communist China's successful nuclear tests in the *hsi pao.* He said he would probably classify the *hai pao* and *hsi pao* in the category of "special" wall posters, for no one is allowed to criticize them.

Some posters, he reported, are used for more practical purposes, such as those asking for information about missing children and lost articles, or those stating that "the headquarters of the So-and-so County Red Guards has moved to Such-and-such a place." In any event, he added, every wall in China, it seems, is plastered with posters of one type or another.

He noted that the posters in Hsian were particularly elaborate. Some of them covered the entire walls up to the second and third floor of multistory apartment buildings. The people who plastered them on the walls probably had a difficult time doing so, but he thought that those who must scrape them off will have even a harder time.

Takagi was taken aback at the bloodthirsty sentiments expressed on the Hsian posters, in characters often as large as two feet square, so that they could be read from passing vehicles. The placards attacking Liu Lantao, first secretary of the Northwest Bureau of the Chinese Communist Party, were emblazoned with demands to "burn him at the stake ... bombard him ... decapitate him and display his head to the public. ..." "The words alone are enough to make any timid person faint with fear," Takagi observed, and then he said, "Below these large posters are the smaller ones. Groups of people wearing clothes made of cotton material cluster in front of these like flies." In an open square near the apartment building, Takagi noted groups of Red Guards holding discussions in large circles, probably criticizing the articles in the wall posters; this has become part of their "study" and "exchange of experiences."

Wall posters were found by the newsmen in every village, however small, at People's Communes, and in factories. When Takagi visited a factory in Shanghai, he was overwhelmed by the display of posters on every wall and partition—wherever there was a flat vertical surface. All of the posters that he saw contained criticisms against factory officials' work and their private lives.

Some of the posters urged the workers to purge undesirables, and to Takagi a dark and oppressive atmosphere seemed to envelop the place.

Generally, it was apparent to the reporter that the Chinese people took a dim view of foreigners reading the posters. Yet, when the Chinese read them, they obviously became unusually excited. Actually, the reporter felt that each item on the posters affected the daily lives of the readers.

But when a foreigner read the posters with a gleam of curiosity in his eyes, the Japanese saw Chinese sneer with obvious distaste. Their expressions suggested that of a man who has caught a stranger stealthily reading one of his private, secret letters. The newsmen could only guess that the Chinese do not want the foreigners to know about any important happenings in their country.

This conclusion seemed to have been confirmed by Premier Chou En-lai, who issued a public denunciation of foreign correspondents who sent the contents of the posters abroad. After Chou's statement it became dangerous for the Japanese reporters to be seen reading the posters, and for a while the Tokyo news media used much less material from this source.

Chapter V

YOUTH ARMY OF THE REVOLUTION

**"LET'S GO TO PEKING WITH TEA LEAVES
ON OUR BACKS"**

Within minutes of their arrival in Peking on the freezing
New Year's Day of 1967, the *Yomiuri* travelers were exercis-
ing their command of the Chinese language among the Red
Guards who thronged the Tien An Men Square.

Residents shivered in the cold wind, with the temperature
at four degrees below zero (Fahrenheit), but the Tien An
Men Square, the mecca of the Red Guards, was teeming with
youth.

During the peak of the Red Guard pilgrimage to Peking,
several months earlier, millions of youths were said to have
occupied the capital. Unable to find lodging in the already
crowded civilian homes, schools, and apartment buildings,
they set up shacks in all parts of the city.

In the terraced gardens that had been the sanctuary of
Ching Dynasty royalty, and on the marble steps where only
the ancient Emperors had been allowed to walk, there were
piles of rush mats and bamboo poles that had been used to
build shacks.

One of the newsmen stopped a troupe of Red Guard

youths about 15 or 16 years of age and asked them where they had come from.

One replied, "From Changchun." Another said, "I come from Shanghai." A third replied, "I walked all the way from Wuhan." Then they asked his nationality. Judging from the way the youngsters crowded around him on being told that he was Japanese, the reporter thought that he was the first foreigner any of them had ever seen.

One youth boldly looked into his notebook as he made a note. In a surprised voice, he said, "Oh, this Japanese can write Chinese!" They probably did not know that the Japanese use Chinese characters.

The Red Guards paid their respects to the "foreign guest who speaks Chinese" by taking off their much-cherished Mao badges and pinning them to his coat. By the time he was ready to leave China, the foreigner had been presented with a sizable collection of the tiny badges, each bearing a printed photo of Mao.

Everywhere the Japanese went they found Red Guard Youths on the march, shouting praises of Mao, covering the walls with their blood-thirsty posters attacking the authority faction and revisionists.

Takuzo Kamai, the *Yomiuri* expert on agricultural communes, traveled to Kwangchow on a train filled with Red Guards.

They were all singing happily, he reported. The tunes were folk songs of Hunan, Manchuria, and other districts, like "Let's Go to Peking with Tea Leaves on Our Backs." It was a beautiful day, and he thoroughly enjoyed basking in the sun pouring through the train windows and listening to the rustic tunes. But he was in for a big shock.

The moment he got off the train at Kwangchow, he saw wall posters written in characters measuring about 60 square centimeters, saying "Bomb the Provincial Commission Office" and "Burn Chao Tzu-yang to Death." The posters were pasted on the walls next to red and purple placards bearing names like "Iron Army of the Central and South China Revolutionary Rebels," "Unit of the Chinese Academy of Sciences Dispatched to the South," and other organizations with equally stirring titles.

He had heard about what was going on in Kwangchow, but it was not until he arrived on this "battlefield" of the Red Guards that he felt the tense atmosphere and understood the importance of their role as standard-bearers of the Cultural Revolution.

In the same city, a Communist shrine, the site of the Peasant Movement Training Center that had been operated by Mao in his youth, was teeming with Red Guards who assembled there from distant provinces.

Here again Nishimura, head of the *Yomiuri* group, was surrounded by a crowd. A girl who claimed that she had walked to Kwangchow all the way from Shanghai spoke to the first foreigner she had ever met in a shy manner but in precise, beautiful Peking dialect.

Nishimura asked her, "When did you leave home? Did not your parents object to your making the trip?"

"No, they just told me to be careful," she said.

"How much money did you bring with you?" he asked.

"My parents gave me fifteen yuan [$6]," she replied.

"I also left home with fifteen yuan," said another youth.

"My parents gave me twenty yuan," said another.

"Did you receive anything from the Government?" asked the reporter.

"I received a subsidy of seven yuan," she said.

"Where did you lodge on your trip up here?"

"At the Red Guard reception center in the People's Communes. They were very kind. We also helped the farmers in the fields and cleaned the rooms and adhered to the Three Main Rules for Discipline and the Eight Points for Attention, which are the guidelines for the workers, the peasants, and the Red Army," the girl replied.

Nishimura explained that the Three Rules and the Eight Points the girls had faithfully observed during their trip were the golden rules established forty years ago by Mao Tse-tung for his revolutionary army.

The rules, made to establish unity and coordination between the revolutionists and the masses, included these: Do not take a single needle or piece of thread from the masses; pay fairly for what you buy, and return everything you borrow. Following these rules, the Red Guards have been welcome throughout rural China, the Japanese were told.

On a trip to Tsung Hua, about 100 kilometers [60 miles] north of Kwangchow, groups of thirty to fifty Red Guards were seen walking along the road in columns. In each half-mile or so there were three or four such groups, some walking away from Kwangchow in a northerly direction and some walking toward the city via Tsung Hua. Some of the groups consisted only of girls.

With a red flag heading the column, these children, holding Mao's book in hand and carrying their bedding on their backs, sometimes walk 1,000 to 2,000 kilometers [600 to 1,200 miles] wearing rubber shoes.

They walk and walk, trying to experience the hardships of the peasants, workers, and soldiers who walked and fought their way on the Long March from Juichen, Kiangsi Province, to northern Shensi Province in a period of about one year.

When Nishimura first encountered the Red Guards, he had thought them "cute and innocent and in high spirits," but as he saw more of the movement its character seemed to change for the Japanese observer.

He talked with a Red Guard who told him that he had just arrived in Kwangchow after leaving Shanghai on foot two months before. Grabbing the reporter by the arm, he said proudly:

"I have climbed mountains and crossed many rivers while walking south from Shanghai for the past two months. The impression I received during my long trek was that China, indeed, is a big country. Everywhere I went, even in the remote provinces, I saw the bust of Chairman Mao, greeting me warmly and encouragingly. It was the first time in my life that I had ever left my home town. And now I am filled with pride for my great fatherland."

"When this boy grows older and reaches the prime of adulthood, I wonder what kind of 'great country' China will be," Nishimura mused in print after recounting this incident. "What merits or faults the Cultural Revolution has I do not know. But I recall gazing at this boy's face with a feeling close to fear."

RED STUDENTS IN BLUE-BLOOD SCHOOLS

According to official history, the Red Guard movement began as a student rebellion at Peking and Chinghua universities. The reporters learned that these top schools had been attacked as cultivating farms for bourgeois and rightist elements.

It is said that only one out of thirty applicants is accepted at these universities. Competition to enter well-known schools is much tougher, it seems, in China than in Japan, *Yomiuri* reported to its readers. College entrance examinations are held in unison throughout the country, and the top scorers are "distributed" to the universities of their choice.

Those doing badly in the entrance examinations are not even allowed to enroll in second- or third-choice universities. Therefore, middle schools or high schools sending the largest number of graduates to Peking and Chinghua become "blue-blood" schools, a situation similar to that in

Japan. In unrestricted student competition, the children of the bourgeois and intellectual classes will naturally have an advantage over those from labor and farm areas.

Therefore, it was only natural, said the authorities, for public opinion in a socialistic society to demand educational priority for the children of farmers, laborers, and soldiers of the Liberation Army. According to this value system, Peking University under the policy set by President Lu Ping had been run on an outdated, feudalistic system. It was considered a "blue-blood school," which placed a one-sided emphasis on knowledge, was strongly conscious of its elitism, and, to anyone who regarded the school through the looking-glass of Maoism, walked the bourgeois line.

Hence it became necessary in Mao-land that there should be a counteroffensive by the proletarian revolutionary students against President Lu and the reactionary instructors who had tried to make Peking University into a stronghold for intellectuals.

President Lu had been the target of criticism several times in the past, but he had managed to suppress the critics by the force of his authority. And then came Miss Nieh Yuantsu and her six comrades, who exposed his organized plot. Miss Nieh Yuan-tsu is one of the heroines of the Great Proletarian Cultural Revolution. She became famous as the woman who put up the first wall poster during the cultural purge. She is an assistant professor in the university's philosophy department and also secretary of the Peking University Communist Party. Miss Nieh criticized the university president as "a typical example of a stubborn, anti-revolutionary fortress."

This exposé appeared on the first wall poster of the Cultural Revolution, which Miss Nieh and her comrades put up in defiance of the authority faction—Liu Shao-chi supporters —who had virtual control of the campus.

These seven people are stout-hearted revolutionists, the

73

reporter thought. But later he learned that he had been too hasty in concluding that this "heroic" deed of putting up the poster had been done voluntarily and at the sole will of the seven people. Later reports revealed that it was not Miss Nieh's original idea to put up the wall poster, but that Mao Tse-tung had personally summoned Miss Nieh and instructed her to criticize President Lu publicly.

This is the story that Mao himself gave to the Communist Party Central Operations Council meeting held six months later, according to an informed source. If this is true, it means that when there were rumors that Mao had been taken seriously ill, he in fact was in the pink of condition and leading the Cultural Revolution.

On the night that the poster criticizing President Lu was put up, the seven comrades held a meeting with the revolutionary members of the philosophy department, at which they were attacked by supporters of President Lu. The authority-faction members, not knowing that the criticism had been made at the direct order of Mao, stormed the meeting.

The following day, *Jenmin Jih Pao* [*People's Daily*] ran an editorial supporting the wall poster's criticism of Peking University. Later, the Communist Party sent a task force to the university. It is said that Mao knew nothing about the dispatch of the task force. In any event, the arrival of the task force, Chairman Mao's personal envoys, changed the entire situation at the university. This time it was the followers of Lu and the authority faction who were persecuted.

These people were forced to wear dunce caps and were dragged about the campus. One week later, Lu was discharged from the post of university president.

It was not clear whether Mao had anything directly to do with the posters that appeared at the Chinghua middle school, reported Takagi. But the fact that Mao later wrote a letter to the school's Red Guard students implies that the posters at this, another "blue-blooded" school, had some authority. Also, in reviewing the various incidents that took place at the school, it can be assumed that students of Chinghua University had some kind of contact with their Peking counterparts.

The first Chinghua poster denounced the middle-school principal, Wan Man-chou, who was identified as coming from the landlord class, Takagi related. It was said that Wan had always hampered the revolutionary students' studies of Mao Tse-tung's works and had suppressed revolutionary ideas.

But the young principal, 38 years old, did not just sit back and meekly take the attack from the posters. After all, he was also a member of the Communist Party's Chinghua University committee. He threatened to expel the students responsible for the posters, signed by the "Federation of Communist Youths."

The students fought back and put up another poster saying, "Let us become Red Guards, the organization which will protect Chairman Mao and smash revisionist and reactionary elements."

The call to organize Red Guards evoked an enthusiastic response from the students. A group of forty Red Guards was organized immediately. This was on May 29, 1966. And this was the birth of the movement, which spread rapidly to schools and universities throughout China.

The mistreatment of school dignitaries, many of whom were known personally to Japanese academic leaders, shocked the scholarly community of Japan. Respect for intellectual rank is deeply ingrained in the Japanese mind through the nation's Confucian tradition, and the university president in Japan is an awesome figure. Professor Yuji Muramatsu, a specialist in Asian—especially Communist Chinese—economic studies at the prestigious Hitotsubashi University in Tokyo, reported on the fate of some of his colleagues in the *Yomiuri* dispatches. One of them was Wang Tao, president

75

of Tungchi University in Shanghai, which was founded in 1915 and was known for its high academic standards in civil engineering, science, and medicine. Wang is still allowed to report for work at the university, Professor Muramatsu found, but he is not permitted to perform his duties as president. His daily routine is to lock himself in his office and spend his day studying the works of Mao Tse-tung. Occasionally he mops his room and corridors, for the sake of exercise. The Japanese educator visited Tungchi University and interviewed about a dozen students belonging to the *Tung Fang Hung* [East Is Red] Red Guard Corps at the university library for about three hours. The following is the students' account of why Wang was denounced as a reactionary:

"Wang, who also served as the first secretary of the Communist Party's university committee, attached too much importance to the teaching of specialized subjects and ignored moral and physical education.

"He failed to recognize the superiority of Mao Tse-tung's thought, and refused to follow the principle that politics takes precedence over the sciences.

"Wang also failed to give precedence to the children of peasant soldiers when selecting students for admission to the university. Instead, he used applicants' scholastic records as the basis for selection. The result was that youths with a bourgeois background constituted the majority of the students enrolled.

"Wang should have carried out a sweeping reform, reorganizing the curriculum along the lines of Mao's thoughts. Instead, he chose to retain Soviet and American elements in the curriculum. As a result, the university tended to follow the reactionary and revisionist lines of thought. The difference between the bourgeois, reactionary, and revisionist type of education and the revolutionary, orthodox, and "reactionary rebel" variety is that the former is not based on

76

the superiority of Mao thought," the Red Guards explained.

Muramatsu noted that the Chinese Communist Party had repeatedly instructed students in Shanghai to criticize the traditional type of university education since about June 1966. The students of Tungchi University had launched the drive against the university authorities shortly after a similar campaign was started at Peking University.

The mushrooming of Red Guard units following the attacks on the schools was accompanied by demands for widespread educational reforms, and one of the first was for elimination of the entrance examination system. Takagi, who had spent so much time investigating Mao's childhood, surmised that some of Mao's sympathy for youthful opposition to the entrance examination system came from memories of his own difficulty in obtaining admission to middle school. Takagi thought that this was one of the reasons why he promoted a reform of the Chinese educational system after students of the Peking No. 1 Girls' Middle School wrote him in a letter in June 1966 demanding changes. The letter said (according to Takagi's translation):

"The present school entrance system places emphasis on educating only talented students. It only serves to revive capitalism. It has become a tool in forging the new bourgeois elements—the bookworms who are only interested in passing examinations."

The coeds' letter contained three proposals:

"Abolish from this year the reactionary school entrance system, which resembles the civil service examinations of the Ching Dynasty.

"Senior middle-school students should become laborers, farmers, and soldiers, and study these trades before advancing to universities or special colleges.

"If universities and special colleges can accept only a limited number of new students this year, the Party central should take direct charge of the entrance examinations and

77

select only 'sound-minded' students from among senior middle-school graduates."

Mao had spent a good part of his revolutionary life as an educator. Therefore, Takagi felt that the complaints contained in the coeds' letter must have hit a harmonious chord in his concept of education.

Mao immediately instructed the Party's Central Committee and the State Council to postpone school entrance examinations. A week later, the Government abolished the examination system completely. Almost all students supported this action. At the time the decision was announced, a mass of middle-school students triumphantly paraded in front of Peking's Tien An Men Square, carrying Mao's bust and placards reading, "*Shuang hei* [double joy]!"

Mao and the middle- and high-school pupils agreed completely on questions concerning the revolution in education. The Red Guards say that they will do "anything that Mao tells us," and Takagi thought that these fanatic followers of Mao have good reason for respecting the man.

HEAVEN-SENT CHILDREN

Takagi devoted considerable time to the history, motivation, and activities of the young Maoists, who were the most visible symbols of the Cultural Revolution. The Red Guards are said to arm themselves with the thoughts of Mao so that they can protect the Mao Tse-tung structure with their lives. "Any person who opposes Chairman Mao, however important and powerful he may be, will be burned to death," the Red Guards say. It was terrifying to Takagi to learn that these youths actually mean what they say. They really mean that their opponents should be burned to death physically.

The Red Guards are called Chairman Mao's "heaven-sent children." But the internationally accepted theory that innocent teen-agers were organized by Mao and his supporters

78

to be used as tools in the power struggle and as a weapon to smash the enemy is not entirely true, Takagi thought.

Nor did he subscribe to Defense Minister Lin Piao's theory that the Red Guards resulted spontaneously from public opinion. The first wall poster, at least, was written by Mao and was displayed at his direct instruction. It was this wall poster that spurred the birth of Red Guard organizations.

But the *Yomiuri* reporter did come to believe that their movement was rooted in seventeen or eighteen years of nourishment on Mao's thoughts, and he found this reflected in their credo.

The "Red Guard Ordinance" was announced on wall posters put up by the "Red Guard Struggle Committee" and said, "Raise high the great red flag of Mao Tse-tung's thought! Our actions must all conform with Mao's thoughts. We must stoutly defend Chairman Mao, the Party Central Committee and the proletarian dictatorship. We must become the red successors of the proletariat."

The most important things for the Red Guards are duty and purpose, which are defined as follows:

"First, struggle; second, criticize, and third, reform. Support the countries helping Vietnam fight against the United States, and build a new world by destroying all types of imperialism and revisionism."

It is only natural that there should be some excesses on the part of the Red Guards, it seemed to Takagi, considering the fact that they have nothing to fear and no one to stop their activities, which have been sanctioned by the "god of the revolution," Mao Tse-tung.

The membership of the "rebel forces" of the Red Guards was originally limited to children of those belonging to the Five Red Classes—workers, farmers, military men, revolutionary officials, and revolutionary heroes. The restriction was later eased, although no one whose parents or friends were counterrevolutionaries is allowed to become a member.

Membership is decided by the respective Red Guard organizations after the applications of prospective members are submitted to "mass discussion."

The average age of the Red Guard youths is 17. This means that most of them were born the year China was liberated, the year the People's Government was born under the direction of Mao Tse-tung and the Communist Party. They learned about the revolutionary war while they were still in their mothers' wombs, for their mothers, at the time of birth, were already working members of the socialist society.

As children, they might have been sent to a nursery where the governess was a veteran hard-core Communist who had fought in underground activities for the Party. Here they would have received instructions on the socialist ways of life from the age of three. And from primary school to middle school they would have been brought up in the fertile soil of Mao's thoughts, which provide the guidelines for education in the new China. Takagi commented that this educational system devised by Mao was, for its purpose, ideal.

The completion of the man-molding structure directly contributed to the birth of the Red Guards, he said. It is in this sense, he pointed out, that the Red Guards are indisputably the product of Mao's thoughts.

LITTLE RED ARMY

Several of the *Yomiuri* team discussed the pattern of youthful involvement in Chinese history. They commented that it is traditional in China for youths to take part in social and political revolutions and reformations and reminded their readers that China has developed tradition and concepts differing from those of other countries.

When the Nationalist Government was formed, the Three-Principle Youth Corps was organized, and the member youths took part in propaganda activities for the "People's New Livelihood" movement. There were other youth organizations that did social welfare work.

When Mao Tse-tung established the government of the Chinese Soviet Republic, teen-agers played more important roles in revolutionary activities. In the Long March from Kiangsi to Yenan, about four hundred youngsters ranging in age from 8 to 15 followed Mao and the Red Army. They worked in communications, as health and hygiene personnel, as messengers, cooks, secretaries, and buglers. They are said to have worked even harder than the adults. Mao had a 16-year-old orderly named Chen Chang-feng. The energy these youths displayed in their work boosted the morale of the adults, who affectionately called them *hsiao kuei* [little devils], *hsiao hungkuei* [little red devils] or *hsiao hungchun* [little red army].

Takagi recalled an incident described by Edgar Snow, the famous American writer on China, in which youths on guard duty refused to let Peng Teh-huai, vice commander of the 18th Army, continue on his way without a pass. After arguing to no avail, Peng had to write out a pass for himself before the youngsters would let him proceed.

Eventually, in the Hsiapei Soviet district, Takagi learned that there were 40,000 members of the Communist Youth League, the Youth Advance Guard Corps, and boys ranging in age from 11 to 17 years, who had participated in the Long March and were later assigned to various military installations of the Eighth Route Army.

Thus, the traditional combination of youth and revolution was maintained. It seemed to Takagi that the Chinese Communists have a special fondness for youth. On the other hand, the young people also love the Red Army and find profound happiness in being treated as adults, or "human equals" of the soldiers.

Most of these boys were the sons of tenant farmers and

81

peasants, and from the day of their birth they had been treated as just another annoyance to the family. They had had to work like horses or oxen for the landlords. From such a downtrodden existence, therefore, it was only natural that they would do their best when they went into the army and were treated like human beings.

HEIRS OF THE REVOLUTION

Younger children have also been organized and indoctrinated in Communist China.

Takagi studied the influence of the nationwide organization, the Child Vanguards, and commented that with their red neckerchiefs they are a familiar sight in Communist China. There are supposed to be 50,000,000 of them throughout the country. The Cultural Revolution led to the disintegration of the Communist Youth Corps, which had guided the Child Vanguards, but the latter organization survived the upheaval, being absorbed into the younger Red Guard groups. The members are now engaging in revolutionary activities more strenuously than ever before.

The history of the Child Vanguards can be traced to the time of the First Internal War—or Revolution—of 1921–1927, when working children's groups were organized in the cities of Wuhan and Hangchow and in the Provinces of Hunan, Hupei, and Kiangsi. These grew into the Communist Children's Groups in the areas under Communist control. During the war against Japan, the Children's Groups and Child Vanguard chapters were established and their members, carrying spears with red tassels, performed sentry and other duties in the Communist-held areas.

Immediately after the Communist regime came to power —on October 13, 1949—these groups were merged into a new national organization called the Chinese Children's Corps. It was renamed the Chinese Child Vanguard Corps in June 1953. For the subsequent thirteen years until the outbreak of the Cultural Revolution, the Corps strove to produce revolutionary children, called "heirs of the revolution."

Chairman Mao has defined the juvenile activities as part of the revolutionary mass movement, Takagi reported. Mao set forth the fundamental principles of child training with the statement that "it is necessary to unify children through the process of the revolutionary movement, and to harden them through education." The statement continued: "Juvenile organizations are schools where children learn Communism. These organizations must grow into large and powerful groups through the process of struggle. We must strive to improve the character, knowledge, and physical constitutions of children in an aggressive and animated manner and lead them to become workers endowed with social consciousness and knowledge. We must produce heirs of the proletarian revolution by strengthening the class consciousness of youths and children."

Kamai also took note of this ideological mobilization of young people. He wrote that while attending primary school, or serving as members of the Child Vanguard Corps, Communist Chinese children learned that their expected goal is "to work for Communism and for the great task of the fatherland." This principle is set forth in two basic education manuals, "Regulations for Primary School Pupils" and "Regulations for Middle School Children."

When they joined the Communist Youth Corps at age 16, they applied themselves to the study of such "textbooks" as *Twelve Chapters for Youths* and ideological guides like *The Communist Party Manifesto* and *Selected Works of Mao Tse-tung*. In a word, they were trained to become qualified as "assistants to members of the Communist Party."

In the current Cultural Revolution, the Communist Youth Corps has been reviled on the ground that it had become a

83

tool of the authority faction. The same fate overtook the Communist Party leadership that had guided the Corps. Until then, however, the C.Y.C. had been a powerful organization with a nationwide membership of 22,000,000, formed around an inner core of 1,300,000. It was considered to be the highest honor for a youth to enter the corps. To be a member was as much distinction as belonging to the Communist Party for an adult.

The C.Y.C. had a network of branches in the universities— the corps committees, the offices established in all departments of each university, and the corps chapters set up in all classes. The C.Y.C. branch office, the Communist Party, and the school authorities formed a trinity to train and educate students along the Communist line of thought.

GOOD GRADES FOR ALL

Takagi collected a number of anecdotes to illustrate the effect of Maoist education on the young people of mainland China.

In the Second Company of the Child Vanguard Corps at the Touyatsaihutung Primary School in Peking, he was told, there were many naughty children who took delight in playing jokes. They often embarrassed teachers by setting other children to laughing during lessons. The harrassed instructors asked the advice of the sober-minded committee members of the Child Vanguard company. The committee suggested that all children in the school join in cultivating the habit of observing classroom discipline. The children agreed that they would refrain from laughing uproariously during classes and would not play jokes while lessons were going on and that offenders would be sent before the committee. The committee members began their drive for better discipline by helping their less capable classmates. Some would sharpen pencils for them during recesses. To improve the habits of absent-minded children, committee members would leave notes in their pencil cases, such as: "Tomorrow we have a lesson in drawing, so please do not forget to bring coloring materials." Children with poor scholastic records were helped in their studies by the company commander, who was chosen for this post by his classmates.

After a year of hard work to reform the "bad" and "lazy" children, the class gained a reputation for good work. Chinese children are taught that they should not be concerned solely with their own school records. Sacrificing their own time, the more successful students remain in classrooms after school and help duller children with their homework. They take the attitude that it serves less purpose if they alone do well in studies, so they are determined to improve the performance of the entire class.

Chairman Mao has popularized a slogan, *Sanhao* [good in three things]—*shenti-hao* [good in physical condition], *hauesi-hao* [good in studies], and *kungtsuohao* [good in manual labor]. Children are told that if a person hardens his body and becomes strong and healthy, he will also do well in his studies; if he does well in his studies, he will do well in manual labor.

Here again, *sanhao* is a goal set for groups, not for individuals, Takagi pointed out. He was told that unless a group as a whole attains *sanhao*, it is meaningless. Emphasis is always placed on groups rather than on individuals, and society rather than one's self. Sober-minded Communist Chinese children, living in groups, make it a point to teach and train each other.

These observations recalled to Takagi a significant statement by Mao when he called for reform of the school examination system. "The present system leaves much to be desired," Mao said. "The teachers present problems and each student gives his own answers. The teacher gives good marks to students who turn in good papers. This means that good papers are monopolized by a few bright students and will not be shared by all. From now on, good papers should be shown to all students during the examination so that everyone in the class can produce ideal work. This is the way that people in a socialist country should engage in studies."

For the benefit of his Japanese readers, who belong to a nation that historically has been deeply interested in educational methods, the *Yomiuri* correspondent interpreted Mao's statement into clearer language.

"It may sound as though the Chairman himself were openly encouraging students to cheat in examinations, but that is not the case," Takagi explained. "If Mao's idea is carried out, there will no longer be the pitiful sight of a student watching for a chance to crib. Nor will there be a student locking himself in his room and cramming for exams with a wet towel around his head."

Among Chinese children there is a widespread belief that the individual should give priority to the public interest, above his own. It must also be noted that the Chinese people have a long-established principle that their children have a duty to serve the general good.

Consequently, boys and girls wearing the red neckerchief of the Child Vanguards are often seen giving their seats to old people in buses and trolleys, or carrying heavy packages for elderly women. Child Vanguards of the Panchang-huting Primary School in Peking appear every day at the Tsienmen bus depot and assist the depot employes in washing the vehicles. The children are never paid for this work.

One day, the Yomiuri Task Force went from the central part of Wuhan to the city's steel complex. As they were about to board a ferry, a Pioneer—the equivalent of a Boy Scout—offered to carry Takagi's heavy traveling bag, and he carried it from the time they boarded the ferry until they caught the bus for the steel mills. Takagi asked if he had been assigned to guide them. "No," the boy answered, "I just wanted to assist you because you are an elderly man."

During his trip across the Chinese mainland, Takagi wrote, he heard from a few Chinese friends that the Cultural Revolution had brought about a revolution in their own homes. Their sons and daughters took leave from their schools and went on long trips to various districts, together with many other children. They came home as changed persons. As they had traveled in large groups, they learned to take care of themselves, without help from their elders. They acquired the habit of doing everything they could for themselves, so that when they came home their parents no longer had to spend time looking after their children. "This kind of discipline cannot be acquired merely by reading books in schools," a friend said.

"So what if the children lose a year of schooling?" the reporters were told. "They are learning from the revolution something that they will never acquire at school." "In today's China," another reporter remarked, "one cannot even take the children lightly any more."

TO "SERVE THE PUBLIC"

To us in the Free World, Takagi commented, it seems that these youths are "being used as tools for politics." But in China, youth is considered the dynamic force and the inheritor of revolution. This is why they are so meticulously trained and are allowed to engage in political activities. *People's Daily* often describes these youngsters as the "little generals of revolution." This description, I believe, is not meant as flattery, but expresses the true feeling of the adults.

The Red Guard young people have practiced and promoted the Cultural Revolution. In so doing, they may have gone to extremes and committed some errors. But their achievements serve as an indication that Communist China, following Chairman Mao's principles of juvenile education, has succeeded in producing "socialistic men."

The effectiveness of the training was demonstrated by an episode a few years ago, when the Shanghai College of Transportation asked its students to list the occupations they preferred. Instead of showing a preference for any particular jobs, 23 students averred that they would go happily to the most distant places to take on the most difficult tasks that must be carried out to achieve the revolution and socialist construction. Students of one class pledged themselves to "strive to remake mountains and rivers that have been won with the blood shed in the revolution."

These youths are so earnest and sincere that one cannot simply write off their actions by saying that they are being subjected to standardization of thought, the reporter said.

Takuzo Kamai, the economic correspondent of *Yomiuri* on the China Task Force, was equally impressed by the young people of all ages who seemed sincere in their desire to further Mao's goals of revolution. He asked each of a group of high-school students in Peking, "What would you like to be?"

A girl said, "Since I was in middle school I have cherished a dream of joining the Liberation Army. If possible, I want to become a surgeon and be like the Canadian doctor, Norman Bethune, who dedicated his life to strengthening ties between nations."

"I would like to enter the Liberation Army, too," said a boy. "I want to take up a gun and overthrow American imperialism."

"I would like to be a scientist," said another boy. "My ambition is to build the highest level of science in the world and teach a lesson to the Soviet revisionists who are elated because they have succeeded in flying space ships."

"I want to become a farmer and build new farms against the backdrop of China's great landscape," a girl said.

A boy declared, "I want to follow the example of Tai Yung-yang and many other heroes and sacrifice my life for my fatherland without fear."

One of the Japanese university professors who was with Kamai marveled at these youngsters and said that they reminded him of students in the military preparatory schools of prewar Japan.

Kamai put the same questions to Red Guard university students in Wuhan, to get the reactions of an older section of Chinese youth. The first answer came from a third-year medical student, the son of an office worker.

"I would like very much to engage in agriculture and assist peasants and middle-class farmers," he said. "But I am not interested in studying a specialized subject at the university hospital after finishing the undergraduate course."

Said a peasant's daughter, who had been working as a nurse since her graduation from a nurses' training institute three years before, "I want to do my best to serve the people, and that is the only thing that occupies my mind. Nurses were despised in bygone years. But we now live in an age when nurses are credited with doing an important work."

"I wish I could go to Peking and meet Chairman Mao, as students do," said a female store clerk in Shanghai. "But we are not supposed to leave our posts until we are ordered to do so by the central Government. Unlike students, we have our job to engage in production and carry out the revolution at our places of employment."

These statements indicated to Kamai that the young people of China have been taught to serve the public—and that this goal is based firmly on their clear-cut ideas of the fatherland, the classes, and the people. They personify the idea expressed in Chinese by the term *po szu li kung*, meaning to destroy self-interest and to give priority to serving the public.

Sometimes, however, Kamai's admiration for the dedication of the Red Guards was tempered by impatience with their standardized rhetoric.

Although well-versed in the Chinese language, he confessed that he occasionally found it difficult to follow the ideological obscurities in the Red Guard utterances. And after a while the repetition began to wear.

A 21-year-old medical student, whom Kamai met at a hospital, spoke in a vein that was to become very familiar. "Chairman Mao and Comrade Lin Piao are always with me," the young man said, pulling a book of quotations from Mao from his pocket. "Whenever I encounter any difficulties, I consult Mao's quotations. Not only I, but every one in China does this." Tears came to his eyes as he described having once seen Mao in Peking.

In Shanghai and in Peking, Kamai listened to these stories until he became tired of them. Each time he could not suppress the thought, "Oh, not again!" But as he patiently listened, he became moved in a different way. Since they were young, he felt that these Red Guards certainly would not shed hypocritical tears. Their devotion to Chairman Mao, he came to believe, was undoubtedly pure and came from the bottom of their hearts.

Mao once said, "Youth is the sun at eight and nine o'clock in the morning. All the hopes of China rest upon you. The world is yours." And in response to these words of Mao's, the young people have reciprocated with a passionate devotion to their leader.

Kamai introduced next a third-year student from the No. 25 High School of Peking, named Li Tung-min, who had this to say: "We are the shock troops who fight against the old world. There are mountains of difficulties blocking our path, but these obstacles can be easily removed because our leader is none other than Chairman Mao. Moreover, we have the undefeatable weapon of Mao's quotations and the sixteen articles on Cultural Revolution which were personally de-

cided by Chairman Mao. We will fight for the Cultural Revolution till the very end and will emerge victorious."

Some of the elderly Chinese might say sarcastically,
"Haven't I heard that before?" Kamai remarked. He understood such sentiments on the part of older Chinese, but felt
that the young people are not being just vainly boastful.
Their words exactly echo Mao Tse-tung's *Problems of Strategy in China's Revolutionary War* and contain Mao's revolutionary optimism.

Miss Lei Kuei-chun from the same school, which was
known to have one of the most aggressive Red Guard units,
said, "My three young sisters have memorized Mao's quotations very well. Occasionally they ask me questions about
Mao's teachings. And if I do not give them an answer, they
become very angry. Therefore, whenever I post any wall
newspaper, I do it after discussing it with my sisters."

The day he arrived in Wuhan, in mid-January, Kamai saw
a group of more than ten children arguing with a doorman
at his hotel. The children were members of hotel employees'
families, and they were telling the doorman, "We know that
this hotel is exclusively for foreign guests and that under
normal conditions we are not allowed to enter. But the
workers of the hotel are now holding a conference, so why
can't we family members come in?" The doorman was un-
moved. Apparently vexed by the endless argument, the children then played their trump card: they began loudly singing a "song of revolution" composed from one of the phrases
of Mao's quotations. In other words, they launched a mass
protest demonstration against what they deemed unequal
treatment by the doorman. Indeed, commented Kamai,
there is no "kid stuff" about the things children do in China.
In fact, he added, the Red Guard High School students are
reared like devils not only by the "authority clique," but
also by the general public.

One day Kamai wondered what these "children of Mao"

do with their time every day. So he asked several Red Guards in Peking what they had done on New Year's Day.

Li Tung-min said, "During the afternoon I participated in a gathering at the Tien An Men Square. I exchanged opinions with my friends after reading the editorials in *Red Flag* [an ideological magazine] and *People's Daily*. We then discussed the general incidents that occurred in the past six months of the Cultural Revolution, talked about the future trend, and discussed how to link the movement with the workers."

Kang Su-chun, of No. 92 Middle School, said, "I took part in a rally to criticize the bourgeoisie at Chungshan Park. Then our school's two Mao Tse-tung Red Guard Propaganda Battalions visited the workers in Chang Tsu-tien in the outskirts of Peking. There we danced and sang songs of our own composition to propagate Mao's thoughts."

Wang Chi-min of Chinghua University Middle School replied, "The university students staged a demonstration march throughout the city, and the high- and middle-school students distributed pamphlets. It was past midnight when I went to bed." Kamai noted the differences between the activities of the college or university students and those from the middle and high schools.

It seemed to him that the college students and the high- and middle-school students of Red Guard groups engaged daily in separate activities. The college students worked in organizations and factories that had recently started forming revolutionary committees. High-school students more or less acted as their assistants. Most of the Red Guards roaming the streets or participating in long marches through the countryside were middle- and high-school students.

He received the impression that the Red Guard college students, key figures in the Cultural Revolution, were engaged in fierce battles beyond the reach of a foreigner's eyes.

The only collegiate Red Guards the reporters saw were those from the few regional organizations that had received "words of praise" from Mao, though in Loyang they did see some university students shouting "Down with Liu Shao-chi and Teng Hsiao-ping" from a propaganda automobile, which had the words "Municipal Public Safety Bureau" on the sides. They also saw some university students in Nanking shouting to "throw out" Chiang Wei-ching, the first secretary of the Communist Party's Kiangsi Provincial Committee.

The people attacked by the Red Guard college students were invariably those holding important posts in the Party. It was likely, Kamai thought, that these students worked under direct instructions from the Party Central Committee, thus laying the groundwork for the activities of Red Guards in the middle schools and high schools.

THE FEARLESS CHILDREN

The fanatic devotion of the Red Guards to the announced goals of the Cultural Revolution has filtered down to the youngest children in China.

Liao Cheng-chih, chairman of the China-Japan Friendship Association in Peking, and the Communist Chinese representative in the unofficial trade relations with Japan, told Takeo Takagi of an encounter with a Red Guard in Peking who was only 8 years old.

Like most Communist Chinese government leaders, Liao is assigned to keep in order one of the reception stations for Red Guards in Peking. It is part of his job to inspect the station several times a day. While making his rounds one day, he spotted a cute little boy who seemed too young to be a Red Guard. Liao thought he was a stray child. Almost every day there are reports of missing Red Guards in Peking;

posters asking people to help locate missing youngsters are sandwiched in between wall newspapers carrying sensational headlines such as "Burn Them to Death," meaning Mao's enemies.

"Where do you come from?" Liao asked the boy.

"Anhwei Province," the child answered.

"How old are you?"

"Eight."

"Oh! And you are a Red Guard?"

"That's right. I have come here to carry out the revolution."

"Fine! Fine! You told that to your father before you left home, I imagine."

Liao got the shock of his life when the boy shook his head, Takagi said, continuing the story. "You mean you left home without telling your folks why you were doing so?"

"Yes."

"They must be worrying about you."

"There is nothing to worry about. I am here for the revolution."

"Let me send a telegram to your father," Liao suggested.

"No, you do not have to do so," the child answered. "They are not worrying about me."

For lack of a better alternative, Liao took the boy to his house, where he had him take a bath and change his underclothes. After having supper, Liao again broached the matter of the boy's family, which worried him.

"We may not have to send a telegram to your family, but you should at least write a letter to your mother saying that you have arrived safely in Peking and are carrying out the revolution," he said.

The boy stared at Liao as if he were trying to figure out why this grown-up man talked such nonsense. Then he said, "Listen, mister! I would rather study the quotations from

Chairman Mao Tse-tung than waste my time writing such a letter! Would you please read the quotations to me?"

"I must admit that I was beaten by that boy," Liao told Takagi, who was impressed that an 8-year-old boy dared to ask a member of the Central Committee of the Chinese Communist Party to study *Quotations from Chairman Mao Tse-tung* with him. To the Chinese themselves, however, Takagi felt that this was not surprising at all. Liao probably said that he was "amazed" at that boy so that his Japanese listeners would understand how different Chinese children are from their foreign counterparts, and that they are not afraid of anything because they believe that they are right.

To illustrate, Takagi told the following anecdote recounted in a book by Yusho Otsuka, *The Story of New China*:

"Every hotel and state-operated store in Communist China has a 'suggestion book,' in which customers write their suggestions or complaints to the management. A group of children made the following entry in the suggestion book at the Sinhua Bookstore in Anshan:

" 'To our comrades in charge of Sinhua Bookstore:

" 'We hereby make a suggestion on a matter which has been thoroughly discussed by us, several children. We want a quick reply.

" 'Why is it that books for children are displayed in glass-covered cases while books for adults are placed in open cases so that customers can take out and read these books at any time?

" 'What is your opinion on the question of how to help children expand their knowledge and enrich their minds?'

"The children's books that the little customers referred to were comic books. Children in Communist China like comics as much as those of other countries. In Communist China there is a kind of comic strip called *lienhuanhua* [serial pictures], which enjoy great popularity among the youngsters.

The bookstore management had apparently placed its *lien-huanhua* books in glass-covered cases to keep them clean. In reply to the children's question, the management made the following entry in the suggestion book:

" 'To our young comrades:

" 'Thank you very much for making such a valuable suggestion. We hereby reply to your question.

"Here is the problem. In the case of books for adults, only a few copies at the top of the pile get dirty, because adults never plant themselves in the store and spend an awful lot of time reading books. But the same thing cannot be said of the children's books. Every child picks up and reads every different copy so that all the books get dirty. It is against the principle of serving people to sell dirty books at list prices. The head office of Sinhua Bookstore is deeply concerned about how to help children expand their knowledge and enrich their minds. Large cities already have Sinhua Bookstores catering exclusively to children. Such a store will be opened shortly in this city also.'

"The management's reply brought a quick response from the children:

" 'To our comrades in charge of the store:

" 'Thanks for a quick reply. We have discussed the matter thoroughly and have reached the following conclusions:

" 'We have committed an error in soiling your books. We will never repeat the same mistake again. But don't you think that we will never get a chance to correct our error if you keep the books in the glass-covered cases? Why is it that you try to shut us out instead of giving us opportunities to improve ourselves?' "

Takagi did not report how the dispute came out, but remarked that every bookstore he had visited in Communist China was crowded with children engrossed in reading books for sale. Store clerks appear to take it for granted, he noted, that children use their shops as libraries.

The same ideological phrases, repeated over and over again by masses of Red Guard students, had an ominous portent for the Japanese professor, Yuji Muramatsu, who found that the celebrated individualism of the Chinese was being replaced in the youth by an enforced sameness of outlook.

Red Guards whom he met in Peking, Shanghai, and Kwangchow were bright and cheerful and full of self-confidence, and he could explain this by the fact that they are children of peasant soldiers who have become a sort of privileged class since the establishment of the Communist regime. However, since they are not old enough to remember the nameless ordeals that their parents had undergone in the pre-Communist days, it is necessary for the Government to give them intensive "class education." Since this kind of education is intended to turn the youths into typical heroes pitted against typical villains, thinking is inevitably stereotyped. The youths accept—and firmly believe in—anything they are taught. They could not receive a red armband and join Red Guard groups if they did not do so.

This absence of individuality reminded Muramatsu of the youth under the ancient Chinese dynasties. The Red Guards endeavor to learn the contents of *Quotations from Chairman Mao Tse-tung* by rote, much as their ancestors in feudal days strove to acquire the knowledge of Confucian principles and ethics in order to pass the Civil Service examinations.

When he crossed the border into Communist China at Shenchuan, Muramatsu recalled, a group of Red Guards had presented him with a small red book of Mao's *Quotations* as "a gift to a friend from Japan." From then until the end of his two-week trip across the country, he was exposed almost constantly to the sight of Red Guards studying Mao Tse-tung's thoughts from the *Quotations*. They begin all their ceremonies, meetings, and dinners by reading aloud passages from the little red book. The professor described the repetitive rite. Someone in the group says, "Open the book at page so-and-so." All youths present open the book at the designated page and read Mao's words in a loud voice. Then another youth says, "Open the book at page so-and-so." Again all present read out the words of Mao in a loud chorus. They go through the same procedure over and over again before they get down to the main business of the meeting, he reported.

Red Guards do not read the *Quotations* to appreciate the anguish that Mao suffered and the ideas he acquired during the years in which he spoke or wrote the words printed in the book, Muramatsu found. They leave this to the scholars appointed by the Communist Party to do such a job. What the masses are instructed to do is to read the *Quotations* aloud, over and over again, until they have every sentence in the book committed to memory and have acquired the ability to think and act in accordance with Mao's teachings without consciously trying to do so.

Muramatsu detected a forewarning of the upheaval called the Cultural Revolution in an incident that happened in the autumn of 1965, when a seemingly minor storm arose over a play written by Wu Han, a historian and deputy mayor of Peking, in which—said Muramatsu—Wu had observed that contemporary Chinese could learn from *chingkuan* [clean government officials] of the feudal dynasties, even though these men had been in the service of the old imperial regimes.

Now pro-Mao "revolutionary rebels" criticize and reject all cultural assets of pre-Communist ages and urge other people to do the same. But despite the fact that Red Guards champion this anti-tradionalist movement, there are some features of their own outlook that remind the Japanese professor of the intellectual bureaucrat in medieval China.

In the ages when China was under the rule of feudal dynasties, he reminded his readers, youths wishing to become Government officials had to pass state examinations which were meant to test their faith in Confucianism and their allegiance to the Emperor. Those were the days when the Chinese Government upheld and protected orthodox Confucianism as a sort of state religion and repressed all other cults and schools of thought as heresies. Youths who passed these examinations and entered the Government service dedicated themselves to the task of protecting and maintaining the power and authority of the Emperor. Under these circumstances objective criticism, which forms a basis of science and ideology, gradually disappeared, and academic research became over-standardized.

If the Red Guards want to become "revolutionary rebels" in the true sense of the expression, Muramatsu thought, they should not bear any similarity to the intellectual bureaucrats of the feudal days. They should be able not only to criticize and rebel against the teachings of the authority faction, he continued, but also to oppose Mao Tse-tung and Lin Piao. They should choose their course by using their own judgment and perspective. If they continue to dissipate their energy in attacking "heretics" under the banner of orthodoxy, Muramatsu predicted, they will end by falling into the same trap as the intellectual bureaucrats who formed the core of Confucian tradition in old China.

Chapter VI

HOW MAO'S THOUGHTS
ARE PUT TO WORK

REMAKING THE LANDSCAPE

The contribution of Mao to the material progress of China is brought home to countless Chinese every day by the visible evidence in their physical surroundings, and Nishimura declared that improvement programs initiated under the Communist regime had changed the appearance of the country so greatly that much of it would hardly be recognizable to a resident of pre-Liberation times who returned today.

In days gone by, he said, the country was for the most part a vast expanse of yellow, parched soil, where it was difficult to find anything blue or green. But now, sheets of water and rows of young trees with green leaves are found anywhere in the country.

About ten years earlier, he visited China for the first time since the end of World War II. During this trip he went from Kwangchow to Tsunghua, a hot-springs resort about 40 kilometers [25 miles] north of the city. En route, he saw a group of laborers planting elm seedlings, each about 30 centimeters [12 inches] long, on the sides of the road. He felt sorry for them, for he knew that only one out of a hundred elm seedlings is likely to take root when they are planted.

100

During the Task Force trip across the Chinese mainland, he took a bus ride along the same route and was astonished to see the road was lined with young elm trees that were already more than five meters tall. The green leaves of the trees cast shadows on the paved road, and he caught glimpses of many artificial lakes through the branches.

A traveler landing at Tungjiao Airport in Peking will see rows of willow trees standing on both sides of the road leading to the central part of the capital, he noted, and the main streets of Changchun in Manchuria, Shanghai, and Nanking are also bordered by trees.

In bygone years, a traveler flying from Peking to Kwangchow saw no water other than the Yellow River before the plane crossed the Hwai River. Now he will spot lakes of different sizes among the hills, and what appear to be dark-brown lines crisscrossing the plains. The lakes are formed by small and medium-sized dams, and the dark-brown lines are irrigation canals.

A traveler driving from Peking to the Great Wall of China will catch glimpses of the Shihsanling Dam through the trees on the righthand side of the road. The dam stores 80 million cubic meters of water. Climbing to the top of the Great Wall, one sees the water of the Kuandling Dam glittering in the sun.

There is an old Chinese saying, "A man who conquers water conquers the nation," and Mao Tse-tung has taken it to heart, Nishimura commented.

Immediately after he assumed power in 1949, one of Mao's announced goals was to "remake the landscape for the benefit of the people." Since then, he has been striving with success to carry out various flood-control and afforestation projects.

Bringing China's rampaging rivers under control has been a great asset to the Communes, and this in turn has helped Mao's image with the farmers.

101

The first riparian work that Mao undertook was that for the Hwai River, running 1,087 kilometers [about 652 miles] through the fertile plains between the Yangtze and the Yellow River, and next only to the Yellow River in the extent of damage that it has caused. When there was heavy rain, the Hwai would breach its banks and send muddy water sweeping through wide areas. When there was a drought, the river would dry up quickly, depriving farmers of irrigation water.

The Hwai River conservation project was divided into three phases: the construction of dams in the mountain areas along the upper reaches of the stream, the building of reservoirs in areas adjacent to the middle stretches of the river, and increasing the amount of water in Hungtse Lake, near the lower end. The Fotzuling Dam and the Meishan Dam, built in tributaries of the Hwai, and the Sanho floodgate constructed in Hungtse Lake, combined to bring the river under control.

The notorious Yellow River, however, still remains unconquered. During the past three thousand years, the 4,845-kilometer [2,907-mile] river has breached its banks 1,500 times and changed its course twenty-six times. According to a plan formulated in October 1954, the Chinese Government will construct forty-six dams to adjust the volume of water, and twenty-four multipurpose dams in the first phase of the Yellow River Utilization Project. But the plan has hit a snag because of the suspension of economic aid by the Soviet Union, among other reasons. It will probably take several more decades for China to conquer the Yellow River, Nishimura thought.

A project has also been launched to develop and utilize the Yangtze, which is said to have latent waterpower 1.6 times that of all the rivers and lakes in the United States together. At the office of the Yangtze Power Utilization Commission in Wuhan, more than three thousand experts are working daily on basic research for a plan to build a huge dam in the gigantic Sanhsia Canyon, between Wuhan and Chungking.

Along with harnessing the rivers, the Government is building reservoirs where there has been no water. Chao Kang, vice director of the People's Commune Bureau, told Nishimura in 1965, "So far, we have completed a hundred large-sized reservoirs, each with more than 100 million cubic meters of water, and a thousand medium-sized reservoirs of more than 10 million cubic meters capacity."

China's afforestation projects are centered on the cultivation of forest reserves used to keep populated areas from turning into deserts. Reserve forests to protect reservoirs and river embankments are also being laid out. The biggest afforestation project carried out so far is the cultivation of a reserve forest 1,100 kilometers [660 miles] long, running from the foot of the Hingan Mountains through Sanhaikwan to Lutai in western Manchuria. This forest, measuring from 200 to 300 kilometers in width, covers an area of 22,950,000 hectares [about 57 million acres] extending over three provinces in Manchuria.

Until this forest was developed, the desert had spread to the western suburbs of the Manchurian capital, Shenyang (formerly Mukden). Railway tracks near the city were often buried in sand. The completion of the forest saved the city from being engulfed.

Along with these Government-sponsored afforestation projects, tree-planting campaigns by People's Communes are promoted. Take, for example, the afforestation drive in Miyan County, adjacent to Peking. Before, the mountains—which cover more than 90 percent of the total area of the county—were bare of trees. Today a large part of the hilly area is covered with fresh verdure.

The afforestation movement has also helped the people to grow orchards in the mountains. In recent months, Peking

103

has achieved self-sufficiency in fruits. Grocery stores in the capital are filled with all kinds of fruits, except bananas, because of the planting by People's Communes near the city.

Nishimura was told Mao Tse-tung aims to cover one-third of the entire country with woods, and he was impressed by the efforts of the Chinese people to achieve this target. Walking along a Peking street, he often saw citizens carrying buckets and putting water on roadside trees.

This remaking of the landscape, the *Yomiuri* force discovered, was only one sign of the recent spurt of progress attributed to the Cultural Revolution.

THE DRAGON WITH NUCLEAR TEETH

Communist China conducted its fifth nuclear test the day the Yomiuri Task Force arrived in Hong Kong, and the Chinese people went wild in celebrating its success. Yoshiro Hoshino, the scientist, recalled it in his report on the progress of technology under Maoism.

The Japanese had their first inkling of the exuberant popular reaction to the successful experiment while they were on the train to Kwangchow the following day. Crying "Good news! Good news!" several railroad workers belonging to a literary group came into their compartment. They were beaming with delight and sang inspirational songs about the Cultural Revolution and extolling Mao's thoughts. Holding up newspaper extras reporting the success of the nuclear test, they cried "*Wantsai!* [Hurrah]" at the top of their voices.

When they reached Kwangchow in the afternoon, the streets were filled with enthusiastic demonstrators celebrating the nuclear achievement. The impression was inescapable that the public related the event to the Cultural Revolution.

To the world outside China, it was almost inexplicable.

Though the scientific principles used in the construction of nuclear weapons and missiles are almost entirely known to the world, to produce these items requires the ability to put together and give full play to highly developed techniques in such industries as machinery, chemicals, and electronics.

The Communist Government had to start from scratch when the new China came into being in 1949. At that time, heavy industries and industrial techniques were almost nonexistent in the country. Chairman Mao described this situation with the Chinese phrase *ichiung erpai,* meaning that the country had nothing in terms of tangible wealth, as well as in terms of culture.

Nevertheless, in the intervening years China was able to develop a technology advanced and sophisticated enough to manufacture not just an atom bomb, but the more complicated uranium type. When the Japanese reporters asked how this great technological progress was achieved, they heard the same answer over and over again.

It went something like this: "By mastering the thoughts of Mao Tse-tung, we can realize technical revolutions and even achieve increases in production, because our spiritual strength can be transformed into material things."

In Nanking, for example, there is an imposing factory called the Nanking Chemical Industry Company, near an inlet of the Yangtze. "Let us energetically carry out the revolution and increase our production" is the slogan of the company. It is the aim of the employes to link the study of Mao's thoughts directly to technical innovation. A Cultural Revolution committee was formed here in October of 1966. Some forty-six committee members, including six officials, were elected by about 10,000 workers of the company. Eleven of the members are persons who hold posts higher than section chief, but none of these is an official of the committee.

The workers here have placed great importance on

thought reform. There was even a sarcastic display of holding a ceremony for the presentation of Mao's books to company officials, who were said to "have a low level of consciousness toward the revolution."

An official of the plant revolutionary committee said, "We have many examples of how the workers have found a breakthrough in technological impasses by studying Mao's thoughts. For instance, we have been carrying out research on how to repair the machine that has been producing synthetic ammonia since August last year. Hitherto, whenever the machine needed repair, we always had to stop the mechanism and wait for the temperature to drop. But this method takes too much work and time. So, we studied—and achieved fine results. We can now repair the machine without lowering the temperature, and it only takes us twelve days instead of the previous twenty. This was a brilliant triumph for the workers, who studied hard and united their strength by following Chairman Mao's teaching that the masses have boundless creative power."

This kind of technological innovation reflected a different approach from that in his own country, the *Yomiuri* scientific expert reported. The Japanese have concentrated on operating facilities, rather than new design. They have made it a point to buy machines from foreign countries and to operate these machines efficiently. The Japanese adopted industrial techniques of other lands on their own initiative and manned the country's industrial facilities with highly qualified men. As a result, the modernization of the country progressed at a rapid rate. But this approach tended to make the Japanese weak in developing new techniques, Hoshino said, and he added that it is a problem which has been discussed frequently in recent years.

The reverse is true of Communist China, he noted. Needless to say, the Chinese are eager to adopt foreign techniques, as is shown by the fact that the country has imported a considerable number of industrial plants from Western European nations during the past several years. But the basic approach of Communist Chinese engineers is to develop their own industrial techniques from basic theoretical research. This may be due partly to the fact that Communist China has had bitter experiences, such as the pressure applied by Chincom—the China Committee on international trade—and the unilateral suspension of technical aid by the Soviet Union.

Hoshino found different stages of progress in different industries. Machinery factories that he visited might have types of machines that had been introduced in Japan as recently as 1962–1963, but there were also old machines of a kind that had been used in Japanese plants back around 1955. The industry still faces a number of problems, he learned, involving the quality of materials used for the machines, the lack of experience in production, defects in the system of keeping stockpiles, and techniques for operation of facilities. Taken as a whole, he concluded, the Communist Chinese machinery industry is lagging behind Japan's by five to ten years.

It must be noted, however, that Communist China has succeeded in producing a highly sophisticated machine called the crooked gear wheel cutting equipment. It is used to make umbrella-shaped cogwheels similar to those used for vehicle gears. Extremely difficult mechanical theories are applied in manufacturing this device, and Hoshino commented that an engineer who could design this piece of equipment could design almost any other machine tool.

In electronic engineering, the Chinese were supposed to be far behind, but this belief no longer holds true, he told *Yomiuri*. Chinese engineers reportedly are depending solely on electronic computers in designing railway bridges now under construction in their country; it was only a few years ago, Hoshino noted, that Japanese engineers began using electronic computers in designing bridges and other structures.

In bygone years, Communist China also lagged far behind other countries in the development of the high polymer industry. But the Chinese have now succeeded in manufacturing heat-proof plastics, including fluorine resins. This field has presumably been cultivated parallel with the development of nuclear devices.

Hoshino gained an impression in his travels through Communist China that Peking was striving mightily to achieve this technological revolution. Although statistics were incomplete in China itself, he was armed with figures from expert Japanese sources that confirmed his estimate.

In 1958, the year of the Great Leap Forward, a blast furnace with a daily production capacity of 2,000 to 3,000 tons was already in operation at the Wuhan steel plant, he reported. In 1965, Communist China's first oxygen supply converter went into operation at the Shihchingshan steel plant near Peking. And in 1968, engineers at the Shihchingshan and Anshan steel plants adopted the method of stoking with coal through the tuyeres—air nozzles—of furnaces.

Of course, he went on, these technical advances have been made only in the forefront of the Chinese steel industry. As a whole, Communist China is still several years behind Japan in its steel production techniques.

Hoshino made it clear, however, that Communist China has much latent power, and that is why it became the fifth nation to acquire nuclear weapons. Taken as a whole, Communist China's industrial techniques are full of defects, and the nation can hardly be called a leader among the manufacturing countries of the world. Nevertheless, it has enough potential to develop such ultra-modern weapons as the nuclear bomb by marshaling its resources.

Where did the potential come from? Hoshino asked. First, he surmised, was the fact that the country received technical aid from the Soviet Union for more than ten years after the establishment of the Communist regime. It must also be noted that Communist China has endeavored to produce highly qualified engineers. In 1962 and 1963, Chinese universities graduated a total of about 200,000 students, of whom 77,000—almost 40 percent—had studied in engineering departments. The figure rises to 60 percent when one includes students in all science faculties; Communist Chinese universities graduated almost twice as many science students as did Japanese universities.

The country's very size gives it great potential in the economic sphere. The annual national income is variously estimated, but it probably amounts to about $70,000,000,000.

Hoshino said that a country usually needs $3,000,000,000 to keep producing uranium-type nuclear missiles and rockets for ten years. The cost presumably is much smaller in Communist China, where personal expenses are lower than in the other nuclear countries. But nuclear missiles are not too expensive for a nation with an annual income of $70,000,000,000.

Many Japanese who visited Communist China told Hoshino that they were surprised to find that the country had made so much progress in the development of nuclear weapons. Hoshino could only wonder why these Japanese underestimated the power of Communist China. He suggested it might be because in the back of their minds there was a deep-rooted sense of superiority toward the Chinese, left over from prewar days.

DO-IT-YOURSELF INDUSTRIALIZATION

In discussing China's potential, Hoshino felt that one must pay attention to the powerful undercurrent of people in action, which runs beneath the surface.

When he talked with farmers at the Huangtukang People's Commune in Peking, the conversation turned to the problem of shortage of fertilizer in Communist China. Capitalistic countries could solve the situation by importing chemical fertilizers from foreign countries, but that is not the case with Communist China.

The farmers said that they had discussed the matter thoroughly and had decided to make fertilizer themselves. The fertilizer they referred to was hog manure. Their approach was based on the principle of self-help, which Communist China also emphasizes in the development of industrial techniques. It is easy to write off the affair by remarking that it simply concerns hog manure, but in fact the action taken by the farmers has great significance in the total fertilizer resources of the country.

Hog manure is not the only kind of fertilizer used in Communist China. The country does have chemical fertilizer plants. The Kirin Chemical Industry complex produces 400,000 tons of synthetic ammonium each year. Facilities to turn out 100,000 tons of ammonium sulphate annually have been completed in the first phase of a project to expand the Wuching chemical plant in Shanghai. A factory to produce 40,000 tons of urea annually is now being built in the second phase of the project.

The point is that the farmers do not want to depend solely upon chemical fertilizers produced at large plants. They are also working hard to obtain hog manure. They are not just sitting back and waiting for their requirements to be delivered, but have created a system of helping themselves—even though the method used is rather unsophisticated.

Hoshino noted in passing that not only has China been able to construct huge plants under a socialistic system, operating under a planned economy, but also that small nitrogen fertilizer factories are now being built in all regions of the country. These small plants fill the gap, so to speak, between the large chemical fertilizer enterprises and the hog manure. In 1965 alone, as many as 146 small nitrogen fertilizer plants were built, or expanded, in various parts of mainland China. Each has an annual capacity of only 2,000 to 5,000 tons, but it is reported that all cities, provinces, and autonomous regions now have this type of facility.

Judged by the yardstick of capitalistic countries, this is not the right way to increase productivity, he commented, and it can be argued that Communist China is turning out large quantities of chemical fertilizer of inferior quality in these small plants. But the scheme pays off, on the basis of the Peking Government's policy of building a socialistic society. Though the fertilizer plants are small, it takes highly developed techniques to produce synthetic ammonium. The point is that the workers, following the principle of self-help, have managed to install such facilities in their plants, which are only slightly larger than those seen in the downtown areas of Japanese cities, he told his readers.

Farmers belonging to People's Communes, using the same principles of self-help, have not only succeeded in attaining self-sufficiency in the supply of fertilizers by collecting animal refuse, but also have carried out large irrigation projects without the aid of such modern equipment as bulldozers. In doing both these things, they have reached beyond the goal of peasants who are good only at tilling the soil. They have improved themselves as human beings and as technicians, too, thereby strengthening the commune system to which they belong. By the same token, Hoshino learned, workers at machinery factories in various parts of the country in solving difficult problems have improved themselves not only as technicians, but also as individuals.

During his trips across the Chinese mainland, Hoshino visited many People's Communes and factories, and asked their members about the progress of production. He was greatly interested in one thing common to all answers. Each Chinese worker he talked to cited figures showing the

111

amount of production and productivity increases. Therefore, his story was certain to be long. He talked in a leisurely
way, but the conversation was never boring, for it concerned
the history of struggle staged at a People's Commune or a
factory. Dramatic and thrilling, the account was a far cry
from the stereotyped reports written by bureaucrats.

The story also struck Hoshino as being something different from that of the Soviet system, under which each worker
is required to attain a "norm," the amount of output fixed by
the state. Needless to say, the figures showing the fruits of
the workers' efforts are important. What is even more important, however, is how people have improved themselves
and how they are seeking to attain a higher goal, and Hoshino was told that is the way people in this socialistic country evaluate their achievements. To act and think in such a
manner is considered to be the short cut—or the best way—
to achieve the goal of establishing a Communistic society;
the best way in terms of human values as well as from the
economic viewpoint.

A SUCCESS STORY IN STEEL

After visiting many factories in different parts of China,
Hoshino felt that the Shanghai Steel Pipe Plant probably
came closest to being a typical example of the kind of technical revolution that he found to be sweeping the country.

As is the case with all other things happening in Communist China, he reported that the Chinese technical revolution differs from those in capitalistic countries. It was noticeable that action was being taken by the laborers, the
"substructure" of the nation's industries.

The semigovernmental Shanghai Steel Pipe Plant typifies
factories in Communist China. Although it is a small concern with only 363 employes, the plant has produced practically all shapes of steel pipes—250 or so types so far. Judg-

ing by the variety and quality of its products, it is a highly capable factory with a high level of technique.

The factory building was such a wretched hovel that Hoshino could not help smiling when he looked at it. This is in spite of the fact that the plant, small as it is, is rated so highly that its achievements are mentioned in the *Semiannual Report on Chinese Industries and Trade,* a well-known and authoritative Japanese publication.

The structure was built basically of brick, but here and there bamboo curtains were used. If a factory in a capitalistic country were in such disrepair, the banks would refuse to lend money to it. Since mainland China is a socialistic country, however, no one seems to care about appearance. Pointing to a bamboo curtain, Hoshino said to his interpreter, "What counts is the machines rather than the building, the men rather than the machines. Isn't that right?" He smiled, and nodded in agreement. The sections shielded by bamboo curtains were lumberyards, and therefore it did not matter at all if the area was exposed to rain, Hoshino discovered, and the factory staff just do not spend time and money on laying bricks at such places.

Since the factory produces various types of steel pipe, the designing of solid-drawn dies is the most important part of its activities. The staff concentrates mainly on this part of their job. Improvement of techniques in other areas is considered less important. There is always a marked contrast, in Communist China, between the "most important" and the "less important."

The factory had started producing seamless steel pipes in 1958, the year of the Great Leap Forward. The enterprise had begun five years earlier with the amalgamation of about twenty tradesmen and artisans, including barbers, tailors, rice dealers, and tricycle manufacturers. It seems almost incredible that this odd assortment succeeded in making steel pipes with their own hands.

They were all inexperienced at this type of work, and among them there were only about five engineers. Needless to say, they accomplished what they did at the request of the state. But they did not even ask the government to assign specialists to their plant. At the time, the country probably had very few men specializing in this field. As usual, the workers solved their own problems. After much debate, they reached a decision: "It is unthinkable that we of a socialist country cannot make steel pipes, when imperialists are doing so." Whereupon, they told the Japanese expert proudly, they resolved to "make steel pipes with their own hands."

But the determined workers admittedly did not know how to go about the job. The project got off to a shaky start when three of the men—one who had made his living by heating the water at a public bath, a tailor, and a common laborer fresh out of primary school—organized what they called the "trial manufacturing group." After many months of painstaking work, they finally managed to fabricate three lengths of steel pipe on a trial basis. This was their first step toward mass production.

The workers racked their brains to solve many technical problems and finally succeeded in putting the project on the right track after repeatedly going through the process of trial and error. Then the state requested the factory to produce more sophisticated types of steel pipes. Some workers suggested that the state be asked to invest money in the project, to make things easier for the staff. But these voices, the Japanese visitor was told, were drowned out by the argument that the workers should continue to attack their problems by themselves. The factory staff then decided to remodel the existing facilities in order to produce the requested new types of pipe.

The state had a very particular reason for asking this factory to turn out advanced types of steel pipes. Communist

eizo Okubo

Yoshiro Hoshino

Takuzo Kamai

*ji Muramatsu
subashi University

*Eisho Mitsuishi, Photographer of Yomiuri,
a member of Yomiuri task force*

*Prof. Tadashi Kawata
of Tokyo University*

ro Nishimura

Mineo Nakajima

Takeo Takagi

Each day 50,000 Red Guards and other Chinese people visit Shaoshan to see the old house where Mao Tse-tung lived in his childhood and the pond where he swam.

The desk and chair Mao used while studying at Changsha.

Red Guards—youth of the Cultural Revolution—marching along a country road on their way to Peking. In the fall of 1967, millions of them occupied the capital.

From all parts of China, the Red Guard converged on cities to overthrow the anti-Maoist factions. With the Red Guard armband, they are seen on the Great Wall.

The 17-year-old editor of a Red Guard newspaper in Peking carrying his book of Mao quotations.

...ntrance to the Shanghai Youth ...ultural Hall. Younger children ...e organized into the Child Vanguards.

Small girl soldiers of a militia corps undergoing training to fire trench mortars in the outskirts of Peking.

Slogans and wall posters criticizing the Shanghai municipal committee that was considered the headquarters of the anti-Maoist "men in authority."

Youths performing their obligatory work to clean the compound of a museum which was formerly a palace. Some work in the fields and some in factories.

A performance at the Tien An Men Square in Peking. Young men and a girl dressed as Americans become objects of accusation by the Chinese masses. Note big noses, a common symbol of Westerners among flat-nosed Orientals.

Even the gates of the houses in Peking are hung with the portrait of Mao.

Demonstrations of workers carrying placards of Mao Tse-tung in Kwangchow.

Educational exhibition hall of the people's commune in Kwang-chow where dolls depicting oppression suffered by farmers under the old regime are shown with slogans: "Do not forget sufferings of farmers under the old society."

In 1968, Chinese soldiers of the liberation army go through hard training in a river on the Chinese-Soviet border.

Typical street scene of Peking: factory workers on bikes on their way to their workshops. Motor buses and trolleys have replaced the old streetcars.

Night view of Peking, a modern city.

A new people's hall which is the biggest building in Peking. The Chinese characters are "Our great leader Mao Tse-tung."

"Great Bridge of Nanking" still incomplete after three years of construction.

Nanking Lake. The site of the lake was a quagmire before it was converted into a man-made lake by the Mao regime. Such lakes are now seen in many parts of China.

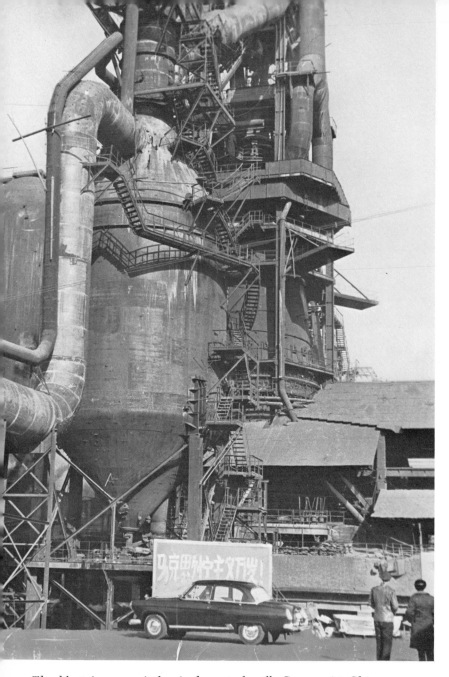

The blast furnace of the Anshan steel mill. Communist China claims that the furnace was built in only four months and three days during the great leap of 1958.

Do-it-yourself industrialization of a farming community. Semi-farm and factory workers working in an agricultural-toolmaking workshop attached to a people's commune in the suburbs of Kwangchow.

University students of Peking assist the work of the people's commune in wheat harvesting in the suburbs of Peking.

China had depended solely upon the Soviet Union for the piping used in heat-exchanging equipment. After the ideological dispute started between the two countries, however, Moscow ceased to export the item to China. A member of the "trial manufacturing group," mentioned before, inspected first-class factories and learned that oil-pressure equipment was required to make the kind of steel pipe ordered. He also found that it would cost 100,000 yuan [$40,000] to make solid-drawn dies for the pipe. Once again, the workers decided to act upon the principle of self-help. They sought and found a new method of manufacturing steel pipes and solid-drawn dies. They made more than forty experiments over a period of eight and a half months in their search for a solution, but finally triumphed. As a result, Hoshino was told, they succeeded in producing steel pipes of a higher quality than those of the Soviet Union. And it had cost them only 5,000 yuan [$2,000] to install the facilities for turning out this kind of pipe.

The story sounded incredible to Hoshino, but it was true, he said. The success of the Shanghai steel plant was due partly to the fact that the equipment was designed on the basis of what the workers actually experienced in their shop, where they studied various methods of treating steel pipes with heat by observing the colors of the furnaces and the steel under various conditions. Another factor was that the designers were not hampered by the rather limited vision of experts, since they were not experts themselves. But the greatest single factor was that the entire factory staff tackled the difficult problem with courage and determination.

The fact that the Communist Chinese Government had succeeded in inspiring the masses with such zeal may be viewed as the principal reason for the triumph of these workers, Hoshino concluded. The Communist Chinese believe that they must master the basic rules of industrial techniques by their own efforts, in order to overcome all sorts of difficulties and create new things. This is what they call "materialization of spirit."

REFORMING THE EXPERTS

Another member of the task force, Keizo Okubo was more skeptical of the claim that all progress could be attributed to the masses armed with Mao's thoughts, nor did he think that all advocates of the Cultural Revolution were ready to do away with educated technocrats, as some of the propaganda implied.

A university student in Wuhan, who was a member of the Red Guard, told Okubo, "What today's China needs is 'red experts' and not 'white experts.'"

Okubo thought he meant that people conforming to the traditional conception of white-collar workers—whether they be economic experts, technicians, or scholars—should not be allowed to exist in Red China. These people do much harm and no good, according to the student. He argued that matters related to industrial techniques and production, or any other subject, will work out well and miracles can be wrought only if experts concerned are armed with the Mao Tse-tung thought and have class consciousness firmly planted in their minds.

It is quite true that the current Cultural Revolution is moving in the direction he described, although the fact remains that even in Red China the out-and-out revolutionaries constitute a minority of the entire population. Only about 18,000,000 of the 700,000,000 people on the Chinese mainland are members of the Communist Party. And it goes without saying that not all Chinese are devoted to the Mao-Lin main-current faction. Okubo wrote about reports that the Maoists were trying to draw intellectuals, including engineers and scholars, into their columns in order to enable them to run the political and economic machinery more easily after they have gained full control of the government.

They recognize the importance particularly of utilizing engineers in production, and presumably hold the view that people who lack revolutionary consciousness should strive to reorganize their thinking while engaging in productive activity.

During his trip across the Chinese mainland, the journalist met a number of plant superintendents and managers who had been engineers before. Some of these men were being criticized publicly and being tried in kangaroo courts by laborers. But they were allowed to keep on working because, it was said, "criticism is criticism and work is work, and one should not stand in the way of the other." There may be some superintendents and managers who are ousted from their plants in the Cultural Revolution, but Okubo felt that the Communist Party's main-current faction presumably is trying to keep the purge of "reactionaries" to a minimum in order to avoid disruption of production activities.

The theoretical organ *Red Flag* said, "In dealing with ranking officials who have committed errors, we should follow the policy of making their mistakes serve as a warning, and save these officials by curing their illness."

The superintendent, named Wang, of a factory that makes ping-pong balls in Kwangchow told Okubo that industry "should depend upon the masses, not upon experts," but the Japanese understood that the statement merely set forth a general principle.

It does not stand to reason that the Maoists will avoid utilizing the specialized knowledge and techniques of experts, Okubo observed. While the success of a Chinese nuclear test may have signalized "the victory of the great Mao thought," as *People's Daily* said, the event must also be viewed, noted Okubo, as an outcome of the constant efforts made by Chinese engineers.

117

In spite of the turmoil caused by the Cultural Revolution, the *Yomiuri* team found that a sense of concrete accomplishment had flowed from the movement on the farms and in the factories of mainland China. Keizo Okubo, the economic specialist, appraised the effects of the Cultural Revolution in the industrial areas of various cities.

The Shanghai Wuching Chemical Industry Company, which makes fertilizer, was one of the first to establish a Cultural Revolution committee, he reported. Selection of the committee members was not made under the candidacy system, but by the so-called Paris Commune method—that is, through a free election by all employes at the factory. The principles of the Paris Commune provided, basically, for the election of delegates by universal suffrage.

The majority of the committee membership was made up of factory workers. These members carried out a thorough "thought investigation" of the plant officials, and relentlessly persecuted those "walking the path of capitalism and revisionism." The committee's work was effective; those who had not adequately reformed their thoughts along the lines of socialism were reprimanded.

He was surprised to learn that in this Shanghai factory alone there were scores of revolutionary organizations, including the Revolutionary Rebel Battalion, the Red Guards —comprising working youths—and the Red Corps of retired soldiers who have an organization separate from the militia.

Wall posters played a big role in boosting the revolutionary spirit among the factory employes. The plant manager, whose name was Kuo, was one of those who had been criticized in the posters. Okubo had visited this factory three years before, and Kuo remembered him. He greeted him with a firm handshake, saying "Welcome, my old friend."

Stifling an expression that looked to Okubo as if he wanted

118

to say, "It is inevitable for me to receive some criticism from the workers," he enthusiastically explained. "This factory not only produces fertilizers to help agriculture; it also has the important duty of producing the heirs of the proletariat. We are planning to make this factory into a college of Mao Tse-tung's thoughts. There have been many changes in this factory, but the biggest has been in the spiritual sense." What he wanted to say, Okubo told his readers, was that although big improvements and expansions had been accomplished on the technical side and in production, the most important improvement in his opinion was in the political activities of the workers. He probably wanted to say that his staff had learned and implemented Mao's thoughts.

What he did say was: "If we raise high the flag of Mao's thoughts, we will surely triumph. It would be a mistake to stay away from under the flag."

In fact, Okubo was told, since the start of the Cultural Revolution in the preceding summer the workers had overcome the scorching heat and had produced more fertilizer than ever before. He was informed that the production goal for 1966 had been attained twenty days ahead of the national target date.

At a medium-sized factory producing seamless steel piping in Shanghai, plant manager Chao proudly said, "The Cultural Revolution had a great influence on production. We achieved a fifty-percent increase last year."

The tide of the Cultural Revolution did not miss the Shanghai Automobile Transport Company, where a man named Lu is employed as a driver. Even here, a Cultural Revolution committee had been established to direct the movement. The role of the committee is to "fight the authority faction who walk the path of imperialism," said Lu.

In the amusement quarter of Shanghai there is an imposing department store called the Tung Fang Hung (East Is Red), on Nanking Road. (It was formerly known as the

Yung An Department Store.) Although the workers here have not yet formed a Cultural Revolution committee, they have a four-hour study program each week on problems of political thought.

If anything profited from the Cultural Revolution, it was the department stores that catered to the vast number of customers who came to Shanghai to take part in the revolutionary movement. Sales soared, and it is said that products with phrases from Mao's teachings on them sold in massive quantities.

Okubo was impressed, as he traveled about the country, by the seemingly unflagging dedication of workers everywhere to the Government goals.

A drive to increase production was at fever pitch in the Wuhan steel complex, he related. Chu, a secretary at the plant's administrative office, said proudly, "We attained the target for 1966 simply by producing more steel than we did in the previous year. This is because the workers have become more eager to boost output as a result of the Cultural Revolution."

Chu's statement was not unique. The slogan "Strive for the Revolution and Increase Production" was displayed at a cotton mill in Chengchow, and in every other plant the economist visited during his trip across the Chinese mainland.

The common view of administrators and workers ran along these lines, he found: Political struggle and the "remaking of thought" are important, but we cannot afford to neglect the economy. We must keep the 700,000,000 people fed, clothed, and housed. We should not sacrifice production for the sake of the Cultural Revolution, because such action would run counter to the purpose of the revolution itself.

The Chinese Communists feel that the current Cultural Revolution must be connected with the actual production and construction work in plants and on farms. The Mao-Lin main-current faction apparently aims to bring about a second Great Leap Forward by using the Cultural Revolution as a springboard.

Farming is as important as revolution, Okubo continued. China must produce at least 180,000,000 to 190,000,000 tons of food each year. At present, the country imports 6,000,000 to 6,500,000 tons of food annually, and is said to have a food reserve of between 5,000,000 and 10,000,000 tons. But it is a tremendous task to feed the population of 700,000,000. The country may be able to get along if the industrial production declines to a certain degree, but it is no easy job to cope with a decrease in agricultural output. Therefore, the main-current faction of the Chinese Communist Party will strive to maintain the present level of food production at any cost.

People's Daily has reported that in 1966 Communist China had the largest food and cotton crop recorded during the seventeen years since the "liberation," and that the country's industrial production rose by more than 20 percent over the previous year. That year had marked the beginning of the third Five-Year Plan. The newspaper declared that the fact that the country had attained and surpassed all its production goals meant "a great new victory of the Mao thought and a brilliant achievement of the Great Proletarian Cultural Revolution." The newspaper's claim was echoed by people at all factories and communes that Okubo visited. They said unanimously that "on the strength of the Cultural Revolution, the revolutionary spirit transformed itself into fact and achieved increased production."

However, Okubo noted, the Chinese Communist Government has not released figures and statistics to substantiate the claim of nationwide bumper crops and increased industrial production. Therefore, it is difficult to verify the official statements. According to an analysis of a Hong Kong economic expert, the 1966 food production in Communist China

121

was about the same as that of 1955, or about 190,000,000 tons (another estimate put the figure at about 180,000,000 tons). The expert said that the *People's Daily* claim that Communist China had achieved the largest food production in seventeen years was doubtful, because the crops had reached the high level of 250,000,000 to 270,000,000 tons in 1958–1959. He said further that industrial output probably had risen by about 10 percent over the previous year's figure.

It seemed to Okubo that Communist China's agricultural and industrial production has remained stable despite all the disorder created by the Cultural Revolution. The Hong Kong expert, for one, believes that considerable production increase has been achieved in certain sectors of the country's industry.

However, the Japanese reporter was not sure that China's economy would continue to remain stable if political upheavals proliferated.

The revolution, which had been led by the Red Guards, was spreading to laborers and farmers, bringing the fervor of the Chinese masses to a high pitch, Okubo thought. The revolution had reached the stage where violent clashes between the main-current faction and the authority faction reportedly were taking place in cities and farming villages, and Liberation Army troops have been mobilized to restore order. Stagnation and disruption of production activities will inevitably result from this situation, the economist concluded.

BOTTLENECK ON WHEELS

As travelers, the members of the Yomiuri Task Force were particularly conscious that one area of the Chinese economy where progress had been made—but much more was needed —was transportation. Again, Okubo was the reporter.

The airplane in which the Japanese flew from Kwangchow

to Peking was a British Viscount, he said. It took them about four hours to reach Peking on the direct flight. Three years earlier, he had made the same trip in a Soviet Ilyushin, and had stopped at Changsha, Wuhan, and Chengchow before arriving at the capital, taking an entire day—from early morning till evening. So, in three years, Communist China saw a great change in air transport.

Also, it was only three years ago, he said, that one saw buses and trucks plodding heavily through the streets of Peking, carrying huge loads of coal gas in containers on their roofs for fuel. It was indeed an awkward sight, but now these outdated vehicles are seen no more in the capital. Since about the middle of 1964, there has been a gradual improvement in the petroleum supply; gasoline has become more plentiful, and this has brought a great change in mainland China's transportation industry, in terms of both quality and quantity.

In Shanghai, old-fashioned streetcars are still seen running through some parts of the city, but in Peking this mode of public transportation has been replaced completely by motor and trolley buses. Construction of an underground railway system is under way in Peking, and soon commuter traffic will be greatly facilitated. It seems that the Chinese have changed their stand on the subway problem, for it was said only two or three years ago that underground transport was not needed in China. However, subways may well be used for military purposes as well as for commuter travel.

The double-decker bus, once a major feature of the street scene in prewar Shankhai, has disappeared. But a double-decker train, named *Huo-che* [firebird], has run once a day between Hangchow and Shanghai since its inauguration in 1964. Railroad officials described the service as "sort of a trial run" for its possible extension throughout China. The cars were made at the Ssu Feng Engine and Coach Company

123

in Tsingtao. A first-class ticket between Shanghai and Hang-chow costs 6.5 yuan [about $2.60].

A project to link the northern and southern provinces in the lower Yangtze River region will open a new era in the national transportation system, Okubo learned. One of the key projects is the Great Bridge of Nanking. The width of the Yangtze in the Nanking vicinity is about 1,500 meters. When he last visited the area, a ferry boat was plying between the northern and southern banks at two-hour intervals. Trains running between Shanghai and Peking also had to cross the river by ferry at this point. Since the Cultural Revolution, the three vessels making the trip were so jammed by masses of young Red Guards that two of them broke down and had to be docked for repairs. When the bridge is completed, the river crossing will be a matter of minutes.

This Great Bridge of Nanking, which will connect Nanking and Pukow, was begun after the completion of the Great Bridge of Wuhau, a monumental structure in the history of China's transportation. When Okubo visited Nanking three years earlier, there were only two or three foundation pillars completed, and he was asked by Communist Chinese authorities not to write about the bridge for a while. But when he recently visited the same place again, he found the bridge structure almost 80 percent finished.

Mr. Chang, the chief of the Nanking bridge construction project, said that the total length of the structure would be 6,670 meters, or about 5,000 meters more than the actual width of the river. The lower span of the multipurpose bridge will have double-tracked rails for trains, and the upper portion will be reserved for motor traffic. The depth of the river is 30 to 40 meters at this point, but it is said that the rock layer serving as the foundation for the bridge is 70 meters below the surface of the water.

The visiting economist was told that the type of bridge

construction adopted here was very rare. The structure will will be so designed that all coastal ships presently using the river will be able to sail under the span, and even 10,000-ton oceangoing vessels will be able to pass beneath if their masts are folded down.

There are nine bridge pillars, each measuring about 400 square meters in cross-section. The bridge will be 110 meters high, measuring from the rock layer below the water surface to the top of the structure.

Soviet technicians played a major role in constructing the Wuhan bridge, but the project at Nanking is an all-Chinese undertaking. However, although Soviet technology learned by Chinese engineers while working with imported experts on the Wuhan bridge has been the basis for the planning of the Nanking structure, no one was heard criticizing the project as being a product of "Soviet revisionism." Construction was begun in 1960, and though there were many difficulties, Chang told the Japanese journalist that the project was to be completed a year ahead of schedule. "This can be done," the engineer said, "because workers are burning with zeal inspired by the Cultural Revolution."

"He was full of confidence, as might be expected of a 'Red engineer,'" Okubo commented.

Despite these evidences of great improvement, Okubo said that the country being as large as it is, the transport system is still not adequate.

Motor vehicles are still generally scarce in Communist China, and automobiles in particular are in short supply. Even in such big cities as Peking and Shanghai, one has difficulty finding a taxi. Cars are far beyond the reach of ordinary citizens. Communist China now makes its automobiles, such as the Red Flag and the Liberation, but the number produced is very small.

Soviet and Eastern European automobiles are seen on the streets of principal cities, and Okubo spotted some Japanese Toyopets and Cedrics. What he thought most interesting was seeing several American-made cars running on the streets of Communist China; it was odd, because Red China has no trade relations with the United States. They were very old models that he thought had probably entered the country through Hong Kong. In Kwangchow, he rode in a sleek microbus made by the Mercedes-Benz company of West Germany and was told that the foreign-made bus was used exclusively to transport foreigners. The scheduled buses on Chinese streets are usually Chinese-made vehicles that have been used for years.

A nationwide austerity campaign can be blamed in part for the rundown condition of the street buses, but the main reason seems to be the fact that Communist China's automotive industry has been unable to catch up with the demand. The buses are always filled to capacity, and long queues line the streets at each stopping place.

Many workers seemed inclined to used bicycles for going to and from work, because of the long lines waiting for the motor buses and trolleys, and the congestion made these a relatively unreliable means of commuter transportation. At about six o'clock in the morning, the reporters could usually see, from the windows of the hotels where they stayed in Shanghai and Peking, masses of bicycles being pedaled through the streets. All working centers, Okubo noted— plants and offices—have "parking lots"—for bicycles.

The Communist Chinese are still far behind in shipbuilding. In 1965, it was reported, the Chinese concluded a three-year agreement with London to charter 150 vessels aggregating 1,000,000 to 1,500,000 tons. Also, Peking tried to purchase a 12,000-ton freighter from the Hitachi Shipbuilding Company of Japan, and though the deal fell through, it is another indication of how badly Communist China needs shipping.

126

Part of the bottleneck in transportation seemed to be due to the disruptions of the Cultural Revolution.

There are already signs that the revolution is affecting foreign trade. Because of a shortage of stevedores, Japanese ships carrying goods to China often remain anchored off-shore in Shanghai and other ports. There has also been a delay in the loading of goods to be exported to Japan. It has been reported frequently that Southeast Asian countries hurriedly placed orders for textiles with Japan after Com-munist China had failed to deliver on schedule.

The Cultural Revolution has also affected public trans-portation services. Okubo was unable to take a morning express from Loyang to Chengchow, a two-hour journey, be-cause the train was too crowded. So he boarded an accommo-dation train, which left Loyang shortly after noon and reached Chengchow more than an hour behind schedule. On another occasion, he had to take a plane from Shanghai to Nanking because there were no trains running.

Even if the revolution does not harm production, he said, the export and import trade is greatly hampered if freight services are disrupted. And when the shipping of raw material cannot be carried on smoothly, production is bound to be affected also.

At one point, Okubo reported, the Maoist authorities placed a limit on free train transportation of Red Guards and took steps to prevent laborers and army men from making trips around the country to "exchange experiences" in the revolution.

It is quite natural that the main-current faction should have shifted the emphasis from the transportation of people to the transportation of goods, in order to alleviate the con-gestion on trains and to prevent a drop in production, the Japanese observer declared. One of the slogans for the third Five-Year Program launched in 1966 was "Strengthen the country's transportation system." The *Yomiuri* groups agreed that modernization and consolidation of transport is one of the most important problems that must be tackled if Communist China is to develop a balanced economy.

INSIDE THE PEOPLE'S COMMUNES

One of the things that surprised Churo Nishimura during his visits to People's Communes was that he could not tell whether they were farm villages or factory zones.

For instance, at the Shuangchia People's Commune, people were working at five different plants every day of the year—plants for making bean curd, wine, pharmaceutical products, and starch, and one for machine repairs. There were other plants and workshops for manufacturing folk art, fodder, medicine for cattle, straw mats. There was even an electrical gilding plant. Although it might be natural for a commune to have factories connected with agricultural products, it was odd to find an electrical gilding plant, which has no connection with farming.

But this type of thing has become increasingly conspicuous in the new commune movement. There were many small factories in the Huashan People's Commune in the suburbs of Kwangchow. A similar tendency was observed at the Taching oil town, which had been made a model industrial settlement. This commune, with a population of about 200,000, is an industrial district as well as a farming area. The families of the oil-field workers have cultivated vast tracts of rice and vegetable fields in order to supply themselves with sufficient food.

The cities seem to be turning increasingly toward agriculture, while the farm villages are being industrialized, Nishimura found—an indication that Mao's dream of "creating a new type of society by eliminating the differences between the cities and the farm villages" is gradually being realized.

128

COUNTERREVOLUTIONARY BICYCLES

But China is still primarily rural and agricultural, and the communes originally were established to socialize the large peasant and farming populations. Rural reform, which had received some severe setbacks during the first disastrous years of the Great Leap Forward, was reactivated by the Cultural Revolution and accompanied by a massive effort to root out remnants of the past.

The great tide of the Cultural Revolution has even swept the farm villages that had been enjoying a tranquil life and a season of abundant harvest unprecedented in history, reported the *Yomiuri* economic specialist.

Various types of revolutionary organizations have been established in the communes, many by the peasants and some by the Red Guards who stopped over during their walking trips and exchanged experiences with the farmers.

The Kangchiao People's Commune in Shanghai and the Ho Ling People's Commune in Nanking have had Cultural Revolution committees since December 1966. In the case of Ho Ling, there were committees for each of the sixteen production battalions, and a consolidated committee to unify activities. There was also a Red Guard organization made up of farm youths and a revolutionary rebel battalion consisting mainly of poor and lower middle-class farmers.

The object of these revolutionary organizations is to root out the "bad guys"—members of the "authority faction walking the path of capitalism and revisionism"—who have hidden themselves within the People's Communes, and to protect the people's reign in the Government by enhancing the popular sense of class consciousness.

Mr. Chou, a secretary of the Ho Ling commune's Consolidated Revolutionary Committee, said sharply:

"We farmers, when we stand in front of our home gates, first of all look toward the Tien An Men Square in Peking.

129

But the bad elements, who hail from the landlord and rich farmer classes, look toward their *tzu liu ti* [private land holdings, the controversial house gardens owned by commune farmers]."

The Cultural Revolution movement had prompt good results, Chou said, reporting that they had uncovered weapons which had been cached away for counterrevolution and found people secretly worshipping Buddha's statue, which, he added, can give them nothing.

The reporter pressed for details about the weapons for counterrevolution.

"We found old bayonets concealed inside cement blocks in toilets, and old military uniforms and coins hidden away by former landlord and rich farmer elements. There was one landlord who had been concealing a bicycle made of precious metal and worth about 500,000 yuan [$200,000]," he replied.

Okubo could not imagine such a valuable bicycle, nor was it conceivable to him that one bicycle could do much in the staging of a counterrevolution. He felt that Chou's description of the weapons and schemes for counterrevolution was grossly distorted, for it was against reason to believe that such a meager supply of arms could start an uprising. The farmers have good reason for their fears, however, when they remember how it used to be.

As described in Pearl Buck's novel *The Good Earth*, the Chinese farmer was once a symbol of the poverty and tribulations of the old China, Okubo reminded his readers. Records show that landowners, who constituted only 10 percent of the agrarian population, abused and exploited the peasants who accounted for the other 90 percent. Tenants were forced, under one pretext or another, to pay the landowners 50 to 90 percent of the proceeds of their tilling.

"Look how we live now!" one commune member said passionately. "The difference is like day and night. Isn't it natural for us to thank Chairman Mao for giving us a good living?" This farmer had benefited from the land reform program of the Communist Chinese Government, under which 300,000,000 landless farmers were given 700,000,000 *mu* [one *mu* equals 6.67 acres].

Until then, he told Okubo, he had been living in a hut belonging to his landlord. Thanks to the land reform, he now had a house of his own. Last year his family of four persons had received approximately 330 kilograms [about 728 pounds] of unhulled rice and 15 kilograms [about 33 pounds] of edible oil. In terms of cash, their monthly income —including earnings from side jobs—totals about 1,000 yuan [$400].

He said that his family, who had barely managed to make a living in bygone years, now has 15 bales of rice in stock and savings equivalent to about 200,000 yen in Japanese currency [about $555]. He added that he used to have two hogs, but had sold one and is keeping the other for the Lunar New Year celebration.

THE BAD OLD DAYS

Everywhere, the Japanese reporters heard stories of terrible hardships that had preceded the Communist reforms.

Takuzo Kamai recounted a conversation with a farmer in a commune along the red clay banks of the Yangtze River, near Nanking. The peasant, said Kamai, began his story by reminiscing about the "bad old pre-liberation days."

"Oh, it was terrible," he told the Japanese journalist. "My father, a tenant farmer, barely managed to eke out a living. As a child, I begged the landowner, in tears, to hire me as a cowherd in return for two meals a day. In winter we would go around selling firewood, which we carried on a pole. It is a wonder that we did not die of starvation."

One cannot travel through rural areas of China without

hearing stories like these about the abject poverty that afflicted Chinese farmers in pre-Communist days. Another sad tale that Kamai heard was about the child of a peasant who was bitten by a dog while guarding a flock of sheep belonging to a landowner. He kicked the animal to defend himself. As luck would have it, the dog died of his injuries. The indignant landlord forced the poor peasant to sell his fields—his only property—to him at an exceptionally low price. The landlord spent his profit on building a fine stone tomb for the dog. What is more, he called a theatrical troupe from a nearby town and held a gala party that lasted for three days to mourn the death of his pet—all at the peasant's expense.

The members of the Huashan People's Commune in Kwangchow had established a "Class Struggle Education Exhibition Hall" in October 1966. Dolls and paintings on display in the hall showed old-time farmers being mistreated by landlords, and the ultimate salvation and victory realized through the efforts of Mao Tse-tung and the Communist Party. The commune members try to emphasize the importance of the Cultural Revolution through endless repetition of propaganda.

At another Huashan People's Commune, 50 kilometers [about 30 miles] northeast of Wuhan [the name is the same as the one in Kwangchow], the Cultural Revolution was being carried out at a feverish pitch.

"The poor and lower middle-class farmers are passionate followers of Mao Tse-tung," the commune president, Mr. Wang, told Kamai. Some of them have voluntarily formed research groups to study Mao's books, because they believe that his works are their staff of life.

Wang said that the grudge felt by the old farmers against the former social order had penetrated their bones and that they would remember the hardships of the old days until they died. They would also hand down this grudge to their children and grandchildren, he declared. Youth in the village are told over and over, "If you forget the hardships of the past, you will not be able to appreciate the present."

In the old days, Wang said, there was a popular elegy that went like this:

"In the months of April, May and June,
We leave the village to seek work elsewhere
And roam about the country, here and there.
In the cold winter of December,
The tears flow and never dry."

As in Mao's native village, December was a month of tears for the farmers, who were usually pressed by the "Three Hardships"—payment of taxes to the bureaucrats, money to the loan sharks, and farm products to the landlord. Today it is their conviction that it was none other than Mao Tse-tung and the Communist Party that liberated their village and allowed them to free themselves from the Three Hardships. As long as the farmers cling to this belief, it is only natural for them to worship Chairman Mao as their "sun that never sets."

"These people have strong class consciousness, because they experienced hardships in the old Chinese society," Wang continued, and explained that it is their belief that China will return to the ways of the old society unless they too stage a Cultural Revolution.

More than seventeen years have passed since the founding of the new China, and eight years since the People's Communes were organized. During this period, the landlord and rich farmer classes, which had been banned from politics and from being qualified as official commune members, steadily began to regain power, particularly during the three consecutive years of natural calamity that began in 1959. They obtained considerable influence after becoming accountants and warehouse superintendents, and were said to have almost succeeded in causing the communes to collapse.

Those who are vigorously promoting the Cultural Revolution want to nip any rebirth of old ideas in the bud, and crush any suspicious tendencies. Since 1963, this aim of the revolutionary sponsors has brought the "Four Purification Movement"—purifying politics, ideas, organizations, and economy—to the farm villages.

However, it seems that the problem of the former landlords and wealthy farmers will remain unsolved for some time, since it is inconceivable that they will apologize and quietly retire from the scene, considering the vigorous nature of the Chinese people.

At another commune, the Cultural Revolution was a continuing inspiration for recovery from recurrent calamities of a more unpredictable kind.

The Huangtukang People's Commune, near Peking, was ravaged by five natural disasters last year—wind, drought, hail, insects, and flood—the vice president, Pien Kung-shin, told the reporter. Twice, hailstones the size of eggs fell on the fields, completely destroying the vegetable crop.

The commune members were most downhearted, Pien said, but they eventually regained their composure and started studying plans to salvage the situation. They finally arrived at the conclusion that although the vegetable fields had been destroyed, the people still lived, and though the heaven causes the hail, it is the people who reap the harvest. So, after replanting with seedlings, the farmers managed to restore their fields to normal in one week, according to the vice president, who added, "we managed to restore our crops because we studied Mao's teachings."

The Japanese visitor thought that restoring the devastated crop to normal within one week was almost a feat of magic, but found that the farmers attribute their success to the omnipotent Mao. Their admiration of the Chairman is close to a religious faith.

The worship of Mao by the farmers in the communes was not an incidental phenomenon, but has been carefully nurtured. Kawai commented on the well-known fact that the Communist Chinese leadership has always derived its strength from the political awakening of the peasants, who constitute the greater proportion of the population. What the government calls the "transformation of the low- and middle-class farmers" applies not only to the years since the Communists came to power, but also to the past four decades since the appearance of the revolutionary forces led by Mao.

The farms in turn have become prime showpieces for Maoism. The *Yomiuri* team was invited to lunch by Mr. Chen, a 42-year-old member of the Hungchiao People's Commune in the suburbs of Shanghai. The family consists of seven members—Chen, his wife, his mother, and four children. His oldest daughter works at a factory; his second daughter was away on a long trip as a middle-school Red Guard.

Chen was originally a poor peasant and had worked for a time at a Shanghai factory during the Japanese occupation. When he told his life story, there was nothing gloomy about the way he talked, in a quiet voice, about the ordeals he had undergone in earlier years.

Now, recounting the family possessions, he reported that he had 1,500 yuan deposited in a bank. "Oh, Grandmother would hate me if I forgot to mention her old chest of drawers, bed, and table," he added, laughing.

The thermos, which had once been the only "fancy" item in the Chen house, had now become so unimportant that it was not even included in the list of family properties. This fact alone illustrates the marked improvement made in the living conditions of farmers in the suburban areas of Shanghai.

135

"We drew 120 yuan from the bank in 1958, and bought a secondhand bed," Chen said, reading entries from the family account book. "In 1958, I bought a wristwatch for 75 yuan. In 1960 we bought a radio for 105 yuan. In 1964, we bought for 189 yuan a bicycle with a lamp attached to it. In 1965 we bought a two-wheeled trailer and a brand-new bed at a total cost of 146 yuan.

"When I get paid by the People's Commune next month, I will make it the first thing to buy furniture for Grandmother. Then I will set aside about 100 yuan to be used as allowances for the children and to buy Sunday suits for family members. I will put the rest of the money in the bank."

Grandmother said happily, "My son gives me a monthly allowance of six yuan."

Kamai wondered what the views of these people were, people who had lived almost like beggars in previous years, but now lead such a blessed life by the old standards. He asked Chen's wife, "What do you like best? And what do you want to do most?"

"What do I like best?" she said quickly. "Why, *Lao Sanpien*, of course." *Lao Sanpien* is Mao's "Three Constantly Read Articles"—"In Memory of Norman Bethune," "Serve the People," and "The Foolish Old Man Who Removed the Mountains."

"I particularly like 'Serve the people,'" she went on. "Before the liberation, I was an illiterate. Since I have started reading *Lao Sanpien*, I have come to realize how good it is to be able to read."

Kamai had heard that she served on the women's committee of the commune's production battalion, and this led him to ask her, "What do you think of the status of women in today's China?" She answered confidently and proudly, "There is no case of a man bullying his wife just because he is a man. Women can do as much work as men."

Chen's wife was not an isolated example of the new farm
136

wife. While traveling through rural districts, he found that the wives of the farmers possessed a high level of political consciousness. But he was taken aback when Mrs. Chen, at one point, prefaced a statement with a reference to "opposition against Japanese militarism."

FEEDING MANY MILLIONS

The increasing prosperity of the communes means more food for China's hungry masses, Kamai pointed out.

At the Yingchuang People's Commune in the northern suburbs of Loyang, the ancient city in Honan Province, he spoke to the director, Mr. Li.

"Look at those fine apple trees on the mountain," Li said, pointing to a young orchard. "When I first suggested that we cultivate the mountainside, the people were opposed, saying that it would be a waste of time to clear such a rocky hill. But I finally convinced them that my plan would work."

The young apple trees, planted on the hillside after the rocks were removed, were Mr. Li's special pride, Kamai related. A canal, 40 kilometers [about 24 miles] long, runs along the foot of the mountain. Fields of yellow clay are soaked in water lifted from wells, some of them about 280 meters deep. Last year the commune earned more than 400,000 yuan [$160,000] from the sale of apples raised in the hillside orchard.

The People's Communes were growing steadily all over the country, Kamai learned. People's Communes were established in the summer of 1958 for the avowed purpose of unifying political and social affairs and combining industries, agriculture, commerce, sciences, and military affairs. During the next several years, the communes were caught in the vicious cycle of natural disasters and the trial-and-error method. They were obliged to abandon the custom of providing free meals to their members. To alleviate these problems, the scope of each commune was reduced gradually, and as each reduced its scope the number of communes increased, until in 1964 there were 74,000, each embracing an average of 1,600 households. In 1965, the number was increased to 80,000, encompassing an average of 1,540 households. Within this basic organization, according to a decision by the central government, a production corps is supposed to include 30 households.

Kamai personally visited six rural communes, near the cities of Peking, Shanghai, Nanking, Loyang, Wuhan, and Kwangchow. The six communities had a combined population of about 160,000 persons, in approximately 35,000 households, on a total land area of 222,000 *mu*, or nearly 1,481,000 acres.

Most communes distribute about 70 percent of their income to members, Kamai was told. Actual rates that he checked were 70 percent at Huangtukang, 54 percent at Hongchiao, 70 percent at Wuhan, and 71 percent at Kwangchow. According to Mr. Neng, vice director of the Kwangchow People's Commune, the amount of tax imposed remains the same if the production increases. In the period immediately after its establishment, the Kwangchow People's Commune paid 10 percent of its income as tax. The ratio declined to 7 percent in 1957, and dropped further to 3.8 percent in 1965. This was because the production of vegetables in this commune had tripled over the years, Mr. Neng explained.

The state allots taxes to the communes, which in turn divide them among the component production units— battalion and corps. The state also imposes taxes on industrial enterprises operated by the communes. However, no tax is imposed on individuals.

The Association of Peasants and Lower and Middle-Class Farmers forms the political basis of the rural communes. But the communes have a big economic reason for existence, in serving as the organs designed to raise the nation's food production. It is difficult to get accurate nationwide figures, but judging by the appearance of people in the Chinese cities and farming villages, there is no doubt that the Chinese are well fed and that the country's food production is progressing smoothly.

The reporters found persuasive evidence attesting to the improvement of the mainland Chinese diet. Now the Chinese people do not smell of garlic as they used to. Foreigners who have lived in China, particularly in the north before the Communists took over, must remember that the streets of Chinese cities were filled with the odor of garlic. But Kamai said that that pungent smell no longer assaults the nose of the traveler. He said he seldom smelled it even in Peking buses filled with laborers, or in trains crowded with the Red Guard youths.

Wowotou, a preparation from corn flour that used to be the daily food of poor people in North China and Manchuria, has disappeared almost completely. Vice director Neng of the Huangtukang People's Commune told him that corn is now used as feed for hogs. While walking along a street on the outskirts of Loyang, he saw a group of commune workers selling baked sweet potatoes—a side job to augment their income. They complained that sweet potatoes do not sell very well nowadays—more evidence that the diet has improved.

In Huangtukang, the yearly production of vegetables rose from 39,500 tons, the output at the time of the establishment of People's Communes, to 80,000 tons in 1966. The amount of food production for one *mu*—6.67 acres—of land increased from 145 kilograms in 1957 to 330 kilograms in 1965. Under a plan formulated in 1963, the area of rice fields at this commune has been expanded by 1,000 *mu* a year and has now reached 4,000 *mu*, with a harvest per *mu* of 335 kilograms [about 740 pounds]. The same commune sells 12,000 hogs each year.

139

At the Huashan commune in Wuhan, the yearly food production jumped from 5,500 tons in 1957 to 6,500 tons in 1965 and 8,500 tons in 1966. The number of cattle here has been increasing by 10,000 head a year. The commune of the same name in Kwangchow showed a rise in food output from 14,850 tons in 1957 to 25,750 tons in 1966. In 1957 this commune had to receive 740 tons of food from the state, but in 1966 the same commune sold more than 11,000 tons to the government. This was in addition to the food distributed to commune members, 225 kilograms for each individual, and 5,000 tons stored as a reserve. In 1957 this commune had 6,898 hogs and 88,000 fowl; in 1966 these figures had risen to 48,500 hogs and 525,000 fowl.

The amount of production in cereals at each of these communes, in terms of kilograms per *mu*, was given as follows: Huangtukang, 333 (rice and other grains); Hongchia, rice 400 and barley 150 (second crop); Muling, 400 average; Yingchuang, 200 average; Huashan (Wuhan), 500 average for rice, 150 for wheat (second crop); Huashan (Kwangchow), 507 average.

Communist China had a 12-year program for development of agriculture, which ended in 1966. According to this plan, the production of rice per *mu* was to be increased by 200 kilograms in North China, 250 in Central China, and 400 in the south. Judging by the production increases described at the six communes Kamai visited in different parts of the country, he thought that the goal had been attained.

He found that the cultivation of rice in North China has been progressing particularly rapidly. According to a *Yomiuri* colleague stationed permanently in Peking, areas along the railway line between Anshan and Shengyang in Manchuria have been turned into rice fields, through the success of the Liao River Conservancy Project. Kamai heard that two yearly crops have become common in areas along

140

the Yangtze River, which have about the same temperate climate as Tokyo.

Another fact that he thought would interest his countrymen was that most of the rice seeds used in Shanghai, Nanking, and Wuhan are imported from Japan. Members of the People's Commune denied this, but he knew that the variety that they called Nung No. 58, mentioned as a high-quality species in those areas, is actually the Japanese Norin No. 58.

The rotation of crops is being practiced widely at various communes, he continued. At the Yingchuan commune near Loyang, for example, farmers raise peas in winter, sweet potatoes or cotton in summer, and wheat and beans in the autumn. Officials of the commune said that they had succeeded in stabilizing and increasing agricultural production by this means.

Lift pumps are rapidly replacing hand-worked wells in the farming villages. Mr. Neng at the Huangtukang commune said that the hand wells, an ancient institution on Chinese farms, would go out of existence in a few years.

However, Communist China still has a long way to go before she attains the goal of utilizing river water and chemical products to the fullest extent possible, and completely mechanizing farm work, Kamai thought. The Communist Chinese Government itself admits that it will take twenty to twenty-five years to achieve this end. It is estimated that only 8,500,000 tons of chemical fertilizers were obtained and used by mainland Chinese farming villages in 1966, although 30,000,000 tons would be needed to give 15 kilograms to each *mu* of field.

On the other hand, Okubo noted the farms and rural villages still depended to a large extent upon primitive methods that have disappeared from most of Japan. In city suburbs and villages he saw the ancient side of China—farmers leading donkey wagons, people pushing one-wheeled carts and carrying baskets on shoulder poles. Farmers still depend a great deal on these age-old means of transportation, he wrote, and he added that although the communes have access to trucks and other modern transport, they are still very scarce.

THE PRIVATE PROPERTY SYNDROME

Kamai pinpointed a controversial feature of the Communist Chinese farm system, in the prevalance of privately owned lands and the practice of taking "side jobs" in order to augment individual income beyond what is derived from sharing the collective earnings of the commune.

Soon after the outbreak of the Cultural Revolution in the summer of 1966, Kamai reported Red Guards came up with the demand that each production corps stop owning commune property. However, this demand is not likely to be realized in the near future.

Red Guards also clamored for the abolition of the system of allowing farmers to have self-retained land—privately owned gardens—but there are no signs that this practice will be abolished, either. Officials of the communes Kamai visited said that there was no need to take up the "self-retained land" from the farmers, since the privately owned acreage amounted to only 5 to 7 percent of the total arable land.

Some American observers, Kamai noted, believe that the food produced from the privately owned plots constituted as much as 20 percent of the total production, but he thought that such a situation may have existed only in 1959 or thereabouts, if it existed at all.

Food that farmers produce individually is sold at free markets that are opened one day in every five. Okubo also heard that the Cultural Revolution created demands that the private land-holding be eliminated.

A farmer named Chu, of the Kangchiao People's Commune, said, "If the water becomes scarce in the large river, the same thing happens in the small river." What he meant was that if the collective economy does not develop smoothly, it is obvious that there must be difficulties also in managing private lands, and that the farmers should concentrate their efforts more in collective work and less in their private enterprises.

Mr. Sha, the vice president of the commune, agreed with Chu's view. "I have already proposed that the authorities rectify the situation concerning private lands, in order to call attention to the attitude of farmers who have become increasingly class-conscious," he said.

However, a final decision on this question has not yet been reached, Okubo found, because some hold that "retained land" helps the farmers to control the rural economy, and that small freedom in a large collective body should be permitted.

There is no doubt, he added, that a movement is afoot to defy, and rectify, the flexible economic policy that has been followed by the Liu-Teng group—the authority faction. But material well-being is also an important element that even the most idealistic revolutionaries cannot overlook. "The elevation of living standards" is one of the much-publicized goals of the third Five-Year Plan, or the second Great Leap Forward, initiated in 1966.

A COMMUNAL COUNTRY

The reporters heard inklings of the extension of the communes into a comprehensive political system. Hoshino predicted, in a discussion meeting after his return to Japan, that the reorganization of farm life under the Communists would eventually progress to a giant federation of communes, embracing both industry and agriculture to create a society different from any known today.

The first step has been to apply the commune principles and methods to industrial organizations.

Hoshino did not visit the Shanghai Glass and Machine Company, but he heard over the Peking radio that a "revolutionary production committee" had been established at the company sometime late in 1966. The forming of this committee was the result of a plan by supporters of Mao and Lin Piao to take over the industries in all cities by applying the Paris Commune style of "people's government" administration in the economic sphere. It was the Peking Municipal Committee that adopted this method and used it in political administration. The committee members in such organizations are uniformly called "servicemen," and there are no titles such as "chief." The committee members are classified as "political servicemen," "production servicemen," and "union servicemen." At the Shanghai Glass and Machine Company, which has 1,200 workers, the revolutionary production committee consisted of 10 "servicemen."

The Peking radio highly commended the revolutionary production committee as "one of the new products born from the great thoughts of Mao. It is the seedling of a new Communistic factory organization."

The regular Cultural Revolution committee in most factories are organizations with the primary aim of applying criticism and thought reform. But the revolutionary production committee is a management body which has as its goal the wresting of supervisory power away from the authority faction.

The same principles have been applied to municipal government. On January 5, 1967, Shanghai became the first city in China to establish—officially—a "commune" or "people's government." It took over the functions previously conducted by the Communist Party's Shanghai Municipal Committee and the municipal government. This is an improved

144

form of the Municipal People's Commune established by Mao in 1958, but which never got off the ground.

The Commune Extraordinary Committee, its supreme authoritative organ, is composed of five workers, two farmers, two military men, one student, and one Party-Government official. The composition of the membership shows that the workers have the largest say in industrial cities, corresponding to the common trend in farm villages where the highest authority is held by poor and lower middle-class growers. Although there is only one representative from the Party-Government organ, this by no means indicates that the influence of the Communist Party has waned. An old friend of the *Yomiuri* reporter, a Party official in Peking, emphasized this point, saying, "It is certain that the new Government structure will have a strong backbone provided by the Party."

The newspapers in Communist China have been calling constantly for a "great alliance of the revolutionary rebel forces"—that is, an alliance of the commune organizations. The Japanese newsman believes that Mao is planning to create a new governing body by forming such an alliance on the foundations of the agricultural and city communes, with the Communist Party forming the core. The National People's Congress, the supreme legislative organ, is expected to be reformed under the same concept.

He asked his friend, "What is to become of the Constitution? Amendments will surely have to be made, but is there not the possibility that the Constitution will be scrapped altogether?" The answer was noncommittal.

"In any event, the Cultural Revolution is one of the greatest experiments of the century, designed to realize Mao's dreams of a Communist society. Only history will answer whether the aims will be realized or not, and whether the Cultural Revolution will be a boon or a curse to peace and human happiness."

Chapter VII

LIVING WELL IN MAO-LAND

SUBURBIA, PEKING STYLE

Though the Japanese reporters, accustomed to the standard of living in Japan, found life in Communist China drab and grim by comparison, they were continuously impressed by the ordinary citizens whom they encountered, in their homes and in fields and factories, who assured the visitors that their lot had improved enormously over what they had known before. This was scarcely news to the members of the Yomiuri Task Force who had lived in the old China as students. The new element was the generally worshipful attitude of the middle and lower classes toward Mao Tse-tung, who was credited with having produced all blessings.

Nishimura's efforts to learn all he could about the life of ordinary citizens in Communist China took him to the Peking suburb of Kangchuwen, and there he met a typical *kanpu* [white-collar] couple, Mr. and Mrs. Chao Hua. Chao was 39 years old and a section chief in a branch of the central Government.

The son of a peasant, Chao had been illiterate when the Communists took over in 1949, Nishimura said. Although his formal education had not begun until he was 22 years old,

146

he has a bright future in the Communist bureaucracy. It seems, according to the account given by Nishimura, that the new Government had singled him out for "ideological excellency" because of his personal background, and had awarded him various scholarships that had enabled him to progress quickly through accelerated courses from elementary-school level through university.

The formula for success in Communist China is different from that followed in a capitalist country, Nishimura explained. In this Communist nation, a person coming from a good family usually finds it difficult to get ahead. What counts is the ideology and the ability of the individual. What school he went to does not make any difference. There are not a few university graduates who remain common clerks after reaching the age of 50. On the other hand, there are a sizable number of middle-school graduates who become section chiefs while in their twenties.

Chao stayed single for many years. He was so absorbed in his work and studies that he did not get around to finding a mate until he was over 30 years old. He finally yielded to the tearful plea of his old mother, who "wanted to have a grandchild." The wedding was held one spring day when the bridegroom was 33 years old.

The bride was Li Ming-hsia, four years younger. The daughter of a middle-class peasant, she worked in the same organization as her husband. She had only a primary-school education, but was second to no other worker in her ability to use an abacus. She was known to have "high ideological standards" and enjoyed a reputation as a woman of strong character.

Li and Chao fell in love while discussing various problems at "study meetings" in the organization. Chao was impressed by this young girl who expressed her well-considered opinions with force and clarity, while Li marveled at his brilliant analysis and criticism of revisionism.

The two found each other irresistible and were united in marriage with the blessings of all the other workers at the organization. It was, so to speak, a marriage born out of the Mao Tse-tung thought.

Nishimura visited the Chaos in their apartment in a building operated by the Government organization for which Chao works.

He and his wife occupy two rooms, of about 15 and 12 square yards, respectively, plus a kitchen. They shared a common bathroom with the other residents of the building. Since this is a new apartment house, Nishimura noted, their kitchen is supplied with gas and tap water. The monthly rent was five yuan [$2], and the maintenance cost less than 10 yuan [$4] a month. Nishimura continued their life story:

In the spring of the year after their wedding, the Chaos had their first child, a daughter. The cute, rosy-cheeked girl was given the nickname "Pinkuo" [apple] by her grandmother, who died four years ago. The child is in her last year of kindergarten, and will go on to primary school next spring.

Three years after Pinkuo was born, Mrs. Chao gave birth to a boy, who is now a third-year pupil at a nursery. When he still had to be fed milk, the Chaos paid a monthly fee of 25 yuan [$10] for keeping him in the nursery, but now they are charged only 12 yuan a month.

Pinkuo lives, eats, and sleeps at the kindergarten at the wish of her parents, who want her to become accustomed to living with other children. The monthly fee for a "live-in pupil" is 17 yuan [$6.80]. Nishimura invited his readers to take a look around the Chao apartment. Hanging on the wall of their living room is a large portrait of Chairman Mao on the snow-covered shore of Chungnankai Lake. It looks as though the Chairman is smiling a welcome to a guest.

At the right there is a large desk on which there are a radio and pens and other writing materials. At the left stands a large bookcase with a glass door. In the left-hand corner there is a double bed covered with a piece of cloth bearing an embroidered flower design, executed by Chao's deceased mother.

The bookcase contains about two hundred books, many of which are ideological works, including the complete works of Mao Tse-tung and Marx and Lenin. There are also a considerable number of books on Chinese history and the revolution, and copies of bestselling novels. Nishimura opened one of the ideological books and found that the pages were filled with red underlining.

"I have read the complete works of Mao Tse-tung thirty times, and my wife has read them at least twenty times. Therefore we know from which articles—and from what pages—the passages in *Quotations from Chairman Mao Tse-tung* are taken," Mr. Chao said.

Aside from the books, the Chao family property consists only of a bicycle, two wristwatches, an alarm clock, padded clothes, overcoats, and holiday outfits—one each for the husband and wife. The bookcase and the bed, the wardrobe, the desk, and other furniture belong to the apartment house. Chao said laughingly, "If we received an order for a transfer in the morning, we could pack up and leave at noon, because we do not have very many things to pack."

The Chaos get up at 6:30 A.M. every day. After washing and having tea, they walk their son to the nursery and then go to a bus stop to catch a bus sent by their organization. They have meals at the dining room where they work, and the children are fed at the kindergarten and the nursery.

The Chaos report to work at the organization at 8 A.M. and take off at 6 P.M. They take a two-hour lunch break at noon and have a 15-minute recess in the morning and in the afternoon, during which time they relieve the stiffening of their shoulders and waists by doing exercises. In winter they cut the lunch period to an hour and a half and go home 30 minutes earlier.

149

Sunday is the day of the week when the Chaos and their children get together and have a good time. They have breakfast consisting of about five dishes—including the favorite foods of northern Chinese, rice gruel and buns and pickled vegetables and eggs. When they go on a picnic, they have their supper at a restaurant.

The study meeting, which forms an integral part of life in Communist China, is held twice a week at the organization where the Chaos work. The employes take half a day off from their jobs and thoroughly study the "Mao thought" and important domestic and international issues, and exchange views on these subjects. But the study meeting apparently has a romantic side to it, Nishimura noted, judging from the way Chao and his wife were brought together.

Noticing the total absence of bars, cabarets, and dance halls, Nishimura wondered what the Chaos did for entertainment besides going on picnics. The country offers much in the way of "wholesome entertainment," particularly movies, dramas, and music, the correspondent said, but added that the theaters and cinema houses were packed to capacity most of the time.

Chao informed him that the department where he works strove for self-sufficiency in entertainment, providing free movies every Saturday night and occasional appearances of theatrical troupes at the organization's expense. He also told Nishimura that he often took extended trips to the provinces to observe and participate in the life of the countryside, a practice encouraged by the Government.

"The year before last, I went on a one-year trip to a People's Commune on the outskirts of Peking," Chao said. "It is so good to stay in a farming village!" he continued. "I am not speaking about fresh air, plenty of food, or anything like that. What I am trying to say is that we have many things to learn from farmers and much to acquire by engaging in manual labor.

"Let me cite an easy example: Intellectuals living in cities eat pork every day, but they do not know anything about what farmers do to fatten up their hogs. When we visit a farming village, we can take lessons from farmers and guide their cultural activities at the same time. In a word, we city people and the farmers teach each other. It is a two-way street, and all to the good.

"Believe me," Chao went on, "the farmers are pure-hearted. During my tour of duty in the People's Commune, I took a vacation and returned to Peking to spend the New Year with my family. When I went back to the farm, I found that the farmers had saved for me dishes that they had prepared for the New Year. I was moved to tears."

Nishimura asked Chao, "What do you want most?" The Chinese answered, "The spirit to serve the people—that is all I want. I want to absorb the proletarian view of the world and the Mao thought more fully. I do not want anything else."

Nishimura learned that Chao received a monthly salary of 100 yuan, his wife 50 yuan. Their apartment rent and other fixed expenses came to 44 yuan, leaving 111 yuan for food, clothing, and other expenditures. The sum, though less than $45, obviously kept the family comfortably as far as the Japanese newsman could see. According to the figures given by Communist Chinese officials, the Chaos were definitely in the middle class; the average wage was put at 60 yuan [$24] a month, and the publicly-announced salary of Mao Tse-tung was 400 yuan [$160]. It was Nishimura's impression that when Chao described himself as contented with his lot, he was telling the truth.

Another kind of success story was described by the *Yomiuri* economist, Okubo.

"Mine is a large family with nine members, but we lead a comfortable and happy life, thanks to Chairman Mao," said Chou Sung-shan, the director of the vegetable section of the Central Market in Wuhan.

Chou, 35 years old, of medium build and clad in a worker's uniform, struck Okubo as an honest and steady person. But his forehead was creased with wrinkles, presumably because he had had a hard life as a child.

Recalling the "bad old days," Chou said, "My father was a factory worker, but he found it hard to support his family. When I was about 10 years old, I started peddling vegetables to supplement the family income. I could not afford to buy rainwear, so I hated to be caught in the rain. I had the bitter experience of being robbed of my vegetables by members of Chiang Kai-shek's Kuonintang Party."

Until four years after the Communists came to power, their was no vegetable market at Wuhan, Okubo continued, so Chou operated his own vegetable store. He did not have to worry about his new customers—Liberation Army troops —for they never failed to pay for their purchases.

In June 1954, Chou started working for the newly organized Mutual Aid Association. He received a monthly salary of 30 yuan [$12]. Later, the association grew into the present state-operated market through the process of collectivization that began in September 1957. As a member of the organization Chou started with a monthly salary of 48 yuan, which has been raised to about 70 today.

Chou's wife also works at a monthly salary of 41 yuan. The couple live with their four children—the oldest is 16 and is in middle school—and the wife's mother and Chou's sister. The sister attends a school where the students divide their time between studies and manual labor. She receives an allowance of 19 yuan a month for her work.

Chou goes to work early in the morning. Being employed in the vegetable section of the market, which opens at 6:30 A.M., he must report at 6. He and his fellow workers study Chairman Mao's works until the market opens. At about 9

A.M. they hold a meeting to discuss their problems and discuss ways of improving service so as to boost sales. Chou is pretty busy in the afternoon, too, performing his duties as chief of the vegetable section and making arrangements to purchase new stock for sale.

Chou regards selling vegetables as a patriotic mission. "This is a life worth living," he said. "I will keep selling vegetables for the sake of society. I used to sell vegetables just to make a living, but now it is a different story. Since I started studying Mao's works, I have come to realize that my first duty is to the people and not to myself."

STABILIZING PRICES

At Chou's market, the reporters were able to see China's price-fixing policy at work. Okubo found that, unlike most countries, Communist China has succeeded in keeping commodity prices at a low level, a great contrast to the old days and an important factor in improving the standard of living.

In the months preceding the fall of Shanghai in 1949, he recalled, residents would wait in a long queue to buy rice, the price of which kept rising day after day. This was when the city was ruled by a son of Generalissimo Chiang Kai-shek.

"Look how it is now," a 25-year-old woman employe of a grocery store in Shanghai said to him. "First-grade rice prices have not changed for quite some time." The prices of dates and some other farm products sold at her store have actually been dropping.

In the pre-Communist days, Okubo recalled from his own years as a young man in Shanghai, there was a saying that "even the price of soil goes up by three fen in the New Year." Nowadays, commodities are sold at a 30 percent discount during the solar and lunar New Year seasons.

A member of the administrative office in the Tienshan

153

Sintsun residential area of Shanghai told him that prices were so stabilized that the cost of essential items such as edible oil, salt, rice, and firewood has remained unchanged for the past ten years.

To avoid any loss to producers, the Government buys goods from producers at a relatively high price and sells them to consumers at a lower figure when it is necessary. The balance is met by the state. To illustrate the point, an official of the Wuhan General Market where Chou worked, said the retail price of meat had been 6 to 8 percent below the wholesale price for months.

The Wuhan Market is one of the state-operated consumer enterprises established in various parts of the Chinese mainland. It purchases vegetables from the People's Communes in nearby farming villages through the procurement station, which is composed of representatives of the communes, central Government agencies, and state-operated markets. In most cases, vegetables are sold to customers at prices 18 to 20 percent below the wholesale cost. Profits are used to keep in stock—and to process—vegetables, and to pay wages to market employees. The Government meets the deficit by subsidies to the market.

The price section of the market fixes the wholesale prices of vegetables after consultations with officials of the procurement station. Even when the communes have produced more vegetables than had been planned, the market buys the entire output at the usual price. When the communes have failed to attain the production target, the market replenishes the shortage by purchasing from communes in other districts. In such cases, the state shoulders the extra cost of transportation, thus keeping the consumer prices undisturbed.

For the state to assume all the cost of keeping prices level would be a heavy drain on the Government exchequer; therefore, the authorities strive to maintain the balance of the national economy by lowering the prices of some goods and lifting the cost of others. Communist China, operating on a planned economy, controls commodity prices in a thoroughgoing manner, Okubo concluded.

A ROOF OVER THEIR HEADS

The Japanese reporters were impressed by the visible evidence of improvements in housing.

The Communist Chinese Government has succeeded in providing people with low-cost houses, Okubo reported. In most cases, houses are built and rented by the state, local public organizations, and business groups, most of which are operated by the central Government.

In Shanghai, now grown into a megalopolis of 10 million people, there is a suburban residential area called Tienshan Sintsun.

There are slightly more than 39,000 people living in Tienshan Sintsun. The buildings in the area have a total floor space of a little over 300,000 square meters. These include middle and primary schools, kindergartens, nurseries, hospitals, public dining halls, restaurants, theaters, libraries, and stores, all of which were built at the expense of the state by the Shanghai Municipal Construction Bureau.

In a concrete apartment house in the area, Okubo found the Yu family and spoke to Mrs. Yu Chu-hsiang, a 49-year-old housewife who lives with her husband, a carpenter at a rubber plant, and their 13-year-old son.

Mr. Yu receives a monthly salary of 94 yuan [$37.60]. Mrs. Yu does not work, because of delicate health. In response to a question, she said that the family pays five yuan and 59 fen [cents] for the room, two yuan for gas, slightly less than one yuan for electricity, 30 fen for tap water, and 30 yuan for food. Of course, the family must also buy clothes and meet unforeseen expenses from time to time, Mrs. Yu said.

155

adding, "But our livelihood is secure, and we can even save money."

Being a small family, the Yus have only one room. It contains beds, wardrobes, a dressing table, a radio, a sewing machine, and other items of furniture. They share a kitchen, a bathroom, and a toilet with another family.

In addition to these residential areas laid out in the style of a modern housing complex, there are living quarters for workers attached to each major factory. The Peking Second Cotton Spinning Factory has a 230,000-square-meter housing development with complete living quarters for married employes and their families, a dormitory for bachelor workers, schools for children, and various welfare facilities.

While visiting this housing project, the reporter dropped in at a two-room apartment of a family with six members—a worker, his wife, his mother, and three children. They pay a monthly rent of two yuan and 60 fen, which is lower than the cost of apartments in Tienshan Sintsun.

The family apparently live in comfort, for there is a total monthly income of 180 yuan, of which 80 yuan is earned by the head of the family, 70 yuan by his wife, and 30 yuan by his son.

According to an official in Kwangchow, the average monthly house rent for workers in that city amounts to only 5 percent of their average monthly salary of 66 yuan. The rate is even lower for those living in housing projects attached to factories.

At the housing project of the Third Cotton Mill in Chengchow, married workers and their families pay a monthly rent of two yuan and five fen, including charges for tap water, electricity, and furniture, as against their average monthly income of 55 yuan. The rent is three yuan for a bachelor employe.

At the employes' living quarters of a tractor plant in Loyang, the rent is two yuan for married workers and their families, and six fen for bachelor employes. The chief of the liaison section of this factory said that commodity prices in the Loyang area have been gradually declining and, therefore, workers are becoming better off, although their salaries remain unchanged.

None of this means that bad housing no longer exists in today's China, Okubo declared. In one section of Tienshan Sintsun, he saw about forty-five old, dilapidated houses that made a strange contrast to the modern apartment buildings surrounding them. They are reminiscent of the abject poverty that had afflicted the laborers of Shanghai in the pre-Communist days. Sun Ping-wen, a 50-year-old employe of a factory that makes spinning machinery, who lives in the same apartment building as the Yu family, said that he used to live in a house with a roof that leaked badly when it rained.

Factories not only provide housing for their workers, but care for their workers' children, enabling the majority of married women to be employed.

At the nursery attached to a paper mill in Kwangchow, 30 governesses look after 413 children. The factory charges parents a monthly fee of only 50 fen for keeping their offspring in the nursery, in addition to food charges of five to eight fen. Other miscellaneous expenses for this care are assumed by the factory.

THE WORST OF ALL SINS

The Japanese correspondents observed that the anxiety to improve the living conditions of the individual without falling into the "revisionist" sin of "economism"—placing material well-being above socialist ideology—constituted a fundamental dilemma for the ruler of Communist China.

"Economism" was one word that Takuzo Kamai heard wherever he went in mainland China.

157

The term first attracted his attention in Shanghai. When he reached Wuhan, it seemed that the streets were filled with this particular word. Wall posters listed countless accusations as examples of economism. One poster said that local leaders had tried to weaken the "revolutionary consciousness" of workers by paying them extra wages and allowances. Another said that local government funds had been used to send large groups of laborers to Peking, under the pretext of promoting the interchange of ideas among "revolutionary masses" of various districts.

This "economism" was obviously the worst of all sins, and *Yomiuri's* economics specialist Okubo noted that this reflected a fundamental conflict between ideals and practicality in the goals of the Cultural Revolution.

Though the Cultural Revolution is aimed at changing the ideological outlook of the masses, the doctrines of Mao and Lin cannot disregard the simple, human desire of the masses to live in comfort, Okubo said.

In early January of 1967, newspapers and the radio charged that in Shanghai and other cities the authority faction was trying to please the laborers by resorting to such tactics as paying extra wages. The mass media said, in effect, that it was outrageous to induce or coax laborers to work harder by giving them material incentives. Such methods, it was charged, are related to revisionism and capitalism.

There was also criticism of the system under which the state granted subsidies to workers through individual enterprises. These subsidies were paid as a reward when workers exceeded target figures. The Maoists contended that whatever the pretext might be for such incentive pay, the system tends to stimulate the earthly desires of the workers and is akin to Soviet revisionism. Judging by the standards fixed in the "Mao Tse-tung thought," this line of approach is the most deviated of all deviations from true socialism, for the

Mao thought attaches prime importance to "spirit" as distinguished from "matter."

Hard-working laborers armed with the Mao thought hate to have others think they are working for subsidies. To be viewed in such a manner is almost as disgraceful as to be taken before a public tribunal, forced to wear a dunce cap, and be subjected to the hisses and boos of the crowd. So, under the impetus of criticism, they began to air the idea of refusing to accept such payments.

But there was one catch: If they declined to take the payments, their incomes suffered, and now they are looking for alternatives. This is a problem that must be solved before Communist China can establish a viable wage system in line with Maoist doctrine.

It is true, Okubo noted, that workers of Communist China are provided the basic requirements for living, whether it be food, clothing, or a residence. The situation is a radical departure from the days when laborers had to live in houses with leaking roofs, wrapped themselves in rags for clothing, and were always facing dire starvation. But at the same time, both the state and the autonomous enterprises have been encouraging them to increase production, so that they can achieve a higher living standard through receiving incentive awards.

The success of the Cultural Revolution in eliminating such awards has been mixed, Okubo discovered. Peng Shui-hsien, chief of the information office of a paper mill in Canton, told him—with an air of enthusiasm—that his plant had abolished incentives because the practice resembled Soviet revisionism. However, the step amounted to an average reduction in the worker's income of 8 percent.

Since the average wage in this mill amounted to about 75 yuan [$30] a month, the end of incentive pay cost a typical worker about six yuan, Okubo noted, questioning the wisdom of such a step as a basis for long-term labor policy. The Japanese investigator discovered that the factory authorities had the same misgivings, so the mill finally decided to adopt in place of the awards a practice of paying supplementary wages equivalent to the amount lost. The difference from the previous method is that the new formula gives extra pay to everyone according to the same percentage formula, whereas previously the awards had been paid according to three different schedules based on the functions and abilities of workers.

Okubo recalled conversations with workers in iron and steel plants of Wuhan and in spinning mills at Chengchow in which he was told, "We do not work just to make money. We work for the establishment of socialism. Therefore, we do not use such terms as "incentive awards," which tend to spread misconceptions. Instead, we pay welfare benefits indirectly by improving the food in company dining halls and supplying edible oil, meat, and other amenities."

He was informed at a spinning plant in Peking, however, that the system of incentive pay was being retained, openly, without such subterfuges as paying equal benefits in another way or under a different name. "The majority of the workers say that they do not want the incentive awards, preferring that the assets of the state be enriched instead," a spokesman assured Okubo, "but we are continuing the system, in the hope that a decision will be made in the matter after discussions in which all workers will participate at a later date."

A Mr. Yuan, manager of a travel agency in Wuhan, told Okubo that he favored—privately—raising wages by an amount equivalent to the incentive awards.

Workers might welcome this plan with open arms, Okubo surmised, but it could pose problems for the state as well as the enterprises concerned. Such awards are generally classified as being in addition to standard wages. If the payments are added to the regular wage scale, the state will have to pay considerably larger retirement pensions.

In Communist China, wages of workers are usually classified in eight categories, he explained. In the case of the paper mill in Canton, the eight-step scale ranged from 49 yuan [$19.60] to 120 yuan [$48]; at the cotton-spinning plant in Peking, from 40 to 100 yuan, and at the Chengchow spinning mill from 30 to 96 yuan. Designated as being outside the eight-step scale are apprentices and semi-skilled workers, who generally receive around 20 yuan [$8]. Similarly, high-class engineers, technicians, and plant chiefs are placed outside the salary framework. Technicians at a chemical plant in Shanghai received a maximum of 250 yuan [$100] a month.

Several factors can be cited as deciding a worker's pay scale, including such considerations as whether he has a firm commitment to socialism, the level of his skill, and the number of hours he works. Since the beginning of the Cultural Revolution, emphasis has been put on the application of "Mao thought" to the job, in the belief that one armed with a sound theology inevitably excels in work, thus converting the spiritual to the material.

However, Okubo thought it might be difficult to measure ideology by a material yardstick in respect to its merits and demerits and suggested that even this system of fixing a wage scale contains elements resembling performance pay.

Differences in wages still exist, he found, despite the establishment of something like a guaranteed minimum income based partly on the size of the household. At the paper mill in Canton, for example, when a breadwinner's earnings divided by the number of dependents yielded a figure of less than 12 yuan a month, the management made up the difference. In effect, then, the mill authorities enforced a minimum individual income of 12 yuan a month for its employes and their families.

161

The differences that do exist produced a mixed reaction from a member of the medical staff in a hospital attached to the Wuhan Medical Institute:

"Differences in wages between university professors and general workers and staff members are exceedingly great, although we hear that the Soviet revisionists are widening the gap. But I am not saying that wages should simply be leveled off among all people equally. Reasonable differences are necessary."

The Government is pushing political measures to wipe out the "Three Forms of Discrimination"—between cities and farms, brain workers and manual workers, factory workers and farmers.

Generally, Okubo found that pay rates have not changed much in recent years; for instance, the average wage of workers at the Wuhan iron and steel complex is 65 yuan, the same as when he visited that city earlier, and at a chemical plant in Nanking the average was 62 yuan, four yuan less than at the time of his previous visit.

In order to raise living standards, it is the Government's policy to lower commodity prices, instead of increasing wages.

However, Okubo was careful to qualify his account of the state of the Communist Chinese economy. When a Chinese worker says that his "livelihood is stabilized," he is speaking in a relative sense, comparing his living conditions with those of the past.

In January 1967 the Communist Chinese Government abolished the coupon system for the sale of stockings, socks, and towels. This was made possible by the bumper cotton crop, but the country still maintains the ration system for staple food, edible oil, and various cotton articles. He was told that these items also are likely to be placed on free sale in the near future.

The price of luxury goods, however, is prohibitively high,

particularly in the case of imported items. Even bicycles are very expensive, although they are a common means of transportation. A middle-aged laborer whom Okubo met in a Peking department store said that he had just bought a bicycle with money that he had taken more than a year to save. The price, he said, was 167 yuan [$66.80], twice or three times the monthly wages of Chinese laborers.

In reviewing the living conditions of Communist Chinese workers, Okubo felt that he had to point out that the living standards are still much below those of their counterparts in Japan and other advanced industrial countries.

DECLINE OF THE LABOR UNIONS

If there are demands for a better standard of living in Communist China, those demands will not come through the traditional labor unions, *Yomiuri's* young historian learned.

Mineo Nakajima, the 30-year-old scholar from the Tokyo Foreign Language University, one of the academic members of the Yomiuri Task Force, had already concluded that the Great Proletarian Cultural Revolution was anything but cultural. Now he discovered that it was not very proletarian, either.

In any case, laborers—who are the proletariat—do not carry much weight in today's China. The All-China Federation of Trade Unions—ACFTU—is the only labor organization with nationwide membership in Communist China, where the modern labor class constitutes only a small segment of the society. And nothing had been heard of the ACFTU for several years until it was reportedly closed down on Dec. 27, 1966—a report not yet confirmed. Wishing to know more about the state of organized labor, he was delighted to hear that representatives of laborers had agreed to talk to the reporters. The place was Shanghai, called "the city of laborers."

163

Three workers, all about 30 years old, came to the Hoping Fantien Hotel on the bank of the Whangpoo River. They identified themselves as Mao Te-ho, an engineer of the Shanghai Acid-Proof Enamel Porcelain Factory; Chou Neng-pang, a worker in charge of revolving furnaces at the Shanghai First Steel Plant, and Su Yin-chen, a woman, vice chairman of the Chiusin Shipyard's labor union.

Nakajima was determined to get answers to many questions concerning Communist Chinese labor that had haunted him for years, but he was baffled at the outset when Mao Te-ho, who appeared to be the senior member of the trio, began the conversation by saying, "Tonight we will tell you how laborers in Shanghai remade themselves by studying Chairman Mao's book, and how they applied their principles to production."

He then launched into a lengthy discourse that might have been entitled "The Mao Tse-tung Thought and the Success Achieved in the Production of Domestic Oxygen Cylinders." His story sounded familiar to the Japanese historian. After returning to Japan, he checked and found that his memory had not been at fault. The same Mao Te-ho, who is a sort of "model laborer," had written a long thesis on the development of oxygen cylinders in the Shanghai *Liberation Daily* in May 1966. The thesis was republished in *People's Daily* and the Japanese translation appeared in the July 26, 1966, issue of *Peking Shuho* [Peking Weekly].

Now, in the Shanghai hotel, Mao went on and on for almost two hours, until Nakajima lost all patience and said, "I know all about it, and I got the point you are trying to make. It is very fortunate for us to be able to meet you tonight. So let us get what we want to get. Besides, it is getting late. So give us time to ask questions."

Finally, he was able to ask what the ACFTU does as a labor union in a socialist country. He got the following answer:

"The ACFTU has three duties: to insure that the Mao thought be studied at all factories; to carry out the struggle for a technical revolution and the mechanization of factories; and to promote the welfare and recreation of laborers. In Communist China there can be no labor struggle concerning wage increases or placement of workers. Wages are fixed through debates in each unit, and the placement of workers is carried out for the purpose of meeting the needs of the state."

Nakajima also asked many questions about the clashes between the Red Guards and laborers, and the problem of "the revolution and production" and the conflict between "Red workers armed with the Mao thought" and specialists who are concerned mainly with the improvement of industrial techniques. The three men answered, in effect, that "all is well with Communist China's labor," adding that the ACFTU is essentially different from labor unions of capitalistic countries.

Nakajima could see that the ACFTU could not be lumped together with such organizations as Japan's Sohyo (General Council of Trade Unions). But there was one question that still remained unanswered. If all was well with labor in Communist China, why was it that the new "rebel" faction had taken over the control of the ACFTU? There were complicated circumstances behind this development, and what the model laborer had told him did not tell the whole story.

Over the years, Nakajima learned, the entrenched leaders of the ACFTU, guided by the Communist Party's Shanghai Municipal Committee, had put up stiff resistance against the Mao-Lin main-current faction by demanding wage increases, a change in the jurisdiction over industrial management, the merger of factories, and a revision in the ownership system, according to *Liberation Daily*. It may appear that demands for higher wages and other changes mentioned

165

here are rightful claims, but in Communist China such demands are considered unjustified.

Clearly, the ACFTU was closed down in a move to eradicate "anti-revolutionary economism."

Paradoxically, the Great Proletarian Cultural Revolution is in fact a movement aimed at eliminating elements that are usually associated with the proletariat, Nakajima decided. ACFTU officials and other labor leaders, as well as officials of the Culture Ministry and the Communist Party Central Propaganda Department, have been attacked one after another in the course of the Cultural Revolution.

Labor Minister Ma Wen-lui and Vice Minister of Labor Li Cheng-ting were severely criticized by Mao's wife and by Red Guard wall posters. Such ACFTU leaders as Chairman Liu Ning-yi, Vice Chairman Ma Chun-ku, Secretary Ku Ta-chun, and Liu Shih, an executive committee member, were criticized successively in the period immediately after the closing of the organization.

Attacks were also leveled against former ACFTU leaders who had retired from politics. Among these men were Li Li-san, the first chairman of ACFTU when the organization was founded in 1925; Chen Yun, the chairman when the federation revived its lawful activities in 1948; and the late Lai Yu-yu, who had succeeded Chen in 1962. The same fate overtook Chen Yung-wen, Kao Li-shung, and Hsing Wen-chun, who had served as first, second, and third editors of the *Laborer's Daily,* the organ of the ACFTU (renamed the *Chinese Laborer's Report,* January 1, 1967). Hsing Wen-chun, the vice chairman of the ACFTU who had played an active role on the international labor front and in the theoretical struggle between Communist China and the Soviet Union, died in January 1967.

Thus the leadership of Communist China's labor, including officials of the 20,000,000-member ACFTU, has now lost its power, Nakajima discovered. Needless to say, the Mao-

Lin faction ousted the labor leaders in order to remove the influence of Liu Shao-chi, who had led the labor movement in China since it came into being in 1925. As a result, the indications are that Maoism will become even more devoid of elements connected with city workers.

Under the circumstances, Nakajima was amused to recall a song—now almost forgotten—that Chinese unionists sang when Liu Shao-chi was their leader more than forty years ago. Called the Song of a Cotton Mill Labor Union, it went as follows:

Laborers have their own chivalrous spirit;

Let us join forces to fight against capitalism;

Follow the orders of the labor union and do not listen to false statements of capitalists;

If we win, our wages will go up;

If we strike one day, our wages will go up that much.

RED MILLIONAIRES

A curious anomaly discovered by the *Yomiuri* team in Communist China was a continued existence of a pampered "capitalist" class, living luxuriously on vast incomes from private fortunes and occupying the same fine homes that they had always inhabited in the former French Concession of Shanghai. Takuzo Kamai went back to that once-fashionable quarter, which he had known well when he was a student at Tungwen University in the pre-Communist era, to investigate this strange survival of another age in the austere Marxian society created by Mao.

There are still some millionaires in Communist China, the journalist reported, like Liu Nien-chih, who receives an annual payment of 1,000,000 yuan [$400,000] as interest on his former assets, and a monthly salary of 525 yuan—much more than Chairman Mao, whose salary is 400 yuan.

Liu leads a luxurious life. He and his family have made

167

sightseeing tours to distant parts of the country, including Manchuria and Sinkiang. His wife serves as a member of the National People's Congress and has traveled overseas several times. Liu himself is a committee member of the Political and Commercial Cooperative Council, an advisory organ to the central Government.

Another well-known capitalist is Yung I-jen, deputy mayor of Shanghai, who receives yearly interest payments totaling 3,000,000 yuan. By any standard this is great wealth, but especially so when compared with the average wage for a laborer or office worker in Communist China of 60 to 70 yuan a month. (Here Kamai explained the value of yuan, in Japanese terms, at one yuan to 350 yen—about 90 cents—or slightly over 150 yen—40 cents—"when the commodity prices and other factors are taken into consideration.") In dollars, 2½ yuan are equivalent to $1.

Liu, Yung, and other capitalists in Shanghai live in large mansions, complete with turfed gardens and tennis courts. They are members of a privileged class that survives in today's China.

The enormous incomes of these millionaires, Kamai explained, comes from the annual interest of 5 percent paid by the Government on private assets donated to the state after the establishment of the Communist regime.

The practice was rationalized by the Government as "repurchasing of capital by the state," he continued. In August 1966, when the Cultural Revolution had reached a feverish pitch, the Red Guards called on the Government to stop paying the interest. There had been theoretical debate earlier as to whether the capitalists were "exploiting" the public by taking revenue from their former properties, but it was not until the outbreak of the Cultural Revolution that the matter became an issue of major public concern.

Naturally, the question Kamai asked is: Why did the Communists see fit to pay remuneration to capitalists in the first place? Here is the answer: Since the early days of its history, the Chinese Communist Party has followed a policy of "using, limiting, and remaking" the existing capitalist. Mao "used" them as engineers and managers, "limited" their activities by making them engage in production, and "remade" them by gradually merging their enterprises into Government agencies and by reforming them along the Communist line of thought.

At the same time, Mao set the principle of bringing profits to both labor and management. He insured that private enterprises obtained profit margins of about 30 percent and that capitalists received bonuses as officials of their respective organizations, in addition to dividends amounting to as much as 8 percent of the total profits.

This formula was followed until 1953, when the Communist Government adopted the policy of dividing the profits equally among the "Four Elements"—the state, private enterprise, labor, and management. And in 1956 the Government placed industrial and commercial organizations under the joint control of the state and private enterprises, and began paying 5 percent interest to capitalists on the holdings that had been absorbed from individual ownership.

At that time, there were 1,140,000 capitalists in the country, and the assets that they had donated to the state were valued at 2,400 million yuan. This means that the Government was paying a yearly interest of 120,000,000 yuan to the former owners. The term for the payment of interest was set originally at seven years, or until 1963, and was extended to nine years. However, the Government was reported to have continued to pay the interest in 1966. We know for sure that the payment was made at least in the first half of that year, Kamai reported. It is small wonder that the Red Guards, inspired by revolutionary fervor, urged the Government to end the practice.

Red Guards also clamored for the dissolution of eight

"democratic groups"—organizations that are composed mainly of capitalists and members of their families. One of these, called the Democratic Society for Establishment of the State, is associated closely with the National Federation of Industrial and Commercial Enterprisers and various other capitalist organizations with nationwide enrollment.

Lately, the agitation for the suspension of interest payments to capitalists and the dissolution of the "democratic groups" has died down, presumably because the demands cannot be met at once, as they would require a revision of the Constitution. But the indications are that the Red Guards will have their way, soon or later, for they are not alone in asserting that capitalists of any kind are an unnecessary evil in Communist China. A truck driver whom Kamai interviewed echoed the views of many others when he declared bluntly, "The capitalists are all the same. There are right-wingers, left-wingers, and middle-of-the-roaders. But the differences between them are a matter of degree. They all have the bourgeois ideology, and that is what is wrong with them."

THE PEOPLE'S BANK

The concept that the payment of interest is somehow antisocial has resulted in the creation of a new kind of banking practice in Communist China, Okubo noted. Banks that pay no interest arose as a result of the Cultural Revolution, he discovered. In August 1966, Shanghai laborers "armed with the Mao thought" proposed that depositors stop receiving interest, arguing that people should put their money in banks for the sole purpose of having it used for the establishment of a socialistic state. It is against the Communist principles, they declared, to take more money out of a bank account than one has put in.

The central Government took no action on the laborers' proposal, but the Shanghai Branch of the People's Bank, acting on its own authority, stopped paying interest to depositors who expressed willingness to forgo this benefit of saving. However, nothing like this has happened in Kwangchow, another Chinese city that Okubo visited. The no-interest deposit system seemed to exist only in places like Shanghai, where there are a large number of citizens imbued with revolutionary fervor.

The ordinary People's Bank pays interest of 3.96 percent annually, or 0.33 percent monthly, on fixed deposits made by individuals. The rates are 2.16 percent a year, 0.18 percent a month, for ordinary deposits by individuals or industrial and commercial organizations. Money deposited by the state yields no interest.

Walking along the streets of Peking, one often sees a sign "Branch Office of the People's Bank," hanging over the door of a small building that obviously had been a residence before being remodeled into offices, the economist reported. These institutions make it their business exclusively to accept, keep, and pay deposits. They do not engage in advancing loans or issuing bills. This is an indication that Communist China depends much on money saved by citizens to finance its plans to build up the national economic strength.

The head office of the state-operated People's Bank engages chiefly in furnishing charter loans, issuing currency, controlling national finance, and providing loans needed to operate various sectors of the nation's economy. In short, this Communist Chinese institution combines the functions of the central and city banks of another country.

The People's Bank, the Agriculture Bank, and the Construction Bank furnish loans at 7.2 percent annual interest —or 0.6 percent a month.

Okubo found that bankers in Communist China take pains to profess the same deep ideological involvement with Maoism that was characteristic of practically everyone the *Yomiuri* reporters interviewed. He talked to Chou Yang-sheng, an official of the Shanghai branch of the People's Bank, who told him, "Our basic task is to carry the red flag of the Mao Tse-tung thought and to help accelerate the industrial and agricultural production, and to facilitate the marketing of commodities. By so doing, we strive to achieve a rapid and balanced progress of the national economy."

Nor were the Communist Chinese bankers free from the anti-Soviet bias that pervaded Mao's China. Criticism of Soviet revisionism cropped up in Chou's account of how the People's Bank operates, Okubo reported. Chou said that, unlike the Soviet banks, the People's Bank makes it a point to extend loans to industrial organizations regardless of their productivity and their financial conditions.

"We are concerned solely with aiding enterprises in boosting production, following Chairman Mao's policy of achieving economic expansion by supplying the enterprises with sufficient funds," Chou went on.

"Members of the bank's charter loan section visit industrial organizations to foster contact with laborers while they are at work on their jobs. They work with the laborers and help them solve various problems. There is no use just sitting at a desk and reading figures in an office. If we are overly conscious of the fact that we are the lenders and become proud of our positions as managers, we will alienate ourselves from enterprises and become isolated from the masses."

Chou further said that the People's Bank issues currency only to keep pace with the production and marketing of commodities. Therefore, he explained, the issuance of currency by the bank never becomes a cause for inflation, and the currency values remain stable for long periods of time.

In addition to the People's Bank, the Agriculture Bank, and the Construction Bank, Communist China also has the Bank of China, which specializes in foreign-exchange transactions; also the Huachiao Bank, with its head office in Singapore, the Siyou Bank of Amoy and the Bank of East Asia in Hong Kong, which are operated by *huachiao* [overseas Chinese] under the guidance of the People's Bank.

The country's financial resources also must take into account money that the overseas Chinese send to their homeland or invest in enterprises in mainland China. The amount from this source has begun to rise again after having shown a decline because of the chaos created by the Cultural Revolution, Okubo reported.

The indications are that the Chinese Communist Government will continue to utilize the financial power of the *huachiao*, though there have been rumors and speculation to the contrary. Officially, this was rationalized by the explanation that the majority of Chinese merchants established overseas are former laborers who fled to foreign countries in order to escape persecution by reactionaries, and the state has taken various steps to assure that these expatriates can send funds to their relatives back home and invest in enterprises in China.

Expert China-watchers in Hong Kong have estimated that remittances to mainland China from her sons abroad run to tens of millions of dollars every year, perhaps hundreds of millions. There is no way of estimating the sum with any accuracy, but there is universal agreement among financial experts in the British Crown Colony—one of the principal sources of such remittances—that this traffic constitutes an extremely important contribution to Communist China's foreign-exchange resources.

Chapter VIII

MAOISM FROM CRADLE TO GRAVE

FIRE-BREATHING WOMEN

In the rapidly changing Chinese society, the Yomiuri Task Force found that Maoism and the Cultural Revolution had put their mark not only on the economy, but on the very fabric of life, affecting all the people, young and old, male and female, in every minute of every day. The Japanese reporters were particularly bemused by the image of politically conscious women manning the barricades of revolution.

Mao's tribute to women of the militia corps took the form of verse:

The gallant figure of a woman carrying a five-foot-long gun,
Standing on the drill ground bathed in the first rays of the morning sun;
Women of China nourish great hopes;
They do not love to wear gay dresses. Instead, they love to carry arms.
—From a poem by Mao Tse-tung, 1961.

"What Mao says in the first three lines of the poem is quite correct, but the fourth and last line shows that the Chairman does not know everything about the women of his country," reported Nishimura, sophisticated Japanese correspondent.

He was willing to accept Mao's conviction that Chinese women love to arm themselves, but would not agree that they do not also love to be gaily dressed.

On May Day, the day of the year when Communist Chinese women are allowed to dress up as much as they wish, Nishimura said that young girls, each wearing the dress of her own preference, are seen in front of mirrors everywhere in Red China, busily applying the powder puff. They are completely engrossed in painting their faces, and do not care if other people are watching them.

"Not that these women are good at making themselves attractive," he added ungallantly. "They put the powder on the tops of their noses, and use so much rouge that their lips are as red as a monkey's anus." At any rate, such scenes led him to doubt the veracity of the aging Chairman's statement that Chinese women do not go in for fancy dresses. However, Nishimura did find that ordinary Chinese women dress up only on special occasions, such as May Day, and usually refrain from using cosmetics. Without a single exception, heavily painted women seen on the streets turn out to be either foreigners or members of the families of Chinese merchants overseas, who have returned to their homeland for a brief visit.

When Nishimura went to Peking as a resident correspondent and took up quarters at the Hsinchiao Fantien Hotel, he saw face powder and rouge displayed for sale at the hotel shop, and they remained unsold when he left for Japan a year later. Women in today's China refrain from wearing gay dresses, or painting their faces, because if they did so they would be severely attacked as revisionists, though a worker in Hangchow told him that she wore silk underclothes beneath her plain cotton dress. The Communist Chinese assert that their women abandoned the habit of dressing up, in order to conform to the lofty ideals of the revolution. One Chinese man told the *Yomiuri* newsman:

175

"Chinese women in the pre-revolution days had no other choice than to sell their personal beauty to the men. Therefore, women who could afford to buy cosmetics spent time painting their faces and arranging their hair day after day. Dressing was, so to speak, the life of women. But now that the equality of the sexes has become an established fact, women no longer find it necessary to curry the favor of men by prettying up."

Nishimura was pleased to discover that this does not imply that the Chinese have lost their sense of feminine beauty.

During a visit to Si-hu [West Lake], a famous scenic spot in Hangchow, he spotted a strikingly beautiful woman whose appearance suggested a Chinese equivalent of Cleopatra. He turned to his interpreter and asked what he thought of her. The sophisticated Japanese visitor was greatly relieved when the interpreter answered that "a beauty is a beauty in everyone's eyes."

Nishimura could not deny, however, that Chinese women have changed much under Communist rule. For one thing, he found them to have a high level of political consciousness, standing head and shoulders above their Japanese counterparts in this respect.

They are very proud of their role in the new society and insist on being addressed properly in the Communist fashion. In Hong Kong, where old Chinese customs are still retained, people use the word *siaota* [miss] as an honorific term for young girls. Even dancehall girls call themselves *wu-siaota*, "dancing miss." But Nishimura got into trouble when he addressed a young woman as *siaota* in Peking.

At the press section of the Communist Chinese Foreign Office, he said, there was a good-looking and talented young woman named Wang Yueh-chin. Since she majored in the Japanese language at Peking University, Miss Wang's job is to keep contact with Japanese reporters stationed in the capital. One day the *Yomiuri* reporter inadvertently called her *Wang Siaota*. She became so angry that she avoided speaking to him for about a month. In Communist China, *siaota* is considered the most degrading word that can be used in addressing a young woman. Only the slovenly and inactive young women following the revisionist line are described as *siaota*, he was told.

In Communist China, professions that feature a woman's glamour have ceased to exist. Women employed in restaurants as waitresses do nothing more than accept orders and bring the dishes desired. They are strictly prohibited from conversing with customers. When asked what occupation they wish to follow, nine out of ten young farm women reply that they would like to become tractor drivers. There are many city women who want to become drivers and, in fact, there are several female taxi drivers in Peking.

Yet glamour has not lost its appeal. Nishimura was intrigued to see that the female members of the Liberation Army's organized cultural troupes are the idols of young women in Communist China. When he saw these groups appearing as choral singers, decked out in dark-blue jackets and skirts—which have been replaced by slacks recently—and wearing golden epaulettes, the starry-eyed young girls gazing from the audience reminded him of Japanese women staring admiringly at performers in the Takarazuka Girls' Opera Troupe. The female cultural organizations have the best of both worlds, "gay dresses" and "arms." They are members of the Liberation Army, and at the same time, as singers, dancers, and actresses, they are officially authorized to wear fancy clothes and use cosmetics.

In today's China, all women—except those who are old or sick—engage in either manual or mental labor. To work is upheld as the supreme virtue, and it is proclaimed that women have largely freed themselves from household chores and have achieved equality with men.

This new feminine freedom is demonstrated by the fact

that the ratio of women in the membership of the National People's Congress, which stood at 11.19 percent—147 members—in the first term, increased to 12.3 percent—150—in the second and has risen further to 17.8 percent, or 542 out of the total membership of 3,404, in the third term.

Tsai Chang, the 72-year-old wife of Deputy Premier Li Fu-chun, who comes from the same province as her old friend Chairman Mao, stood at the apex of Communist Chinese womanhood until recently. She is a member of the Chinese Communist Party Central Committee and chairman of the All-China Democratic Women's Federation, and is ranked eleventh—directly above her husband—among party leaders. Tsai is one of the thirty women members of the Chinese Communist Party who accompanied Mao on the Long March to Yenan. However, she is likely to retire from active politics in the near future because of her age and declining health.

Another leading feminine figure is Soong Ching-ling, 76, honorary chairman of the All-China Democratic Women's Federation, widow of Dr. Sun Yat-sen and sister of Mme. Chiang Kai-shek. Other prominent women are also related, by marriage or family, to male leaders in the Government. Famous feminine personalities include Ho Hsiang-ning, 89-year-old mother of Liao Cheng-chih, chairman of the China-Japan Friendship Association and architect of the unofficial trade between Japan and Communist China; Li Te-chuan, 78, widow of the "Christian General," Feng Yu-hsiang; Teng Ying-chao, 65, wife of Premier Chou En-lai; Hsu Kuang-ping, widow of Lu Hsun, the famous writer and essayist; Shih Liang, 59, a heroine of the war against Japan; and Kang Ke-ching, 53, wife of Chu Tei and herself a veteran of the Long March.

These women have now reached an advanced age, Nishimura pointed out, and must soon be replaced by younger feminine leaders. Mrs. Teng, a gray-haired woman with a
178

Dutch cut, looks like Premier Chou's mother when she stands beside her husband, who looks much younger than he is. When he interviewed Mrs. Li Te-chuan about ten years ago, she kept falling asleep in her chair. She retired from politics several years ago, presumably because she could no longer stand the strain of her duties.

It will be noticed that Nishimura did not include Chiang Ching, the wife of Chairman Mao, in his list of the most notable women of Communist China. This one-time motion picture actress who became a central figure in the Cultural Revolution is so well-known abroad that the correspondent did not feel it necessary to add much more to what had already been said in all the Japanese newspapers, including his own, about this formidable woman. He did, however, take pains to differ with the popular Japanese view—at least among the men—that Mme. Chiang Ching is a person to be derided rather than respected for her activities.

The Japanese usually speak in derogatory terms of Chiang Ching, calling her "the hen that eggs on the rooster," he wrote in *Yomiuri*. "To do so, however," he continued, "is to underrate this dedicated Communist woman, who has taken an active part in the revolution since the days when the party had its headquarters in the caves of Yenan. She has also rendered meritorious national service in reforming the traditional drama."

It fell to Takeo Takagi, *Yomiuri's* senior writer on Chinese Communist affairs, to inform his paper's readers further on the extraordinary career of Mao's wife.

Chiang Ching is more talked about in other countries than in China, wrote Takagi, although some Chinese call her "the red Tse Tien," after an Empress of the Tang period. She suddenly came into the limelight in August 1966, when a Red Guard wall poster reported that she had become deputy chairman of the Great Proletarian Cultural Revolution Committee. She became linked with the movement not only because she was the wife of Mao, but also because she was one of those most responsible for kindling the fires of the Cultural Revolution. Takagi told the story of his involvement with theater reform.

In 1958, when Communist China was in the throes of the ill-fated Great Leap Forward, a group of revolutionary students and instructors at the Shanghai Theatrical Academy responded to Mao's call by launching a new art education movement aimed at serving the workers, peasants, and soldiers.

The first thing they did was to transfer the school from Shanghai to a farm village on the city's outskirts, called Tung Wan Tou. There the instructors and students then took up the "Three Sames" movement—to eat the same food as the farmers, do the same work, and live in the same place. They worked under the Maoist principle of laboring in the fields for half a day and pursuing studies the other half. They converted a pigsty into a classroom, cleared a bamboo thicket for a sports ground, and dug a well with their own hands.

The method of instruction was completely revolutionized. The former practice of dividing various aspects of theatrical studies into separate academic departments was abolished; all the departments were consolidated into one, so that there would be no specialized training among the students. Under the new system, all were required to learn the arts of directing, scenario writing, dancing, acting, and story-telling. The main objective was to train "proletarian" actors capable of doing everything concerned with the theater.

However, this new educational method in the performing arts was immediately condemned by the Communist Party propaganda and cultural departments.

"You have become pragmatists and are catering to vulgar public tastes," said one editorial attack on the new venture.

"In spite of the fact that your school is one of China's two most important training institutes for actors, you have neglected your studies by whiling away your precious hours in the fields."

The authorities ordered the students to close down the classroom at the farm village and return to the school's former site in Shanghai. But the revolutionary instructors and students decided to stick by the Maoist line. On the advice of Ke Cheng-shih, then mayor of Shanghai, they went to work for a factory whose management was sympathetic. There the aspiring artists studied labor conditions, continued their education under the ideal of "serving the people," and discussed the eradication of the "Four Old" evils from the theater.

In the three-year period from 1960 through 1962, the young theatrical students and their sympathetic instructors fought a campaign against what they called "the mass production of poor plays." Finally, they established contact with Mme. Chiang Ching, who had acquired considerable renown in revolutionary circles for her contribution to the "modernization" of the Peking Opera troupe, the elimination of bourgeois drama featuring emperors, court beauties, and ancient geniuses.

Inspired by Mao's wife, the students began a study looking toward reforms in their own institution in line with Maoist Shanghai drama teachings. The East China District Action Drama Competition, held in Shanghai from December 25, 1963, to January 22, 1964, was perhaps the breakthrough for the Cultural Revolution in theatrical circles. Mayor Ko of Shanghai made a speech encouraging the performance of dramas for the advancement of socialism.

Mao's wife adopted the name Chiang Ching after she married the Communist Party Chairman. Her maiden name was Li Ching-yun. She is said to be the daughter of a land-

181

lord in Chuchan, Shantung Province. At the age of two or three she lost her parents and was adopted by her maternal grandfather, who was dean of the Tsinan Middle School.

Takagi had the opportunity of meeting a certain educator, who had taught under Dean Li. This person, who now lives in Hong Kong, told him something of how Chiang Ching had lived in her childhood. As a girl, she loved the theater, and whenever a drama troupe arrived in town she was seldom to be found at home. In other words Ching was, in the Chinese idiom, a *hsi mi*—a stagestruck girl.

She was an avid fan of the Peking Opera in her childhood. Later she went to Shanghai, where she became a film actress and eventually joined the Communist Party after she had developed an interest in politics. She went to Yenan and there became an instructor in theater arts at the Lu Hsan Academy.

With her abundant experience in the theater, Takagi felt it was appropriate that she become the adviser on the Cultural Revolution for the Army after the Peking Opera was incorporated into the military organization.

THE GREAT SHOE POLISH SAGA

Takagi related a true parable to illustrate how the housewives responded to Mao's call for women to participate in the Great Leap Forward. He heard the story from a woman named Liang Yu-ying, 48 years old, when he visited the factory in Taiyuan that makes the well-known shoe polish cream known as *Hu Tieh* [Butterfly Brand]. The story begins eight years ago, when Chairman Mao called on the nation's housewives to join the revolution with those words:

"Now, the peoples of China have begun to take a Great Leap Forward under the Three Red Banners. In such times, should the housewives content themselves with only guarding their kitchens? The women of China are a valuable human resource for the construction of a socialist country. Let us study how we can socialize the housewives."

The housewives in Liang Yu-ying's neighborhood studied Mao's words and decided, "Let us also take a Great Leap Forward." But it was more easily said than done. For the housewives—eleven of them, ranging in age from 35 to 40 years—did not know how to take the Great Leap. After a conference beside a neighborhood well, they decided that the best way was to make something that had not been made by anyone else in Taiyuan. The women agreed unanimously to make shoe polish.

"Yes, that's right, let us do it," said one after another. "We will be serving the people," they agreed.

But they had neither the knowledge nor the money to start a factory. What they had were the "three things too old and three things too little." There were many women, many old people, and many uncultural assets, but not enough men, youths, and cultural assets. They also lacked four very important requirements—funds, a building, machinery, and technology.

"What shall we do?" they asked each other. Then one of the women said, "Chairman Mao says that people are the most important element."

"You are right," the others agreed. "We have no money, but we have manpower, eleven people in all. This is where we start."

So, instead of looking for funds, they went outside the town to look for the sand that is used in making bricks. Then they went to various construction sites and collected waste lumber which was still usable as beams and pillars for the factory building they planned. For the site of the factory, the women obtained rent-free a dump yard filled with mud and junk on the outskirts of Taiyuan. They got tiles for the roof where an old castle wall was being demolished.

183

Now the framework of the factory was complete, but they had nothing with which to make the walls. One woman suggested that money to buy the walls and machinery be obtained in a bank loan. But Liang Yu-ying quoted a passage from one of Mao's writings: "We must reconstruct through our own power. We welcome aid from the outside, but we must not depend on it. Let us depend on our own efforts and ideas."

To the housewives attempting a Great Leap Forward, the words of Mao were like the voice of God. There was no more talk of a loan.

After working for one year, they finally had the incomplete skeleton of a factory. Then they began manufacturing shoe polish. "Manufacture" may not be the exact word, for all they did was to use their ingenuity and find a way to make shoe polish by solidifying a liquid containing carbon and petroleum boiled together. They packed the polish into boxes and sold it to department stores. Later, however, they began to receive complaints from customers who said that their black shoes turned gray after they had used the cream. The customers demanded money for new shoes, and the department stores canceled their orders.

The housewives did not know what to do, until they recalled another of Mao's sayings: "It serves no purpose to pretend that you understand something when you do not actually understand it. If there is something you do not understand, ask the experts."

Accordingly, a representative of the housewives went to Peking and studied the process of making shoe polish at a large factory. After observing the procedures for twenty days, she saw what was wrong. The housewives had been using the wrong method of mixing the materials.

They tried again, and sold the new shoe cream under the brand name of *Ting Shan Hsieh Tu* [Top Grade Shoe Cream]. But again they were plagued with complaints. Some

184

customers declared that the shoe polish melted in the containers as they carried it home in their pockets, and leaked out and soiled their clothes. They demanded that the women pay for the stained garments.

The first impulse of the women was to ask, "Why don't they just wash out the stains?" But then they remembered another saying of Mao: "Let us not be arrogant and haughty. Accept criticism and rectify the faults."

This time, one of the housewives was sent to observe the operation of a factory in Shanghai. The next shoe cream that the housewives turned out was called *Chin Shih Tzu* [Golden Lion]. The polish seemed to be of good quality, so they printed the name of their factory—"Taiyuan City No. 3 Chemical Industry Joint Production Company"—on the container.

But again they had failed. The cream melted during the hot summer, and hardened like stone during cold weather. Panic reigned among the housewives. Because they had printed the name of the company on their product, angry customers brought their complaints direct to the factory, and the women had to pay compensation for ruined clothes and shoes. Moreover, a Government agency ordered the company to suspend production. By then, the housewives had expanded into four buildings, including a warehouse and company offices. But the structures now served no purpose. Alas, had the housewives' Great Leap Forward transformed itself into a great defeat?

Once more they had recourse to the sayings of Mao, and found this: "Any problem can be easily solved if the most important contradiction is discovered."

Their troubles, they judged, were the result of an accumulation of contradictions. But what was the most important contradiction? they asked each other. Obviously, it was the poor quality of the shoe cream, they concluded; the essential problem lay in the fact that they were making a product

185

unsuitable for the climate. So they set about studying thermal effects on shoe polish.

But there was a danger involved in experimenting with heat on a substance containing petroleum. None of the women was willing to undertake the delicate task until Mrs. Liang volunteered, declaring that a patriotic Chinese woman should be willing to risk her life "to serve the people." When Mrs. Liang said that, all the others likewise volunteered.

After about 600 experiments, they finally produced a satisfactory shoe polish. Overjoyed by their success, the eleven housewives took their merchandise to department stores. But the stores refused to buy, for the shoe cream made by the housewives had now acquired a bad reputation. The women changed the brand name to "Butterfly," and guaranteed to take back any unsatisfactory merchandise and pay compensation for any ruined shoes. Still the wary department store managers refused to handle the product. Undaunted, the housewives started a chain of shoe-shine businesses on various street corners to advertise their polish. The move was a success. Shoes shone brightly, and the cream did not soil clothes. The polish began selling rapidly.

While shining shoes on the streets, the housewives sang the following song:

"Though we work at the factory, our eyes are looking at the Tien An Men Square.

"Though we work at the factory, our eyes are looking at the world.

"Our hearts think about our fatherland, but our eyes are looking at the world."

The song they sang was not simply empty words, for they actually planned to sell their shoe polish on the overseas markets.

But Takagi thought he had detected an ideological inconsistency here.

The original intention had been to serve the people of

China. Why, then, had they thought of exporting the polish?

"Because it irritates us when the Soviet revisionists tell lies about China," Mrs. Liang answered. "They say that China's Great Leap Forward is nothing but a hoax and that the Chinese are destroying things instead of building them. That is why we decided to show the products of the Great Leap to the world."

But problems persisted. Their determination was truly heroic, Takagi observed, but yet, how were they going to go about exporting the shoe polish? Although they might have their "eyes on the world," they could not very well sell poor-quality products on the world market. The housewives embarked upon a project to make a shoe polish that would measure up to international standards. After more than 100 experiments, the women turned out a product that they considered fairly good.

The Chinese trade corporation found the housewives a foreign outlet, but to export they needed solid wooden boxes for packing. They decided to make their own boxes, and sent a 40-year-old woman to a carpenter to study the trade for fifteen days. On her return, the housewives collected unwanted boards from the public and constructed the boxes.

The woman carpenter made other things besides the boxes, Mrs. Liang told Takagi. "For instance, the chair you are sitting on is one of them."

He looked at the chair and noticed that although it was well made, the material was an assortment of old boards.

The export destinations chosen for the Butterfly brand shoe polish were the Middle East and Africa, including Syria, Iran, Guinea, and the Sudan. Eight years after the founding of the company, the eleven housewives had built four plants and were making candles and naphthalene in addition to shoe polish.

As he talked with Mrs. Liang in the factory, Takagi
187

noticed one of the other women lifting heavy boxes. It was Mrs. Chen Min, the carpenter.

"All women in this company have powerful muscles," she told the Japanese visitor. "Any woman here can easily carry a load of up to about 70 kilograms [154 pounds].

"We must show those American imperialists the true worth of the liberated Chinese women," she added.

Takagi thought that these women must indeed breathe fire. But invariably they were very cheerful when they spoke to him, and unlike most Chinese of today, they were humorous and frequently laughed.

He asked them whether they were members of the militia.

"Of course!" they replied in chorus. "Our leader is now out on the street shining shoes," one of the women said, "but let us show this foreigner some of our drill."

Casually grabbing their rifles, they formed ranks and marched out of the plant. Outside, they put on a demonstration of their military marching exercises, and the Japanese correspondent could only stare in amazement.

TOO MANY CHILDREN

Surrounded on all sides by the remarkable children who become such passionate Red Guards, the *Yomiuri* team found that their very numbers were symptomatic of one problem the Cultural Revolution has not been able to solve.

Kamai noted that all foreign travelers find they are always running into hordes of children in Communist China. In every alley, a visitor is so engulfed that he finds it hard to move about.

When Kamai visited Tienshan Sintsun, a residential area for workers in the suburbs of Shanghai, he ran into large groups of youngsters who followed him everywhere to welcome the *waipin* [foreign guest] with cheers.

"By nature and tradition, the Chinese like to have many

188

children," he said. "A house bursting at the seams with children and grandchildren" is an expression that people in the country use to describe what they consider one of the greatest blessings in life, and this long-established tradition is still very much alive in China today." The truth of the statement that "one in every four people in the world is Chinese" strikes home in Chinese cities, towns, and villages.

Exactly how many people are living in Communist China is unknown. Though a census has presumably been taken several times in recent years, the Communist Government has not released any official figures since it announced in 1957 that the country then had a population of 656,300,000.

However, an official of the central government told a colleague of Kamai's in August 1965 that China's population had been increasing by 2 percent a year and had passed the 700,000,000 mark. If this rate of increase in maintained, mainland China's population will exceed 1,000 million in 1980. But even this is a modest estimate in the eyes of some experts. In a recent report to a Congressional committee, an American population expert predicted that the number of people in Communist China would reach 1,000 million no later than in 1975.

Some scholars are skeptical about such predictions, Kamai reported, and he cited an authority who surmises that a lower birth rate and a higher death rate have resulted from the great famine that afflicted Communist China for three years from 1959.

But regardless of exact numbers, it is certain that China has a huge population and that Chinese leaders are faced with the problem of how to feed the teeming millions inhabiting the land. There are indications that the country is not producing enough food to keep its people well nourished. A report submitted to the U.S. Congress in February 1966 showed that Communist China's per capita grain production was 285 kilograms in 1963, 274 kilograms in 1964, and 275 kilograms in 1965, as compared with the all-time high of 320 kilograms set in the prewar period.

These are certainly not impressive figures, according to the *Yomiuri* reporter. At one time Teng Tzu-hui, former deputy premier and chief of the agricultural districts organizing group, said that a minimum per capita grain production of 300 kilograms was required to feed a population of 600,000,000. It is known that Communist China has been importing five to six million tons of wheat each year, presumably in order to replenish the shortage of the grain on the domestic market, but it is also possible, Kamai thought, that the Government might be trying to establish a balance between the prices of wheat and rice by purchasing wheat from foreign countries.

Officially, the Communist Chinese say, "More people mean a better and stronger country." Yung Lung-kui, an economist and vice chairman of the National Committee for Promotion of International Trade, went so far as to say that a large country like China can go on feeding its population as long as two-thirds of its arable land yields heavy crops, even if no harvest is reaped from the remaining third.

But this is regarded as an over-optimistic view even among Communist Chinese. The truth of the matter, Kamai learned, is that Chinese leaders are deeply concerned about the problem of the "population explosion." In 1965 Premier Chou told Edgar Snow that he wished to reduce the rate of the population increase in China to the level of Japan's—less than one percent.

Until the outbreak of the Cultural Revolution, Chinese Government leaders were caught up in a debate over whether or not they should encourage people to practice birth control. Now the Government has established a new population policy under which married couples are advised to regulate the size of their families in order to alleviate the burden of the mothers and give them enough time to engage

190

in production and studies, and also to give sufficient education to the children.

This is a fine way to combine the lofty ideals of Maoism with practical considerations, thought Kamai, and he noted that as a means of carrying out this policy, the Government is encouraging late marriages, saying that "the most suitable age" is 28 years for men and 25 for women.

Birth control, however, is still the most effective way to check further increase in population, and Government leaders are fully aware of this fact. A Japanese who made a prolonged trip through Communist China in 1966 has reported that meetings to familiarize the people with methods of birth control were held frequently in various parts of the country, despite the fact that the Cultural Revolution was going at full blast everywhere.

In Communist China, abortion is a simple and easy matter. The operation is performed in less than twenty minutes, and doctors do not even ask their patients whether they are married. Birth-control equipment is also readily available.

However, Kamai concluded, "planned parenthood" is not practiced widely in the rural areas. "Farmers have difficulty mastering the various methods of birth control, and they cling to the notion that it would be going against the will of their forefathers not to have many children."

SERVE MAO NOW—MARRY LATER

If the young people the newsmen met were representative, the campaign to postpone marriage seemed to be having some success, particularly since it could be combined with an appeal to their patriotism. In a romantic mood, Kamai wondered how young people raised in a Communist strait-jacket felt about love and marriage. Their answers were a tribute to their indoctrination and evidence that late marriage is a new virtue in the Maoist morality.

191

The young women he questioned liked to use the expression "dedicate our youth to the country." This Kamai learned from his interviews with Miss Yu and Miss Siao, who work at a dress counter in the same department store in the Nankinglu district of Shanghai, several young women working at a spinning mill in Chengchow, and a nurse and a medical student in Wuhan.

These girls had one and the same answer to his questions. They declared, "This is no time for us to talk about love. We will dedicate our youth to the country."

"People of different classes have different outlooks on love and marriage," said Miss Yu Tsui-hua, a high-school graduate who manages a small department store in Shanghai. ("She is a lovely young girl—a far cry from the popular conception of a manager," Kamai noted.)

"I have neither husband nor lover," she told the Japanese writer. "Chairman Mao has often said that 'youth is the most valuable thing,' but he does not mean that young people should find mates and get married before it is too late. I am not contemplating marriage at the moment," she went on, "though I do not intend to stay single forever. Working to build up the country is a matter of prime importance. I am determined to stay at my present place of employment and work my hardest for the sake of the people."

Kamai found a high degree of patriotic motivation and social consciousness among the young women with whom he talked in several cities.

They are certainly dedicated young women, he decided, but he added that this does not imply that they are totally indifferent to men and marriage. One evening he was pleased to see several pairs of young lovers braving cold winds to stroll along the shores of Lake Ksuanwu in Shanghai.

While talking to him, the young women factory workers in Chengchow looked at each other and agreed smilingly that they would get married after reaching the age of 25 or 26 years. Miss Yu of Shanghai, who was 25 years old, blushed violently when she was asked, "What is your concept of an ideal husband?" Prefacing her remarks with the cautious statement "If I can marry such a man . . ." Miss Yu went on to describe the type of mate she wanted:

"A man who has the same views as I—the kind of man who devotes his heart and soul to the task of serving the people of the entire world, as is described in Chairman Mao's book, *In Memory of Norman Bethune.*"

Young men and women in Communist China seem to feel shy when they are asked to discuss love, marriage, and sex, the romantic reporter discovered. The youths whom he questioned on these subjects were so bashful that he felt sorry for them. Miss Yu spoke in a trembling voice when she expressed her ideas on marriage, though her statements may seem bold enough in print, and Kamai said that the medical student in Wuhan blushed deeply and kept her head lowered when the conversation turned to the subject of romance.

Wu Chiang-shan, a handsome 29-year-old interpreter with the International Tourist Bureau and a graduate of the Shanghai Foreign Language Academy, also was visibly abashed when he admitted, while riding in a bus with Kamai, that he had a sweetheart.

Kamai was quick to add that this did not mean that all of the hundred-odd million youths in Communist China are unspoiled and sober-minded, for he was aware of reports of delinquents among them. At one time, women's magazines in Communist China carried articles about a young man who seduced a girl who had fallen in love with him at first sight. *People's Daily* once discussed the problem of youth in large cities who refuse to take jobs or attend schools. Young people who are absorbed in pornographic books and try to act like the heroes of popular novels exist even in the country where they are constantly urged to accept discipline, and Kamai concluded that youth problems will continue to be a major concern in Communist China, too.

A LAND OF VIRTUE

Officially, the Communists claim that crime has been completely eliminated under the new regime, and from the visible evidence, Nishimura had to agree.

The Chinese used to say *nantao nuchang*, meaning "men can turn thieves and women can turn prostitutes," when they were discussing the government's failure to improve their living conditions. What they meant, he told his Japanese readers, was that men had to steal and women had to sell their flesh because they could not make a living otherwise.

There were certainly many Chinese who could not help stealing, the correspondent acknowledged, recalling some of the scenes he had witnessed while living in Shanghai about seventeen years earlier, such as the following:

A truck, carrying a load of raw cotton to a textile factory, is running slowly down the street. Suddenly, a barefooted boy with a sagging belly runs up to the truck and climbs into the back. A guard riding in the rear whips him with a leather belt. Undaunted, the boy plucks a piece of cotton, jumps down from the truck and runs off, holding the loot tightly in his hands. Apparently his parents had told him to steal pieces of cotton, which they would sell.

But those days are gone, Nishimura could say happily. What he saw in today's China was almost too good to be true. Banks have no steel bars, because there is no likelihood of robbery. At the bank office in a hotel, bundles of bills are piled up high on the counter where a passerby could easily reach out and take them. Sometimes bank employes working there leave the office without removing the bills from the counter.

Hotel staffs are always eager to return to guests any article

194

left in a room when checking out. Once, when he was about to leave Peking on a train, a hotel employe came to the railway station in a hired car to hand him a comb that he had forgotten in the hotel room.

There are still locks on the doors of hotel rooms, however. When he checked into one hotel, he said to an employe, "I guess I don't need a key. I won't have to lock my room, because there are no thieves in China." After a moment of hesitation the clerk said, "Yes, but there are some foreigners staying in the hotel." The Japanese reporter blushed.

It would be untrue to say that there are *no* thieves in Communist China, he added, but it is safe to say that there are very few. He had heard reports that Chinese do not steal because they would be imprisoned for twenty or thirty years if caught, but if the Communist Chinese Public Safety Law is any guide, he found, the courts cannot impose such heavy penalties.

Although the legal code examined by Nishimura provided only modest fines or a jail sentence of up to fifteen days for petty theft, the penalty for narcotics violations was death, he said, recalling that 37 persons had been executed during a twelve-month period in 1950 and 1951 for such offenses. This, he added, was at a time when the newly established Communist regime was conducting a nationwide drive to eradicate narcotics addiction.

There are no dope addicts in China now, Nishimura declared, deducing that this is one reason for the sharp decline in crime rates.

The other social evils that plagued China in bygone years in addition to theft were gambling and prostitution, Nishimura recalled, and they too have vanished almost completely.

The practice of gambling at mahjong and other games used to be widespread, not only among adults, but among children, he remembered. A group of children squatting on a road and playing some game for money was a familiar sight in Chinese cities. But those days are gone. Nishimura was told that Chinese nowadays play mahjong only for fun, and only on such occasions as a get-together of relatives during the Lunar New Year holidays. Of course, gambling is outlawed, and the penalty is confinement for up to seven days, or a fine not exceeding 14 yuan [$5.60].

Nishimura could not say that the practice of gambling has been completely eradicated in Communist China. At public parks in Peking, he often saw several men sitting in the shade of a tree absorbed in a card game, and judging by the serious expressions on their faces, he thought that they were not playing the game just for fun.

Nishimura advanced three reasons why Communist China is almost entirely free of gambling, theft, and prostitution.

First, the country has succeeded in stamping out poverty, which was a major factor behind the high crime rate. The Chinese nowadays are fed, clothed, and housed adequately, even though their living standards still remain low.

Second, the Communist Government has adopted and carried out policies well calculated to induce the people to abide by the law.

Third, he found that people have been cooperating fully with the Government in bringing down the crime rate. He cited an example: The chief of the Peking Bureau of a certain Japanese newspaper went to a seal maker and ordered a rubber stamp showing his name and title. The seal maker said that he could not accept the order unless the reporter brought a paper certifying that he was indeed the Peking correspondent of the newspaper.

The result has been a country where people can go anywhere without worrying about being victimized by robbers, hoodlums, or rapists, Nishimura said. And he told how he often ran across groups of middle-school girls trekking to Peking and other cities, several thousand miles away from their home towns, in order to take part in the Cultural Revolution. They were not accompanied by men. Young girls traveling so freely through China in earlier years could not have stayed alive, the reporter declared.

Not that rape has disappeared from Communist China, either. Nishimura describes a poster, seen on a street in Kwangchow, with the photograph of a primary-school principal accused of raping a pupil.

The correspondent noted, in a candid dispatch, that the new wave of virtue in Communist China had its drawbacks from a visitor's point of view. "We foreigners find life in China boring," he confessed. "The only worldly pleasure that we get in Peking is to eat delicious Chinese foods offered at low prices. Chinese radio and television programs are extremely uninteresting to foreigners. The Chinese Government is considerate enough to invite us to shows, movies, and parties occasionally, but the shows and movies are far from interesting, and at parties we are bored to death by long-winded speeches by our hosts, about the overthrow of American imperialism.

"What dismayed me most," Nishimura added, "was the fact that the Chinese, once known for their eagerness to play host, have stopped inviting foreigners to their homes. During my one-year residence in Peking as a *Yomiuri* correspondent, I was never invited to a Chinese home. Therefore, I could not have a Chinese friend to whom I could talk frankly."

CONFUCIUS IS NOT COMPLETELY DEAD

Okubo observed that the traditional Chinese respect for the aged was still as strong in present-day Communist China as he had found it when a young student long before Mao came to power, in spite of the fact that a movement to destroy the "Four Olds"—old thought, old culture, old customs, and old manners—is sweeping the country. The Chinese Communists are quick to say, he noted, that the spirit of respecting the aged as taught by Confucius does not fall under any of these "evil" categories.

In fact, the Communists have a set of policies for improving the welfare of old people. Like "welfare states" in the West, the Government makes it a cardinal principle to look after its citizens "from the cradle to the grave."

Retired workers in Communist China receive old-age pensions corresponding to 50 percent to 70 percent of their former wages. Retirement is mandatory under an age-limit system. In the case of factory employes, the retirement age is 60 years for men, 55 for women doing office work, and 50 for female factory hands. These last are required to retire earlier than other workers because the state is concerned about the strain of manual labor on women, according to the explanation given by officials of the Second Spinning Plant in Peking.

At this spinning mill visited by Okubo, retired workers and their families were permitted to continue living in the residential quarters, maintained by the plant, that they had occupied when working. The Japanese writer interviewed a 60-year-old grandmother who shared a two-room apartment with her daughter and son-in-law, who work at the plant, and their two children. The room that she shares with the children is decorated with a photograph of Chairman Mao, Okubo reported. The walls are plastered with paper whose design consists of passages from Mao's *Quotations*.

"In the years before the Liberation, I barely managed to eke out a living," she said. "But now I live comfortably and have such a fine room, thanks to Chairman Mao."

Though she used to work at the plant, this elderly woman does not receive an old-age pension, because she was dismissed because of illness before the Communist regime was established and the factory came under the control of the state. Her daughter pays her 10 yuan a month for looking after the children while the young mother works.

In most cases, old people do live with their children. This may be due in part to the shortage of housing, but the main factor is the unwillingness of young people to live apart from their aged parents, according to a 25-year-old girl who worked as a clerk in a store in Shanghai.

"Chairman Mao says that people should help and protect each other," she told Okubo. "That is the way it should be in the home as well as in public. We want to live with our parents so that we can help and protect them."

He asked her if there were cases of old women and their daughters-in-law failing to get along, and she answered quickly, "In-law trouble does exist in our country, but it is much less evident than it was in bygone years."

In each neighborhood in Chinese cities, towns, and villages, people take turns looking after the welfare of the aged who are without relatives. People's Communes in farming villages have established a system of granting financial aid to families with a large number of old folks and children. Old people wishing to enter state-supported homes are permitted to do so if they meet certain qualifications. To accommodate such persons, the Government has established a chain of old people's homes, called *Chinglaoyuan*—literally, "Respect for the Aged" Institutions—in various parts of the country.

At Tienshan Sintsun, the residential quarter for workers on the outskirts of Shanghai, there is an institute called the Cultural Station, which is designed to provide entertainment for retired workers and help them to acquire "culture." There Okubo met a 56-year-old woman who used to work at a spinning plant in Shanghai. She draws an old-age pension of 56 yuan a month, and occupies herself assisting public-health workers in the neighborhood. She typifies the old people of China who earnestly serve—and are served by —the public, he said.

The Communist authorities consider that the conspicuous

presence of elderly people serves an important purpose as living testimony to the evils of the old society, the reporter was told. A case in point was Chang Hsih-han, the 81-year-old curator of the February Seventh Memorial Hall in Wuhan—a museum that houses various items connected with a strike of railway workers in the city forty-four years ago. Chang, who speaks standard Chinese—the Peking dialect—with machine-gun rapidity, makes it his task to explain to visitors how the railway men rose against the Nationalist Government. He had been one of the leaders of the strike.

At the Huashan People's Commune in Wuhan, Okubo saw a group of old men exhorting young people "not to forget the tribulations of the old society." A spokesman was saying, "If we unbend our minds and forget the ordeals that the farmers underwent in pre-Liberation years, our society will revert to revisionism or capitalism, and we will end up turning the clock back to the bad old days. This is why we must study and absorb the teachings of Chairman Mao, and carry out the Cultural Revolution."

THE FOUR CALAMITIES

Like others who had lived in China in earlier times, Nishimura was surprised to find that a marked change had occurred in sanitary conditions since the advent of the Communists. Chinese towns he had known in his younger days had been really filthy, he recalled, describing piles of refuse in the streets and the pervasive odor of human waste, opium, and garlic.

When Peking was liberated, there were 600,000 tons of garbage in the city, the *Yomiuri* reporters were told by Chou Yung-yuan, vice director of the Peking Municipal Planning Bureau.

Today Nishimura could report that flies and mosquitos

are almost nonexistent in China. Once in a while, he saw a fly in the dining room of a hotel for foreigners in Peking, but when they are found, flies are sure to be chased and killed by hotel employes armed with fly-swatters. Fly-killing campaigns are conducted in early spring in North China and all the year round in South China. In Peking the Municipal Public Health Bureau carries out a fly-killing campaign every year at the end of March, before the first generation of flies for the year is hatched.

Mosquitos were a more difficult problem, but Nishimura was informed that these pests had been wiped out in Peking by concerted civic action. Breeding places were eliminated, he was told, by filling in stagnant ponds and streams (or, alternatively, by digging them deeper to create a swifter flow), and eliminating potholes in the streets where rain water accumulated.

However, he could not say that bodily uncleanliness has disappeared completely. He noted that some of the children whom he had seen playing in the streets of Peking, stripped to the waist during the hot summer days, looked as though they had not taken a bath for more than a month. The correspondent observed that facilities for bathing were still inadequate. Apartment houses built in recent years have bathrooms, he said, but this does not apply to the older apartment houses. Nor are there enough public bathhouses to fill the need. So he could not conclude that there are no lice in China. He remarked also that there must still be a lot of rats, since he had seen occasional newspaper reports that a new kind of trap in a factory somewhere had eliminated hundreds of the rodents.

Rats, flies, mosquitos, and bugs have been designated by the Government as the "Four Calamities," Nishimura learned. People are encouraged to kill them wherever they are found. The success in this endeavor impressed Nishimura, but it would be asking too much, he said, to expect the Chinese to exterminate flies in the plains of Mongolia, where there are many cows and horses that relieve themselves on the ground.

MEDICINE, OLD AND NEW

The noticeable improvement in sanitary conditions is a contributing factor to the obvious progress being made in health care. When one of the *Yomiuri* men became ill with a high fever in Loyang, he was taken to one of the largest hospitals in the region. His colleagues were pleased to discover, Kamai reported, that the doctors and nurses treated him admirably, and when it was all over, the charge for the entire hospital expense was only about 600 yen [approximately $1.50]. Kamai thereupon began a reportorial study of the state of medical science under the Chinese Communists.

Late in 1966, he recalled, Communist China drew international attention in medical circles when it was announced that the Chinese had succeeded in making synthetic insulin. Communist China's medical community has presented other interesting topics to the scientific world in the past few years. It was reported that doctors had succeeded in reviving a laborer who had been medically dead for at least 16 minutes. Another instance was the successful treatment of a patient who had suffered burns over 90 percent of his body.

In Chengchow Province, Kamai heard how a youthful doctor, just out of medical school, had successfully sewn all five fingers back onto the bloody stump of a hand after a farmer had severed them in an accident while cutting cattle fodder. He was told that there had been more than 10 cases in which doctors in China had successfully sewed back severed hands and arms.

As usually happened whenever the Japanese correspondents encountered an instance of material progress in Communist China, someone was ready with a stereotyped ideological explanation. In recounting his exploration of Communist Chinese medicine, Kamai recorded these claims without comment.

Mr. Li, an official of the Chengchow office of the International Travel Bureau, told the reporter that the youthful doctor of humble peasant origin had succeeded in the intricate finger surgery because he and the entire hospital staff had responded resolutely to Mao's call to "serve the people."

"Skill alone does not make a good doctor," the chief surgeon of the Lunghua Hospital in Shanghai assured the Japanese reporter. "What really counts," he went on, "is the spirit of serving the people."

The Chinese Medical Society's campaign to "serve the people" was launched in 1963, Kamai learned. Since then, Communist Chinese medical policy has placed primary importance on the farming villages. He was told that close to one-third of the staff of the Lunghua Hospital, and the hospital affiliated with the Wuhan Medical Institute, were out in the "field," serving the people of the rural villages.

The itinerant medical teams touring the countryside even include some of China's top medical experts, such as Dr. Heng Chia-su, president of China Medical University and chief surgeon of the country's supreme medical organ, the Medical Science Institute. Another famous medical expert on one of the traveling units is Dr. Chang Hsiao-chien, vice president of China Medical University and head physician of the renowned Hsieh Ho Hospital.

During the past seventeen years, the new China has succeeded in controlling smallpox and other serious diseases that once were common. The Government is now trying to improve the medical personnel structure in the provinces by organizing two three-month training courses as health aides for some of the bright middle-school graduates in the farm villages, and having them accompany the traveling teams. As a result of this program, rural clinics are now so well staffed that patients with minor injuries need not be sent to town hospitals.

Kamai observed the rural medical program at work in the Huashan People's Commune in the outskirts of Wuhan, the great steel center. The Huashan settlement, he said, consisted of 3,800 households with a total population of 17,000. At the commune's hospital, he reported, there were five doctors, including two experts in Chinese traditional medicine. He was told that the hospital had both the facilities and the skill to conduct surgical operations as well as to deliver babies.

Medicine in Communist China is an amalgamation of the ancient Chinese system and the modern scientific practices of the West. The Lunghua Hospital, affiliated with Shanghai Medical Institute, depends upon Chinese indigenous methods to a considerable extent, but Western science is also used in diagnosis and treatment. At this hospital there were seventy practitioners of traditional medicine, but they were also well acquainted with modern medical science. On the other hand, there were thirty "modern" physicians, and all of them had taken at least two years of training in Chinese medicine.

Officials of the Lunghua Hospital assured the Japanese reporter that acute appendicitis could be cured completely in five or six days through the application of traditional Chinese treatment. One of the systems in use was acupuncture, or treatment by pressing needles into the tissues, a system widely known in Japan also. Kamai was told that an acupuncturist can cure dysentery and diarrhea much more quickly than Western medicine can, and that persons suffering partial paralysis following a stroke have recovered the ability to walk within 35 days under acupuncture treatment.

One of the advantages of ancient Chiness medicine, he learned, is that the practitioner can obtain the necessary herbs wherever he is.

But the Communist Chinese are also proud of the fact that they are able to manufacture sophisticated medical apparatus and drugs at relatively low cost, because of the progress made in production methods. A few years ago, a terramycin tablet of 250,000 units cost 0.5 yuan [20 cents]; now the price is down to 0.08 yuan [about 3 cents].

Under the "cradle to grave" philosophy, China has developed a fine social-medicine system, the *Yomiuri* correspondent said. In Wuhan, the Government pays all medical expenses of poor or lower middle-class farmers, revolutionary soldiers and officials, students and labor unionists. If a laborer is hospitalized, his only expense is the cost of his food. If he is hospitalized for a long period, he is assured of receiving 60 to 100 percent of his salary for the first six months, and 40 to 60 percent after that. In the old China, the entire family had to go begging in the streets if the breadwinner ever fell ill. Today, a family left without income because of illness receives Government aid.

Since the Communists came to power, the country has turned out 600,000 doctors, including medical technicians and practitioners of traditional medicine, Kamai was informed. Even in this field, however, the new wave of fanatical Maoism had an upsetting effect on established methods. During the Cultural Revolution, China's medical education system came under severe criticism, Kamai learned. Critics charged that adherence to the Soviet style of medical education had led educators to place too much emphasis on textbooks at the expense of practical clinical training.

"I have read about 650 pages of textbooks here, and about 450 pages were utterly useless," a Red Guard told him at the Wuhan Medical Institute. "Medical schools, which now give five to six years of instruction, should reduce the cur-

205

riculum to three or four years and give the students clinical training from the beginning. Medical education must also follow the principle of 'serving the people.'"

A distinguished physician whom Kamai met on a plane going from Hangchow to Shanghai agreed at least partially with the curriculum reforms proposed by the Red Guard.

"I believe that it is necessary to maintain the eight-year system at the China Medical University in Peking, as an academic research organ," said Dr. Wang Yung-a, vice president of the Anhwei Medical Institute. "But as far as the five-year and six-year medical institutes are concerned, the study years could be cut to four. The first year should be devoted to basic academic subjects. Students in the second and third years should divide their time between classrooms and hospitals. In the fourth year they should be sent to rural areas, and continue their studies while working on the farms. In my ophthalmology class I have ninety students, divided into nine groups," the doctor went on. "We are now trying to organize a study program that would send each group in turn, accompanied by instructors from other medical fields, into farm areas to study and work. The students have all expressed their support for this plan, as well as the instructors from the nose and ear department, and gynecology, obstetrics, internal medicine, and surgery."

Kamai refrained from comment on the technical and ideological aspects of Communist Chinese medicine, as argued by the young Red Guard, Dr. Wang, and others. But, thinking of the conditions he had observed as a student in Shanghai, the correspondent was deeply impressed with the improvement in the quantity and quality of medical service now available to ordinary Chinese citizens.

"In short," he declared, "the state of Communist Chinese medicine can be summed up in two words: progress and service."

Chapter IX

MAO'S WAR MACHINE

AN INHERITANCE FROM JAPANESE IMPERIALISM

The Tokyo reporters were startled to discover that the cult of Maoism acquired much of its strength from the battles against Japanese imperialism a generation ago. The Chinese believe that their nationalistic spirit, the proletarian culture, and their socialist politics and economy are all products of the conflict with Japan.

If Japanese imperialism became the teacher by accident in the construction of the new China, the classrooms were the oddly shaped mountains and hills of Yenan Province. Here flourished the Anti-Japanese Military and Political College called Kangta by the Chinese.

Tens of thousands of its graduates now occupy important posts in the Party, the Government, and the army. Needless to say, some of these people have become the targets of criticism, but the great majority of those leading the Cultural Revolution are soldiers-turned-politician who were nurtured in this school.

"Revert to the spirit of Kangta" was a slogan of the Cultural Revolution that Takagi heard frequently, and his search into the spiritual heritage of Maoism that had taken him to Mao's birthplace now led him to the mountainous province of Yenan, the holy land of Chinese Communism. Only the summits are cultivated, and the sides of the hills are reddish, steep slopes, he found. A bird's-eye view of the cultivated mountain fields from a plane gives the impression that the hills and mountains are wearing grey berets.

In the valleys between these hills he saw long columns of Red Guard youths on their own "long march" from various provinces to this classroom of the revolution.

An old friend, pointing to the fields on top of the hills, told Takagi about the days of the war against Japan, about the revolutionary farmers' struggle in cultivated areas, and of the tillers who migrated to this southern land from the barren soil of Hsiapei in responding to Chairman Mao's call for "regeneration through one's own efforts."

In 1936, the year after the Red Army completed its Long March, the China Anti-Japanese Red Army College was founded in Wa Yu Pao, in Northern Hsiasi Province, to train officers for the national war against Japan. The school was transferred to Yenan in 1937 and was renamed Anti-Japanese Military and Political College. During a nine-year period it turned out more than 10,000 revolutionary officials.

Mao personally took over the chairmanship of the college's education board and then appointed his "intimate comrade in arms," Lin Piao, as president of the college. For the post of head educator he selected Lo Jui-ching, who later became Chief of the General Staff and was recently purged. The education of Kangta was stated in three principles: "To obtain a resolute and accurate political direction, to acquire a simple personality that will enable one to endure all kinds of hardships, and to learn swift, mobile tactics and strategies of war." At the front entrance of the college four plaques are inscribed with the words "unity," "tension," "austerity," and "vigor."

Thousands of persons, burning with the passionate mission of saving China from Japanese imperialism, thronged to the school in Yenan—college students, university professors, literary people, sons of merchants, and overseas Chinese students who had abandoned their studies abroad to come to the aid of their homeland.

When they entered, the students were given the "Three Treasured Weapons"—a rifle, a hoe, and a pen. With the hoe, the students were to clear the wilderness for school buildings, and with the pen they were to acquire knowledge of Marxist theory and culture.

The problem was that 80 percent of them were what the Communists called "argumentative intellectuals talking nonsense about how to save the nation."

According to Kangta tradition, Mao the educator wondered, "How shall I remold these arrogant petit bourgeois intellectual rascals, who are only skillful talkers?"

He then asked them, "Can you eat millet?"

"Yes, we can," they replied thinking that Mao was only humoring them.

"Very well," said Mao, "you students, who came here to join the revolution, must study Marxism-Leninism. You must learn first of all that Marxism-Leninism is to eat millet, climb the hills wearing straw sandals, and cultivate the barren land."

They all merely gazed blankly at him, these actors, writers, college students, and middle-school instructors. But there was more to come.

President Lin Piao appeared in front of them and, pointing to a yellow, bald mountain, said, "That is your classroom." Not a single house graced the top of the barren peak. Lin continued, "In our college, there is a course that is not listed in the curriculum. The course is a study of how to overcome hardships and difficulties through struggle."

Each of the talkers, actors, college students, and poets was given a pair of sandals and a shovel. They then climbed the bald mountain, where they dug caves all day. Sweat flowed freely from their brows, blisters formed on their hands, and their legs and backs ached.

"Is this a study of Marxism-Leninism? We are just like convicts doing forced labor," a few muttered. They were immediately dragged before a kangaroo court. The hole-digging operation finally came to an end at about the time the setting sun colored the mountain peaks red. But the students were so fatigued that they could hardly utter a word. As they stretched their limbs and backs, thinking that at last they could rest, they were told to fetch wood for fuel. After that, they were ordered to do kitchen duty. Finally they were given a meal of millet gruel, which they ate sitting on the ground.

The pale-faced intellectuals were no longer inclined to start any discussions. They only wanted to sleep like logs. But morning came and they were ordered out of their beds at 6 A.M. They wanted to wash their faces, but there was no water.

"The water is over there," they were told. "There is plenty of water over there."

They looked, and indeed found water. Soon a number of senior college students were seen washing their faces in the cold water of the Yenho River. After the students had washed, they were ordered to clean the toilet. Clenching their teeth, the students—who had walked 200 miles from Sian to the mountains of Yenan filled with the desire to save China from Japan—donned their sandals and again climbed the bare hills. As they climbed, they muttered among themselves, "Overcome hardships and difficulties through arduous struggle!"—the name of the new course that was not listed in the college curriculum.

The students of Kangta were obliged to make for themselves everything they needed, in the spirit of Mao's slogan, "Regeneration through one's own efforts." They dug their cave classrooms, converted a cattle barn into an auditorium, and made blackboards and desks. Thus, by their own efforts, Takagi learned, the students overcame various handicaps—lack of funds, lack of school buildings, and lack of classroom materials. At one point, all students and instructors joined in a concerted drive to construct school buildings and put up 175 classrooms in fifteen days. Meanwhile, they studied Mao's works in the caves.

Mao taught classes personally. Lectures were given on his theoretical writings—such as his essays, "On Practice" and "On Contradictions"—which later were made into books. Other teaching material used by Mao from his own works included his "Strategic Problems in the Anti-Japanese Guerrilla War," "The Chinese Revolution and the Chinese Communist Party," "On New Democracy," "On Coalition Government," and "Combat Liberalism."

The list of these Mao writings may give the impression that the college curriculum was quite difficult, Takagi told his readers, but, he added, Mao's lectures were easy to understand.

For example, in his lecture on "Activities of Party Members," Mao would use the analogy of the famous horse *Pai Lung* [White Dragon], which was the priest San Tsang's constant companion in the ancient novel *Hsi Yu Chi.* "You must not think that this story is about an ordinary horse," Mao would say. "This horse wanted neither fame nor money, and carried the priest San Tsang all the way to India to obtain the Buddhist scriptures. Let us say, for example, that our work involves carrying luggage. If there is one parcel weighing 20 kilograms and another weighing 50 kilograms, we must try to carry the heavier load. This is the simplest and best way to work. It is this type of attitude we must cultivate with regard to our work."

The course at the Anti-Japanese Military and Political College was short. One could graduate after six to eight months. However, the *Yomiuri* reporter said, it would be a

211

mistake to jump to the conclusion that schooling at the college was similar to the "instant education" system which he said is used by some schools in Japan. Although the study period was short, the students at the Kangta college learned a great deal, because the education policy was based on the principle of combining theory with practice.

After a lecture on "Protracted War" at Liu Ya Lou, which later became the command headquarters of the Liberation Army, the students would sit around a Korean stove table and discuss the day's lecture. Shortly after going to bed they would be awakened by the roar of guns and explosives. The students would scramble frantically to the mountain top, only to have a roll-call taken.

"That is all for the drill!" an instructor would shout. Relieved that the tumult was merely an exercise, one of the students would ask, "Why was the drill held?" The instructor would answer, "Have you forgotten already? Only yesterday you learned about night tactics in protracted war." Theory, followed by immediate practice—this was the spirit of Kangta college. And it was this spirit, Takagi noted, that was inherited by the Red Guards who thirty years later put theory into practice in the Cultural Revolution's rebel activities.

Since the founding of the Kangta college, it has been Mao's aim to reforge intellectuals into proletarian, class-conscious revolutionaries.

Emphasis was placed on political training and thought reform, so that the Communist Party could absorb many intellectual elements in order to increase its fighting force. Therefore, the first thing Mao did was to crush any illusions among the new students about the nature of the college. He said, "Each entering class at Kangta college is a training ground to turn out officers for the Eighth Route Army, which is under the direction of the Communist Party. The Kangta college is the blast furnace of the revolution. You students are going to be tempered in the furnace—that is, you will study on one hand and produce on the other, you will fight on one hand and produce on the other."

Under the principle of "study and fight," after the fifth month in school the students were sent to the front lines to receive on-the-spot guerrilla training. They were instructed in *kung shih ching yeh* [empty the rooms and purify the fields] tactics, a guerrilla strategy to nullify invasion by hiding food and all other material that the enemy might use.

But as future leaders of the revolution they were expected to do more than fight. They were also instructed to take part in local movements to reduce land rentals and the interest rates on loans, a project fostered by the Communists before they launched their land reform. The students participated in propaganda work, and armed and organized the masses for the revolution. All these activities, in effect, were part of the examination for graduation from Kangta. The most important consideration in this examination was to determine whether the students could manage to fight the revolution by maintaining close contact with farmers and workers.

Kangta students were also in the forefront of the Cheng Feng movement launched in 1942 to rectify Party activities and the ideology of its members. The campaign in effect was a reeducation drive to eliminate subjectivism, sectarianism, and the use of difficult written expressions among the Party members, thus advancing Mao's interpretation of Marxism-Leninism.

The weapons of criticism and self-criticism were used to cleanse the ideology of Party members and the masses, foreshadowing the present Cultural Revolution. The students of Kangta participated in the campaign in the region of Shenkanning, and also in the "Great Production Movement" inaugurated by Mao in the spirit of "regeneration through one's own efforts."

213

On the production front, the students not only raised food, but also made toothbrushes, soap, clothing, and leather goods in the Sopei district, which was under an economic blockade. The production activities of the students covered a wide area, including the fabrication of guns and munitions by the use of crude earth furnaces for making steel. These activities were inherited by the leaders of the Great Leap Forward, who fostered the construction of the backyard steel plants.

"Thus we established the foundations for our ideology and the material things that enabled us to stage a great counteroffensive and win the revolution on a nationwide scale," said Mao in calling upon participants in the Cultural Revolution to go back to the Yenan days and remember the spirit of Kangta college.

FIGHTERS OF THE PEOPLE'S WAR

The lesson learned at Kangta bore fruit during the guerrilla war against Japanese invaders. Takuzo Kamai found that today's vast militia forces are trained to emulate the successful harassment of Japanese troops in occupied villages. When he went to visit a vinyl plant, the first, and at that time, the only large industrial installation that Japan exported to Communist China, he found his countrymen remembered for other reasons.

Driving for an hour in a northeasterly direction from Peking, through farming villages presenting desolate wintry scenes in which the predominant color is that of yellow clay, he reached Shuni County and Tsiaochuanghu, called "the village of the people's war." At first sight it is just an ordinary village with about 260 households and 1,200 or so residents. Yet the place is so well-known in Peking that it attracts more than a thousand visitors daily from the capital city.

The villagers of Tsiaochuanghu resisted the Japanese op-

214

erations to clear the countryside by entrenching themselves in a tunnel three kilometers [about 1.8 miles] long, dug in secret by all the inhabitants, including old folks and children, under the guidance of the Chinese Communist forces. During the third civil war between the Nationalists and Communists, the villagers harassed the Nationalist troops by operating once again from the tunnel, which had been lengthened to slightly over 11 kilometers [about 6.6 miles]. At the time, the Central Committee of the Communist Party had presented to this community a battle flag and the title of "first fortress of the people"— distinctions that remain the pride of the village.

Tsiaochuanghu is not an isolated example; Kamai learned that in the territories where the Communist forces directed operations against the Japanese, there were many villages where all inhabitants—men and women, young and old— acted in concert to resist the invaders from Japan.

In a typical story that Kamai reported, Japanese troops would hear that a Chinese army contingent had been spotted at a nearby village. The Japanese would immediately rush to the scene, only to find that the village had been vacated. They would see clouds of dust rising several kilometers away, where the villagers were running through a covered trench to another village. All they would hear was the neighing of donkeys and the oinking of pigs, which sounded as though the animals were ridiculing the slow-witted Japanese soldiers.

Arriving at another village, a group of Japanese soldiers would open the door to a house and would be blown up. The same would happen upon lifting the lid of an oven. While running down a road, a soldier would be hit by a bullet coming from the supposedly deserted village; the shot, it would be discovered, had been fired by a sniper shooting through a hole in a tunnel.

Out of such episodes, the "people's war" and the Chinese
215

militia were created to foster the Mao Tse-tung strategy of swallowing up the enemy in the "vast ocean" of firmly united hamlets and people, and of isolating the cities by surrounding them with farming villages owing allegiance to the Communist Party.

This is the same idea on which today Lin Piao bases his appeal to countries in Asia, Africa, and Latin America to surround the United States aggressor, commented Kamai.

The militia has become an integral part of Communist China's war machinery. Neither the end of the hostilities with Japan nor the "liberation" of China brought about the abolition of the militia system. Article 23 of the Communist Party statutes explicitly stipulates the maintenance of the militia as a basis of national mobilization and a prerequisite to the enforcement of compulsory military service.

When the outbreak of the Korean War in June 1950 and attacks on the Chinese mainland by Nationalist guerrillas created a need for mobilization of militia corps, the Communist Chinese Government acted quickly to meet this need. More than 5,000,000 Chinese citizens were formed into militia units in October 1950; the number rose to 12,000,000 at the end of the next year and to 20,000,000 in 1953.

The enforcement of universal military conscription has led to the development of the largest militia corps in history—a 220,000,000-member army organized around the "skeleton" core of 30,000,000 militiamen, a formidable source of manpower to supplement the Regular Army.

Militia forces are considered to be necessary for other than purely military reasons.

Kamai learned that Chairman Mao has defined the militia corps as a military and labor organization which is also designed to promote mental and physical education.

There are signs that the majority of Communist Chinese leaders dwelt upon the idea of employing the militia as production units as suggested by Lo Jui-ching at the militia-men's conference held in April 1960, immediately after he had been appointed Chief of the General Staff. Lo, who has now been branded as a reactionary element and has been dragged about the streets wearing a triangular cap forced upon him by his captors, said in that speech that the main function of the militia was to engage in production and to help build up the nation.

This line of thinking was reflected also in the *People's Daily* editorial hailing the conference as a significant event, and in a congratulatory address to the conference by Marshal Ho Lung, as representative of the Communist Party Central Committee.

The first article of the 10-article proclamation issued immediately after the conference called on the militia to "become shock troops on the production front." The strengthening of national defense by the militia is not mentioned until Article 4. Lin Piao, the father of the corps, was the only speaker who stressed the importance of militia activities as part of "the people's armed forces."

The role of the militia has in fact been at stake in the Cultural Revolution. Lin's appeal for the development and strengthening of militia corps to fight the people's war prevailed at a later conference in 1964, and militiamen were hailed as "spiritual atom bombs."

TRAINING THE MILITIA

Militia units were in view wherever the Task Force traveled.

During his trip across the China mainland, Kamai saw signs reading "The Armed People's Department" on buildings in Kwangchow and several other cities. He learned that these departments, each covering a city or a county, were terminal organizations for the education of militia members.

217

They form the lowest stratum leading upward to military subdistrict headquarters, military district headquarters, and the General Political Department of the People's Liberation Army.

Factories, people's communes, and schools under the command of a municipal or county Armed People's Department make up a Militia Division. In the case of the Hungchiao People's Commune in the suburbs of Shanghai, the Armed People's Department is set up at the commune headquarters and each militia company at its production battalion.

The composition of a militia company is identical to that of a Liberation Army company, each consisting of a commander, vice commander, political instructors, and ordinary officers and soldiers. Militia company leaders are never plant superintendents or comune presidents. The majority of militia company leaders are retired Liberation Army officers who are highly qualified for their jobs. Liberation Army troops serve as drill instructors when militia members take time out from their production activities to undergo military training. Drills include rifle practice, mining operations, and training for intercepting paratroopers. Militia companies also hold maneuvers once or twice a year.

Militia members include ordinary militiamen and "skeleton" militiamen, Kamai continued. "Skeleton" militiamen are chosen from among people between 16 and 30 years of age, while the others include those in the 31-to-45 age group and the young men who were not selected for the "skeleton" forces. Some of the "skeleton" militiamen are allowed to keep weapons at home. In some cases, weapons are placed under the care of a division commander.

Most of the weapons are light firearms such as rifles and submachine guns, but militiamen also handle mortars and antiaircraft guns. Use of antiaircraft weapons was observed among militia units in and around large cities, apparently

218

in order to prepare for air raids. Militiamen also operate radios and lay telephone wire, but jobs requiring difficult mathematical calculations are presumably done only by men who have formerly served in the Liberation Army.

The militia is extolled as "an instrument to defend the country from acts of aggression by imperialists and to practice proletarian dictatorship in the country." Kamai was convinced, however, that Mao and Lin could not have put up a bold front in the Cultural Revolution if militiamen in rural areas had not been "hardened" by the movement to study Mao's thoughts and the drive to clean out "harmful elements" that was begun in 1963.

He was not aware, however, during his trip of militiamen training hard from early morning, presumably because they did not have much time for military activity while the Cultural Revolution was going on at full blast.

But the *Yomiuri* group did see an impressive demonstration of riflery by the barefoot militia—men, women, and children—of the Huatung People's Commune in Kwangtung Province. In keeping with the spirit of the Cultural Revolution, it was combined with an ideological lecture directed at the visiting Japanese, who were more than a little discomfited by it.

Takagi described the program that began with a cacophony of gongs and drums, "arousing a festive mood befitting peasants."

"The festive mood in itself was understandable," Takagi declared, "but we Japanese needed considerable patience to tolerate the lengthy explanations of Japan's economy being exploited by 'U.S. imperialism' and capitalists, and speeches sympathizing with the 'unhappy conditions' of the Japanese people." Possibly reflecting on the luxurious life of most Japanese compared to that of the average Chinese whom he saw, Takagi added, "It certainly would have contributed to promoting Japan-China friendship a step forward if we could have explained the actual conditions in Japan ourselves to a Communist Party secretary stationed in such a rustic area on the outskirts of Canton."

But the Japanese had to remain painfully silent, Takagi said, while the Communists distorted the facts of life in their country. Then the visitors were told that they were about to see something splendid.

At a warning signal, three families of barefoot people, including a 10-year-old child and a 51-year-old father, rushed in to the accompaniment of a gong and drum. Using ten semiautomatic rifles and an equal number of ordinary rifles, they fired three shots each at twenty steel targets placed 100 meters [about 110 yards] ahead. A mother knocked down a target, amid great applause, that a father had missed. Five-member teams of girls had a contest with boys' teams in bursting balloons 25 centimeters [about 10 inches] in diameter, with six shots each. In a shooting contest between the couples, the women outshot their male teammates. Another shooting contest between the Kaochi Battalion Militia and the Hsiangshan Battalion Women's Corps, handling two machine guns and twelve rifles, also was won by the women, reminding Takagi of songs composed by Mao praising female soldiers.

The culmination of the program was a barefoot chorus singing a song called "Become Militiamen of Communism," while each member waved a red-covered copy of *Quotations from Chairman Mao Tse-tung*.

THE CLASSLESS ARMY

The concept of a people's war as the road to a fully Communistic society rests firmly on Mao's greatest source of strength in today's China, the People's Liberation Army, which has been gradually replacing the Red Guards as the main force in the Cultural Revolution.

The majority of its 2,500,000 members come from the rural areas, where Mao has always had his strongest following among the peasants. Men who serve in the People's Liberation Army are armed to the teeth with Mao Tse-tung's thought, the reporters were told, and they think nothing of the modern weapons of their enemies.

Yet there are leaders in China who feel that the army should have weapons other than words and ideas, and this controversy is one of the most divisive issues today, according to the Yomiuri Task Force.

The argument over modernization of the ground forces began immediately after the end of the Korean War in 1953 and ended with the dismissal of Defense Minister Peng Teh-huai and the Chief of the General Staff, Huang Ke-cheng in 1959.

Peng Teh-huai had assumed command of the Communist Chinese forces in Korea after his predecessor, Lin Piao, was wounded in battle. Peng must have learned many lessons from this war, in which the Chinese inaugurated the "human sea" tactics against the well-equipped United States troops. The Chinese Government itself learned from the Korean conflict, and took a series of steps to improve the national defense. The establishment of the Ministry of National Defense in 1954 was followed in the next year by the enforcement of compulsory military service, the conferring of military ranks, the paying of monthly salaries, and the awarding of decorations to members of the armed forces.

In 1956, however, the Political Bureau of the Chinese Communist Party Central Committee decided to utilize the People's Liberation Army in the movement to develop agriculture by forming and operating People's Communes. Needless to say, said Takagi, the decision reflected the will of Chairman Mao. But the action came as a great shock to Defense Minister Peng, who felt that the country's war potential would be weakened if troops engaged only in agriculture.

Peng Teh-huai was a seasoned military professional. After serving as a low-ranking officer belonging to the old military clique of the Kuomintang Party, according to Takagi, he participated in an uprising against the Nationalist Government and then entered the Red Army. He fought with Mao during the time that the Communist leader was entrenching himself at Chingkangshan. Later he saw action in the Long March, the guerrilla war against Japan, the modern war against Japan, and the war against U.S. forces in Korea.

He never imagined, the reporter felt, that he was destined to be purged from this army on the ground that he followed an anti-Party, bourgeois line of thought.

In military affairs, Peng had been Mao's right-hand man, one of his most trusted generals. Like Mao, Peng is a native of Hunan Province and comes from a peasant family. He gave up his heart and soul to Mao's writings when he was an officer with the Kuomintang and joined him with his own troops. Since then, he had always sided with Mao on every question. The last thing Peng would do was to criticize or oppose his mentor. In a word, said Takagi, he was a soldier who devoted his life to the man named Mao, rather than to the revolution itself.

It was Lin Piao, then vice chairman of the Chinese Communist Party Central Committee and also of the National Defense Council, who defied and castigated Peng's idea of modernizing the army in the controversy that lasted for the next three years. The weapons in Lin's hands were the Mao military theory, which attaches the greatest importance to guerrilla warfare, and the other Maoist doctrine that stresses the "supremacy of politics."

Lin launched his attacks on Peng by having his close associate, Air Force Chief Lin Ya-lou, write a thesis entitled "Let Us Study the Mao Tse-tung Military Thought in

Real Earnest!" In this thesis, Lin Ya-lou said ironically, referring to Peng's admiration for the Soviet Army, that "there is a man who believes that the military experiences of a foreign country are all good and that our own experiences are behind the times.... This man is not trying to learn from the Soviet Union in an objective manner. Instead, he is trying to follow the example of the Soviet Union mechanically, without considering the history and conditions of our country."

He went on to say, "Under all circumstances, men are the decisive factor. In all cases, it is politics that assume supreme command. Do not forget that all weapons, and the work of preparing for war, are in the hands of men!" To illustrate his point, he cited the case of a teen-aged pilot with a flying record of only 100 hours, who shot down a veteran American pilot who had logged more than 3,000 hours of flying.

In September 1959, Lin gave the coup de grace to Peng in a statement saying, "As the People's Liberation Army is a tool for political struggle, revolutionary soldiers should not divorce themselves from politics. Army commanders and soldiers can deepen their interest in politics by engaging in the work to build up the country, and taking part in the mass movement.

"Some comrades [Peng and Huang] have the wrong idea that military drill is the only kind of training which army troops must undergo, and that troops are wasting their time and energy by assisting people in production."

After the dismissal of Peng and Huang, Lin Piao became Defense Minister and appointed Lo Jui-ching as Chief of the General Staff. Lo, who was to be purged in the course of the Cultural Revolution, had been Lin's close associate since the two men were serving at the Anti-Japanese Political and Military College (Kangta).

Mao avoided antagonizing Peng too much by keeping

him in his vice chairmanships of the National Defense Council and the State Council, and by appointing him a member of the committee for the funeral service of Lin Po-chu. For the same reason, he appointed Huang vice governor of Shansi.

A SOBER, SILENT MAN

Takagi tried to learn something about the victor in this struggle, the man whose name is linked with Mao's in the Cultural Revolution.

Lin is a tall man with a pale face, thick eyebrows, and a bow-shaped nose, according to Takagi's description, who always seems calm and does not talk very much. The Chinese say that Lin's face brings to their minds the saying "When he is in heaven, he is a cunning bird; when he is on earth, he is nothing but a man from Hupei."

Lin, the second most powerful man in Communist China, next only to Mao himself, is not a very sociable man. He does not drink or smoke and has no hobby and no friends. It is said that he leads a lonely and simple life and goes through his dry daily routines like a machine.

Takagi told the following story which, he said, tells much about Lin's personality:

When he served in the administrative office of the Eighth Route Army Headquarters in Chungking during the war, Lin used to lock himself in his room and read books all day long. Chou En-lai wished to do something to make Lin more cheerful. He tried to induce him to take dancing lessons from Anna, the German wife of Wang Ping-nan, who later became the Communist Chinese Ambassador to Poland. Anna did her best to teach dancing to Lin for some time, but she finally gave up, saying that he was hopeless.

Lin keeps himself aloof from other people because he is in delicate health. But the rumor that he has tuberculosis is groundless, Takagi learned. The truth is that he has, however, suffered from a nervous breakdown and has had a gastric ailment for more than twenty years.

Recalling the time when Lin's 115th Division dealt a crushing defeat to the transport corps of General Itagaki's Fifth Division, at Pingshingkuan, Vice Chief of Staff Li Tien-yu wrote that during the battle the lean Chinese general was lying on a *kang* [stove] with a "brain tonic" band wrapped around his head. Lin, then 31 years old, was suffering from insomnia. When he had trouble going to sleep, he would munch popped beans that he kept in a bag.

"Come to think of it," Takagi interjected, "Lin's Moscow-born daughter is named Tao-tao, which means 'bean-bean.'" Tao-tao, now 25 years old, established herself as a writer when she composed an obituary to Communist Chinese Air Force Chief Lin Ya-lou, who died of a disease in Shanghai in 1965. The Air Force commander had been Lin Piao's close associate since early days in the Fourth Field Army. Wu Fa-hsien, who succeeded to the command of the Air Force, had been a member of the political committee of the Fourth Field Army. This means that the Air Force has been completely controlled by men close to Lin Piao.

Lin gained Mao's confidence not only because he was a genius in military strategy, Takagi reported, but also because he always studied hard to try to broaden his views as a Communist. He had not had much schooling, having gone from the Wu Tai Middle School in Wuhan into the Whampoa Military Academy. But he was always eager to learn. Even after he became a commander, Lin continued to be absorbed in the books of Marx, Lenin, and Mao when his troops were not in action.

More importantly, he applied his knowledge to military tactics. One of his famous principles of attack was to "do three things fast and one thing slowly," meaning, Takagi told his readers, that troops should march rapidly, break

225

quickly through enemy lines, immediately enlarge the fruits of battle and pursue the foe swiftly—but take plenty of time to prepare the initial assault. This is considered an application of Mao thought to military methods.

After Lin was wounded in the war with Japan, Mao visited him in the hospital and sent him to the Soviet Union for recuperation. Lin remained in Moscow for four years, during which time he studied tirelessly to absorb Soviet military science. But Lin is not an admirer of the Soviet Union. On one occasion, Mao is said to have handed him a Soviet manual on guerrilla warfare and asked him what he thought of it. After looking over the manual Lin commented scoffingly, "If we had operated as this textbook says, we would have been exterminated by our enemies ten years ago."

Since the days when Communist China was uncompromisingly pro-Moscow, Lin has been antagonistic to the Soviet Union and advocated a get-tough policy toward that country. When Lin's troops were stationed in Manchuria around 1949, the territory was occupied also by Soviet forces commanded by Marshal Rodion Y. Malinovsky. But the commanders of the two Communist armies did not cooperate well with each other. The Chinese deeply resented the fact that the Soviet troops had seized and taken away industrial facilities in Manchuria valued at $2,000,000,000.

At any rate, Lin's Northeast (Manchuria) Liberation Army grew into the largest and best-equipped force in the People's Liberation Army by arming itself with weapons seized from the Japanese forces in Manchuria at the end of World War II. Later the Northeast Liberation Army was renamed the Fourth Field Army, and the leaders of this force now constitute the main current in the Communist Chinese Army.

Among key military figures in Communist China today who had formerly held top positions under Lin Piao in the army, Takagi listed Yang Chen-wu, the deputy chief of staff; Hsiao Kua, director of the General Political Department of the Liberation Army; Li Tien-yu, another deputy chief of staff, and Hsiao Ching-kuang, commander of the Communist Chinese naval forces. Among the twenty-five military areas in Red China, former leaders of the Fourth Field Army under Lin Piao constitute the majority of army troops stationed in Hopeh, Shansi, Shantung, Kiangsu, Chekiang, Anhwei, Fukien, Kiangsi, Kwangtung, Kwangsi, Hunan, Hupeh, and Honan, Takagi said. Exceptions are the troop commanders in Chengtu, Kunming, Tibet, Sinkiang, Inner Mongolia, and Manchuria. Studying records of the Central Military Committee of the Army, Takagi calculated that 188 of the 365 leading commanders—51 percent—had served previously under Lin.

Lin's tenure as Defense Minister began under very difficult circumstances, noted Takagi. At that time, the men of the Liberation Army were bitter and disillusioned. It may seem impossible that there was ever such a time, Takagi commented, but it is a blot left on the history of the Communist Chinese military establishment.

The time was the summer of 1960, he wrote, when the country was being hit by natural disasters and a great famine that lasted for three years. The story of these times is typified by events in the Chengtu Military Area in Szechwan, where Li Ching-chuan, now being criticized as a leader of the authority faction, served as the first political commissioner. Takagi related the details:

Liu Kuan-hsien, a member of the First Squad, First Company, First Battalion of the First Regiment, was singing a folk song that went like this: "Soldiers are lucky. At the sound of the bugle they go to the mess hall and have a bowl of rice. Pretty soon they get hungry again and walk with reeling feet."

The daily per capita food ration for soldiers had been cut

from 0.75 to 0.6 kilograms [about 1.32 pounds]. This was hard on the soldiers, who have large appetites at their age. The First Company was a model unit, honored as the "steel sword company" for distinguished service in the Korean War. Members of this elite group were heard to say during study hours, "What has happened to our food? Maybe the Government has seized it all. The food was sent ahead of the troops, and the soldiers cannot move because they are hungry. The folks back home must be having a really hard time, considering how rations have been cut even in the army. Is it all because of the People's Communes that we are so hungry? This is what the Three Red Banners have brought about."

During rifle practice one September day, Liu Sheng-hua, vice chief of the Eighth Squad, said suddenly, "When I get out of the army I will take a rifle with me, and that is all I need!"

"Are you going to eat the rifle?" a comrade asked.

"No, I am going to start a rebellion against the Communist Party," Liu answered. Liu came from a peasant family who had died from illnesses caused by lack of proper nourishment.

Cheng Wen-kan and Kuo Shu-yuan, adjutants of the Chief of the General Staff of the People's Liberation Army, inspected the barracks of the First Company and made the following report:

"The company consists of three infantry platoons and one machine-gun platoon, comprising personnel temporarily attached to the unit. The company has nine officers, including warrant officers, 18 noncommissioned officers, and 60 enlisted men—of whom 18 are Communist Party members and 33 are members of the Communist Party Young Men's Association.

"Of the 87 men in the company, 62 come from peasant families, 24 from middle-class farm families, and one from a small landowner's family. Forty-eight joined the army in 1960. All 60 enlisted men are natives of Szechwan Province. Twenty-four have reported that their families were suffering very much from the famine. Ten enlisted men lost a total of sixteen relatives between May and December of 1960."

As the enlisted men became bitter and disillusioned, company commanders began to treat their men harshly. The men began to disobey orders, and a tense atmosphere prevailed in the barracks. Three members of the 55th Regiment —Kung Ho-yu and Wang Yu-tsui of the Third Battalion and Chen Fan-ting, assistant squad leader of the machine-gun company—committed suicide between September and December of 1960. These men had become despondent because they were mistreated, and also because their families were suffering greatly in the famine.

Alarmed by the situation, Lo Jui-ching—then the Chief of the General Staff—made an inspection tour of army barracks in Kunming, Chengtu, Chungking, Wuhan, and other areas from the beginning of 1961 and reported that the percentage of soldiers coming from disaster areas was extremely high in some army units. Such soldiers constituted 16 to 71 percent of the members of companies in the Wuhan Military Area.

The most outstanding example was the Engineer Battalion of the 3953rd Regiment, where 480 of its 600 members were from famine-stricken families.

These findings must have been a big headache to army leaders, Takagi surmised. The situation was aggravated further when nearly 2,000 Soviet engineers left China without finishing work on modern industrial facilities, as if they were unconcerned about the natural calamities and the great famine that plagued the country.

Army authorities then initiated a campaign to "correct" its members, with emphasis on political and ideological education. They began by carrying out a movement aimed at "recalling two types of suffering and examining three elements." This program was a combination of two different campaigns: an educational drive to enable soldiers "to grasp the present situation by looking back on the suffering of the Chinese race in the past and the suffering of the working classes," and the "rectification campaign" to examine and criticize class-consciousness, struggle, and activities of individual officers and soldiers.

From April 1961 the army conducted an additional campaign to develop "four-hao [good or excellent] units." "Four-hao" units were companies that combined the "four right methods" of political thought, military techniques, styles of work, and way of living in accordance with Mao's teachings. A "new look" in the army was sought by combining study of Maoist thought with the actual putting of these principles into practice through work.

The movement proved to be very successful, Takagi was told. As the majority of soldiers were farmers themselves, they earnestly studied such subjects as the People's Communes. More than a dozen "people's heroes" were born among soldiers of the Liberation Army, and they served as models for the people.

Thus the Communist Chinese Government was able to assert, Takagi indicated, that "the Liberation Army has succeeded in becoming an armed force to serve the people, and a 'spiritual pivot of society.' Needless to say," he added, "it was Defense Minister Lin Piao, heir apparent of Mao Tse-tung, who was credited with having administered spiritual education to revitalize the Liberation Army."

FIGHTING THE PAPER TIGER

The military policy of Communist China reflects a thesis expounded by Lin Piao in an article published in September

1965 in connection with the observance of the twentieth anniversary of the defeat of Japan.

"The monster called war will ultimately be made to disappear by the development of human society," the Communist Chinese Defense Minister wrote, "and it will not be very long before this happens. However, there is only one way to make it disappear; that is, to fight war with war and to fight an anti-revolutionary war with a revolutionary war."

On the Communist Chinese confrontation with the United States, Lin had this to say, "We have full confidence in bringing down American imperialism in the near future by forming a united front with the peoples of Asia, Africa, and Latin America. There is only one way to achieve this. That is by war.

"There has never been an instance in the history of the East or West, in ancient times or in modern days, where the intruder has admitted, 'I was wrong, so I will discontinue the invasion.' Compromise or negotiation with the intruder is tantamount to giving him time, to permitting him to become stronger. The only way to stop him and chase him out is to resort to war. . . ."

The strategy and tactics of Communist China are constructed on the basic philosophy outlined in the 1965 article by Lin Piao, wrote Nishimura. "The strategy is severe and stern, allowing absolutely no room for compromise.

"With the relationship between the Soviet Union and China having deteriorated to where it stands today," Nishimura said, "Communist China should be prepared for a war on two fronts, against the United States and against the Soviet Union, and it is not too far off the mark to assume that Red China today is mapping out strategy and tactics accordingly.

"What we cannot disregard when we look at the Chinese strategy and tactics is how they intend to utilize the experience gained in various struggles since their war against

231

Japan. Since Chairman Mao said 'an atomic bomb is nothing but a paper tiger,' it is obvious that their strategy and tactics are not centered on nuclear weapons," Nishimura wrote. Lin Piao, in his thesis entitled "Hail to the Victory of People's War," stated that "no matter what advances are made in modern weapons and no matter how complex modern warfare might become, the ultimate victory in a war will be determined by the continuous battles of the ground forces, by hand-to-hand fighting on the battle-grounds, by the self-consciousness, courage, and spirit of sacrifice of the people."

Lin added, "In this respect, American imperialism is fully exposing its weakness. The spiritual bomb of the revolutionary people is far stronger and more effective than the materialistic atomic bomb."

The major difference in strategy between the Communist Chinese who fought the Japanese a few decades ago and the Communist China of today is the shifting of the enemy and the change in the battleground, said the veteran newsman. In those days, the objective was to defeat Japanese imperialism, and the battleground was the mainland itself. Today, the strategy is directed against American imperialism, and the front has spread from China to the whole world, including Asia, Africa, and Latin America. In other words, the strategy has been escalated from "emancipation of China" to "liberation of the oppressed people of the world."

"In the war against Japan, the Communist Chinese first strengthened the rural areas, isolated the Japanese army in cities, and then crushed the enemy and retook the cities. Lin Piao has simply evolved this into a world strategy, by postulating as follows: 'If we look at the world, North America and Europe are the cities. Asia, Africa, and Latin America are the villages. The world revolution that is going to take place will eventually assume the form of the villages encircling the cities. World revolution will eventually be led by the revolutionary struggles of the people of Asia, Africa, and Latin America, which have the overwhelming majority of the world's population.'"

But Lin Piao does not say that Red China will dispatch troops to help these people of Asia, Africa, and Latin America in their wars of emancipation, Nishimura pointed out. The Maoists contend, "A revolution is something that some foreign nation should help or should carry out in the form of a contract. However, this does not preclude the possibility of sympathizing and offering assistance."

These statements indicated to Nishimura the attitude of Communist China toward the Vietnam war. The tactics that the Red Chinese employed in the war against Japan are regarded as a sample of the strategy for "liberating the world." As a matter of fact, they are being used by the Vietcong today.

Nishimura recalled another statement by Lin, addressed to the United States: "The large human sea that will be created by hundreds of millions of Chinese people will engulf you American intruders, who will number several million at the most."

Judging from that statement, the Japanese newsman assumed that in a war with the United States, what the Chinese would welcome most is to have the well-equipped Americans land on the mainland and come deep into the interior. If this happens, the Chinese strategy will be to preserve the Regular Army as long as they can by having these regular troops retreat, call an all-out mobilization of the militiamen, encircle the invading American troops, and threaten a supply line that will have been stretched to the limit. They would counter the American air raids by moving underground. As they did in the Korean War, and as the Vietcong are doing today, they would dig deep holes and move factories, schools, and other organs and facilities there. In a war, such tactics constitute guerrilla warfare. They would eventually mobilize the Regular Army (held in reserve until then), take advantage of their overwhelming numerical superiority, encircle the small American units, and isolate and crush them by utilizing the mobility that the Chinese troops have to their advantage on their home front.

But the Chinese most likely would try to avoid as much as possible having tens of thousands of their men coming face to face with an appreciable number of American troops. One outstanding characteristic of Mao's tactics is never to wage a war or fight a battle except when 100 percent certain he can win. He will never risk the "fate of the fatherland" in an all-out clash unless it is certain that the outcome will be in his favor.

Against American strategy backed by material superiority the Communist Chinese intend to counter with spiritual strategy. To challenge the American nuclear power, the Chinese will develop nuclear bombs and missiles as "political weapons."

The Liberation Army—that is, the Regular Army—is 2,700,000 strong, mostly infantry. Other than these, Communist China has a militia of 200,000,000 that can carry out "human sea" tactics. Communist China has not developed large bombers, aircraft carriers, or warships, considered essential for modern warfare. The Navy consists mostly of submarines, numbering approximately thirty; a few of the submarines are equipped with missile-launching devices. As for the Air Force, emphasis is being placed on fighter planes that will be used to intercept intruders. Hence the weapons are generally defensive in nature, rather than offensive.

"Communist China, which takes the stand that 'a revolution should be conducted by the people of that nation,' does not believe in possessing offensive weapons," Nishimura asserted. This is based on the line that there is no possibility of Communist China's attacking other countries in any near future, although nobody can tell what lies ahead.

One of the reasons for this stand, the reporter pointed out, is China's weak industrial power. With the manufacturing capability it has today, it cannot develop atomic and hydrogen bombs as well as arm itself with modern weapons effectively. Nishimura wondered what would happen if a war between the United States and Red China developed into a Third World War, with Japan occupied by Communist Chinese troops. The Chinese could not maintain the occupation with their present capabilities, he said, because they do not have the transportation power to supply the colossal amount of materials needed to carry out the operation, or the Navy to protect the supply line. But, he warned his countrymen, we cannot state categorically that Communist China would leave Japan alone if a war with the United States broke out.

During his trip through Communist China, he asked one influential person, "Can we be assured that you will not attack Japan, even if a war occurs between China and the United States?" The Chinese replied, "I cannot guarantee that you can feel at ease. It would depend on the attitude and the moves of Japan. If Japan became too involved by siding with America, there would be no assurance that the safety of Japan would be guaranteed."

DEPLOYMENT OF FORCES

The two major recent events in China—the Great Proletarian Cultural Revolution and the tension between Moscow and Peking—have not caused the Regular Army to do anything noteworthy, reported Nishimura. According to the estimates of the so-called military experts, the only Chinese move was the addition of some 100,000 troops to the Manchurian area.

As for the actual deployment of the Regular Army, he thought he could obtain quite reliable figures by studying the distribution or the number of the military representatives who attended the third National People's Congress held toward the end of 1964. He cited the following figures: 224,000 troops directly under Mao; 316,000 in the Shenyang (Fengtien) area; 270,000 in the Peking area; 157,000 in the Tsinan (Shantung Province) area; 157,000 in the Foochow (Fukien Province) area; 248,000 in the Nanking area; 89,000 in the Chengtu, (Szechwan Province) area; 157,000 in the Kunming (Yunnan Province) area; 113,000 in the Lanchow area; 113,000 in the Wuhan (Hupeh Province) area; 68,000 in Inner Mongolia; 133,000 in Sinkiang-Uighur, and 68,000 in Tibet. Red China also has a naval force of 135,000 men, an Air Force of 202,000, and a police force of 500,000.

As these figures indicate, the Japanese reporter explained, Communist China has 316,000 troops stationed in the northeastern area, even in peacetime, ready for any incident that might occur with the United Nations forces now stationed in the Republic of Korea [South Korea]. The distribution also reveals that Communist China is placing emphasis on deployment along the seacoast, which includes Tsinan, Foochow, Nanking, and Canton. These troops are in a state of readiness to repel any attack from the outside.

The Air Force has most of its power stationed in the Honan district to be ready for an attack by the U.S. Air Force, while the Navy has most of its strength deployed along the coast facing the Formosa [Taiwan] Strait and around the island of Hainan.

The defense setup in the northwestern area is particularly strong, Nishimura thought. Well-informed sources believe that between 400,000 and 500,000 troops equipped with modern weapons are deployed along the 3,000-kilometer border with the Soviet Union, running parallel to the Yalu

River, the Ussuri River, and the Amur River. According to these sources, fortresses that the Japanese built thirty years ago, along the route used by the Russians for the invasion of Manchuria toward the end of World War II, are being used more and more. Today, Chinese troops are positioned strategically in these installations, which lie mainly in the Tungning area facing Khabarovsk, the Aigun area facing Blagoveschchensk and the Hailar-Manchuli area.

The northeastern area is the model district for industry and farming in China. Therefore, it is very important for Peking to protect this sector from a Soviet attack in the event of hostilities with that country, as well as having a vantage point to watch closely the moves of United Nations troops in South Korea.

It appears to be common sense to regard Sinkiang Province as second in strategic importance, judging from the way minor clashes have been taking place between the Soviet Union and Communist China. However, military critics do not concur with this thinking, Nishimura found. The experts believe that China would give up most of Sinkiang Province and withdraw its defense line to Hami and Turtan if Soviet troops moved in. One of the reasons is that Sinkiang Province is too far from central China. Another reason is that there is only the Lansin railroad that can be depended upon as a supply line.

Besides, because of deserts like Takla Makan and many large prairies that dot this area, the smooth movement of big armies is extremely difficult. In other words, Sinkiang Province is hard to defend and is not suitable for the mobile tactics practiced by the Liberation Army. It is said that it requires about 200 tons of supplies a day to support one Chinese division of 10,000 to 12,000 men, in contrast to one ton a day for every U.S. soldier. Even if this is so, the supply of this minimum of 200 tons a day for a division might be jeopardized if the Lansin railway, the one and only supply line for the Red Chinese Army in the area, were exposed to bombing by the Soviet Air Force.

If that happened, there is a possibility that even a well-trained regular Communist Chinese Army would not be able to carry out its tactics. It would seem to be better strategy to retreat to the east, set up a defense line to the west of Lop Nor, where the nuclear tests were held, attack the Soviet Army from behind—using guerrilla warfare after its supply line has been stretched out—and crush the enemy after they have become exhausted, Nishimura surmised.

In the southern Honan district, facing Vietnam, Communist China has a defense line set up between Kunming and Yunnan, and has a good stock of war matériel on hand. However, it is a fact that the installations themselves are nothing but a row of trenches; the number of men deployed there is said to be not more than 200,000 to 300,000. Hence it can be said that the Chinese are only keeping prepared for an emergency here and have no active intention of attacking.

Nishimura also looked into the problem of the army in relation to the fluidity of the Great Proletarian Cultural Revolution and found that hardly any movement of the army has been seen in this connection. Each military district is capable of carrying out its own tactics, so there will be no major movement of troops unless something really serious occurs. In mainland China, where transportation capability is quite limited, the relocation of any appreciable number of divisions would immediately tell on the private demand for transport facilities.

"There is one final question," Nishimura continued, "Is the Communist Chinese Army strong or weak?" The answers to this question by military experts were intriguing to Nishimura. Some state categorically that the Red Chinese Army is the strongest in the world, without question, while others, more reserved, say that the Red Chinese forces are "strong against outside aggression, but weak against internal strife." One critic declared, "Just as there is a limit to American strategy depending upon material superiority, there is equally a limit to spiritual weapons. For instance, U.S. Air Force pilots ordinarily undergo flight training for an average of two hours a day, while Red Chinese pilots have a chance to fly only four hours a month. With this kind of training, it is next to impossible for Chinese Air Force fighter pilots to down American planes.

"You might wonder at this point," the military expert said, "how we evaluate the ability of the Communist Chinese military that enabled them to shoot down a Nationalist Chinese U-2 high-altitude reconnaissance plane. To this question, we would reply that this U-2 was downed while it was forced to fly low after running out of fuel."

At this stage the military strength of Communist China is still largely an unknown quantity, Nishimura concluded.

Chapter X

CHINA AND THE WORLD

DERIDING THE SOVIET BIG NOSES

One of the dominant factors of the Cultural Revolution has been the breakdown in relations between Communist China and the Soviet Union. The *Yomiuri* reporters found that voicing anti-Russian sentiments had become a popular pastime. Nishimura recalled with amusement a tour of Manchuria that he had made while he was the *Yomiuri* resident correspondent in Peking in 1965.

"It proved to be a rather unusual journey," he said. "It seemed that I made the trip just to listen to the people of the region speaking ill of the Soviet Union."

In Changchung, the Japanese journalist spoke to a worker in an automobile factory on the subject of economic assistance by Moscow and was told that everyone had been jubilant when they received a shipment of press machines. These were the lifeblood of their plant. But then they were surprised to find that they were damaged, secondhand goods; the workers said they were no good, and did not take three days before they broke down. The plant suffered a great loss by purchasing those machines.

Said the vice superintendent of an electrical equipment factory in Harbin, "We were made to pay through the nose for Soviet machines. In some cases, they cost us seven times the prevailing international market prices. We were lucky if we got the stuff at all. Often the Russians did not even bother to deliver the items after getting the money for them. This is the way the Soviet revisionists operate. Khrushchev is a thief, and Kosygin is a swindler."

Nishimura noted that Moscow had not made any serious attempt to answer such charges by Communist Chinese.

The Soviet Union may have made money by granting aid and exporting goods to Communist China, but, the reporter said, undeniably the Soviets have lost the friendship of the Chinese. He remembered vividly the happy smile on the face of Liao Cheng-chih, chairman of the China-Japan Friendship Association, when he announced to newsmen in Peking that the Chinese had paid their debts to the Soviet Union.

He also remembered how Chinese officials treated Premier Kosygin of the Soviet Union when he stopped at Peking while en route to Hanoi at the time the United States started bombing North Vietnam in February 1965. It was to Nishimura a typical example of hosts insulting their guest while seemingly receiving him with courtesy.

And then there was the time that the New China News Agency reporters and Soviet correspondents argued hotly and came close to exchanging blows at Tungpu Airport while covering the arrival of Chinese students who reportedly had been manhandled by Soviet policemen for staging anti-American demonstrations in Moscow. Nishimura saw similar scenes so often that he finally came to the conclusion that Communist China and the Soviet Union would never reestablish friendly relations, even though some observers in Tokyo and Moscow still did not believe that relations between the two countries had deteriorated hopelessly.

When Prime Minister Chou En-lai visited Moscow immediately after Khrushchev's fall from power, there was speculation that a thaw had started in the cold war between Moscow and Peking. The belief that the two Communist powers would become friends again was so widespread, Nishimura noted, that an article he sent from Peking, entitled "Spilt Water Will Never Be Gathered Again," was never printed.

But the thaw never materialized, and the deterioration of relations between the two countries had reached the stage by 1967 where he could say that Communist China simply despises the Soviet Union, without hatred.

This anti-Soviet feeling among the Chinese people is by no means a new phenomenon, the reporter said. Immediately after the Communists came to power, the new Government in Peking established the China-Soviet Friendship Association. Headed by Soong Ching-ling—Mme. Sun Yat-sen—the organization had as many as 100,000,000 members. But this did not mean that the Chinese and the Russians were on good terms with each other. Rather, the whole affair serves as an indication that the people of the two nations were on extremely bad terms, and the Chinese Government found it necessary to improve the public image of the Soviet Union in Red China by establishing a "friendship association" with 100,000,000 members.

Despite these efforts, however, the people have come to regard the Soviet Union with greater hostility since the Communist takeover, Nishimura reported. The official verdict is that the blame for the situation lies solely with the Kremlin leaders and that in spite of this, the people of the two countries remain eternal comrades, but he thought that the people themselves are engaged in such mudslinging and regard each other with such great contempt that even if the two Governments should settle their differences, it would take many years for the Chinese and Soviet masses to restore their old relationship as comrades.

On ideological grounds, the direct confrontation and antagonism is between two countries that both avowedly follow Marxism-Leninism. Communist China brands the Soviet doctrines and policies as revisionism, while the Soviet Union denounces the Chinese position as doctrinaire and adventurist.

Nishimura composed an imaginary message that a Communist Chinese official spokesman might address to the Moscow leadership if he were to state Peking's point of view in earthier terms than the usual high-flown clichés of Communist invective. It was meant to clarify the conflict for Japanese readers in simple language, and read as follows:

"Gentlemen in the Kremlin! You make it a point to talk about peaceful competition and peaceful transition. Do you really believe that the differences between the two diametrically opposite systems of socialism and capitalism can be automatically eliminated by 'economic competition' and that a 'warless' new world, marked by full cooperation between nations, will come into being? If so, you have turned your backs on Marxism. You claim to be the legitimate successors to Lenin, but this is nonsense. Have you ever thought seriously about what the world's Communist fighters have done, seen, and experienced, and about the profits, goals, and duties of the international Communist movement?

"Gentlemen in the Kremlin!" the message continued. "You talk so much about the state for all people, the party for all people, and the classless society! Do you really think that there can be a state or a society that has nothing to do with classes and which exists beyond and above the classes? As long as there is a state, there are classes. When society no longer has classes, there will be no state. Your concept of the state for all people is a mock imitation of the bourgeois doctrine of the state. You should ponder the fact that the

243

social system of Yugoslavia has changed in the wrong way since that country adopted such a doctrine."

The ideological differences between Peking and Moscow have affected the entire spectrum of their relations, Nishimura said, and their differences on the Vietnam conflict are particularly strong.

Communist China is not rapping the Soviet Union just because Moscow has supplied North Vietnam only with a small number of missiles and outdated airplanes, as Nishimura analyzed the situation. In the eyes of the Chinese, this is a small matter. Communist China's principal objection to the Soviet policy in Vietnam is stated in the familiar charge that "the Kremlin is in collusion with the United States to repress the struggle against American imperialism being waged by North Vietnam and the South Vietnamese National Liberation Front [Vietcong]."

What Communist China wants the Soviet Union to do, Nishimura gathered, is to act on the assumption that the Vietnam conflict is "a war between socialist countries and imperialist countries," with great significance in global strategy. In concrete terms the Chinese believe that the Soviet Union should cause the United States to divert troops from Vietnam to Europe by starting a conflict in Berlin. The Communist Chinese, themselves, have a brilliant record of struggles staged to achieve such a strategic purpose.

For example, the Communist Chinese feel that in 1950 they saved North Korea by sending a volunteer army to the peninsula to fight the American forces. And when President Eisenhower dispatched troops to the crisis-ridden Middle East in 1958, Peking responded by bombarding Quemoy, diverting American attention to the Formosa Strait.

Communist China is saying, Nishimura suggested, "Now that imperialism is on the verge of destruction, China, the Soviet Union, and all other socialist countries should join forces against the American imperialists. It is such a pity that the Kremlin at this time is in collusion with the United States to suppress the war of liberation in Vietnam!"

The discord and antagonism between Communist China and the Soviet Union are deep-rooted, indeed, he reported. The complexity of the problem stems partly from the fact that the two countries, like a divorced couple, know each other very well. Because the two nations have a long common border, they are plagued by territorial issues and other problems arising from a conflict of interests. The biggest problem is that each side firmly believes that its position is right and refuses to budge an inch from its stand.

Nishimura concluded with the comment that he is still standing on his earlier conclusion that "spilt water will never be gathered again."

AN INSOLUBLE CONFLICT

Revisiting Communist China for the first time in eleven years, Takeo Takagi also was astonished by the overt reversal of attitude toward the Soviet "Big Brothers." Traveling around the country, he searched for reasons to explain the underlying animosity between the Chinese and Soviet people that Nishimura had noticed.

He found that the two people distrust, hate, and fear each other. In a typical incident, a textile technician in Shanghai told Takagi what happened when groups of Soviet technicians were sent to state-operated factories and spinning mills in that city in the spring of 1952.

"We are textile technicians in our own right," he said, "so we had nothing to learn from Soviet spinning techniques. But we wanted to size up the Soviet technicians, so we asked them many questions dealing with delicate points in textile manufacture. These *tapitzu* [Big Noses] could hardly answer our questions, and, while they were here, we did not follow their instructions at all. They packed up and left after three months."

The Chinese technician ended his story with a hearty laugh. Takagi discovered that many Chinese disrespectfully called Soviet engineers "Big Noses" when talking among themselves.

However, there had been a time when the Communist Chinese Government encouraged the people to learn from the Soviet Union. When he visited China in 1955, Takagi saw posters saying "Follow the Example of Our Big Brothers" plastered all over the walls of factories. Posters inviting enrollment in Russian language courses were seen on the streets of Peking.

But even in those days when the two Governments were honeymooning, Takagi heard that Russians and Chinese took a hostile attitude toward each other on many occasions and at many places when they were unable to control their pent-up feelings. In fact, anti-Soviet attitude of the masses was the reason that the Chinese Communist Party Central Committee ordered posters put up advising citizens to "learn from the experience of the Soviet Union."

A cursory glance at history, Takagi found, shows that the two countries have spent more time in snarling, bickering, and fighting than in being friendly toward each other.

In the eyes of the Chinese the Russians are a crude and uncivilized race. They regard them as "white barbarians," the cousins of the Huns—the northern tribe that invaded China proper from time to time over the past several thousand years. The Russians, for their part, believe that the Chinese are an impertinent and conceited people who are prone to find fault with Russia despite the fact that they are a "yellow race" with a "low level of culture." The Russian attitude is akin to the doctrine of the "Yellow Peril," Takagi told *Yomiuri* readers.

On their side, Chinese cite the massacre of their people
246

by Russian troops at the time of the Boxer Uprising in 1900. The most appalling fact of this mass killing, said Takagi, was that it took place at Aigun, a town on the northern border, and not in Peking, where the Boxers were threatening the lives of foreigners. About 3,000 Chinese, including women and children, are supposed to have been butchered by the Russian soldiers who stormed into the town. According to one description, the battered bodies of the victims floated down the Amur River like so many logs. The invading Russians completely destroyed the town, which had played an important role as a frontier outpost under the Ch'ing Dynasty. As a result, Aigun was displaced by Taiheiho, the famous gold-mining center, as the most prosperous community in the region.

Aigun appears in history as the site of a treaty allowing both countries to use the Amur River. But in 1900 Russia arbitrarily banned Chinese vessels from the river. This caused Chinese troops to bombard Blagoveshchenks, a Russian town situated on the border. Russian troops seized the excuse to cross the Amur and lay siege to Aigun. The massacre followed.

The Chinese claim that the Maritime Provinces and other parts of Siberia originally belonged to China, and that these territories had been invaded and annexed by the "Big Noses" over the centuries. In the eyes of the Chinese, the Sino-Soviet Border Treaty is a typical example of an unequal pact. In March 1963, the Communist Chinese Government issued a statement calling for a revision of the treaties of Aigun, Tientsin, and Ili.

There have been other clashes, the reporter said, reviewing history. In 1921, Soviet forces pursuing White Russian troops invaded and occupied Ulan Bator in Outer Mongolia, where the Soviet Union established a puppet regime called the People's Government. This blatant act of aggression ran

247

counter to the statement of 1919 renouncing Soviet rights in Mongolia.

The Soviet actions in Mongolia have been a series of contradictions. In May 1924, the Soviet Government issued a statement acknowledging that Outer Mongolia is part of China. Two months later, Moscow established the People's Republic of Mongolia and made this new country its own satellite nation. China has never reconciled itself to the status of the Outer Mongolian republic.

The Soviet Union caused a political upheaval in Sinkiang in April 1933 and later appointed Cheng Shih-tsuai as governor of the province. When Ma Chung-ying's forces laid siege to Tihwa, the capital, in January 1934, the Soviet Union dispatched troops to the city. In the following month, Russian troops marched on Hami and brought the entire northwest of China under the control of the Soviet Union.

Memories of Soviet actions in Mongolia and Sinkiang simply jar upon the nerves of the Chinese, said Takagi. With this background in mind, he found it easy to understand the eagerness with which the Chinese engineers and factory officials whom he interviewed expressed widespread dissatisfaction with the quality of machinery supplied by the Soviet Union.

At the Taiyuan chemical fertilizer plant he was shown two gas compressors—one large and the other small—being operated side by side. The large one is a Soviet-made machine that was brought to the factory under the Soviet technical aid program for Communist China. Soviet engineers who transported the parts left without assembling and installing the machine. Chinese engineers managed to put the parts together and get the machine into operation, but they complained that it had been made back in the 1940s and that the Soviet Government had sold it at an exorbitant price. Later, the Chinese engineers—following the principle of self-help—made a smaller but more efficient compressor and put it into operation alongside the Soviet machine. The factory staff proudly tell visitors, "Ours is seventy percent more efficient than the Soviet model."

Something like this happened also at the high-pressure electrical equipment factory in Sian, Takagi reported. Soviet engineers went home without completing a high-temperature tunnel furnace to be used to burn insulators. They also left unfinished the task of installing four rock pulverizers. The Soviet engineers took with them the blueprints and other papers containing information needed for installing the machines. The factory staff was at a loss, because there were no Chinese engineers who could do the job. Soon after, they discovered a paper—forgotten by the Soviet engineers —which showed that the Soviet Union had purchased the machines in question from East Germany. The Chinese were furious when they found that the machines had been purchased by the Soviet Union for 153,000 rubles and then resold to Communist China for 218,000 rubles. A Chinese engineer told Takagi indignantly that the Soviet practice had been even more dishonest than that of the capitalists who make money by charging commissions, adding that at the same time, the country was in the throes of natural disasters that lasted for three years. "The Soviets took mean advantage of our helpless condition," said the engineer. "We can hardly call the Soviet Union a friendly nation."

Mineo Nakajima, looking at the Sino-Soviet rift from the point of view of a scholar specializing in modern Chinese history, examined the implications of the clash in the realm of world affairs. What effect, he asked, will the conflict have on the rivalry between Communism and democracy?

It will be extremely difficult to end the Sino-Soviet confrontation, Nakajima declared, since it involves three different factors—theoretical struggle, racial and national antagonism, and the competition for leadership in the international Communist movement—all closely interwoven. If the present situation stemmed wholly from a clash of national interests and the antagonism between the two races, it would be quite possible that a shift in the tide of international politics would make the enemies of yesterday the friends of today, as has happened frequently in world history. But the fact is that these two factors are not the only ones involved.

The theoretical struggle relates to the change in the Communist direction growing out of the fact that the destruction of colonialism in the period following World War II was accompanied by the rise of socialism as a form of government. The basic lineup of nations has been completely altered since the world itself has become divided into the two different camps of capitalism and socialism.

It was necessary for the Soviet Union to set forth daring new doctrines in order to adapt Marxism-Leninism to the needs of the new era. Thus Moscow came up with the idea of peaceful coexistence, the possibility of averting wars between the two groups of nations with different social systems, and the multifariousness of revolutions.

The Soviet leaders went so far as to theorize that their country, which has formerly been ruled by a proletarian dictatorship, has now grown into a state for all people, which will eventually turn into a classless society, the dream of Marxists. This theory is based on the assumption that socialism has already won a complete victory and that the opposition between different classes has been eliminated in the Soviet Union. These new doctrines, which were advanced by the official denunciation of Stalin, have been approved by the Communist parties of many countries and have won international recognition.

But the Chinese believe that the only way to inherit and uphold Marxism-Leninism in the present age is to recognize the absolute value of Maoism and the experience of the Chinese Communist revolution, and in their judgment, the new Kremlin stand is the detested "modern revisionism."

While resisting the opposing forces in the international movement, the Chinese strengthened their desire to have their own view of the state accepted widely. Their own internal political upheavals led to a hardening of their inflexible view of the revolution.

At the Moscow conference in the autumn of 1957, Mao came out with the slogan that "East Wind" prevails over the "West Wind," and proposed that Communist countries wage a "quick, decisive battle" to overthrow imperialism. But this suggestion was rejected by the Soviet Union and other Communist countries.

The Soviet Union expressed its disapproval of the People's Commune movement of 1959 by refusing to comment on the subject. Moscow also took an airy attitude toward the Sino-Indian border dispute in 1959. The Russians antagonized the Chinese further by holding direct negotiations with the United States at Camp David. And in June 1959 the Soviet Union abrogated the new Sino-Soviet military agreement and rejected Communist China's request for a sample of an atomic bomb, with the technical data needed to create the weapon. The Soviet refusal to supply Red China with these items was based on Moscow's policy of preventing the proliferation of nuclear arms. At the same time, however, Communist China had just finished formulating its nuclear warfare strategy. Therefore, the Soviet attitude on this point brought the Sino-Soviet tension to a high pitch. With the withdrawal of Soviet engineers from Communist China in 1960, the dispute acquired the status of a direct confrontation between the two countries. Since then, Communist China has been advocating—and acting on—the principle of self-help.

Now the Mao-Lin main-current group is emphasizing that the "bourgeois authority faction" headed by Liu Shao-chi and Teng Hsiao-ping is related to the Soviet revisionists. As has been stated before in the *Yomiuri* dispatches, however,

251

the Liu-Teng faction is not exactly pro-Soviet. To be sure, Liu and Teng and their followers frown on the Mao-Lin line of regarding the Soviet Union as a foe. Nevertheless, the Liu-Teng group has been extremely active in criticizing "modern revisionism" in Moscow.

What the Mao-Lin faction fears most is the possibility that the Khrushchev line of thought might take root in China, too. The reason is simple, said Nakajima. Communist China has enough ideological weapons—the Mao Tse-tung thought and Marxism-Leninism—to keep its people from being influenced by the ideologies of capitalist countries, but it is difficult to arrest the spread of the Khrushchev doctrine, which might be born in Communist China at any moment under the banner of Marxism-Leninism. This is one of the reasons why the Sino-Soviet controversy has assumed the proportions of a life-or-death struggle for the Mao-Lin group.

AMERICAMANIA IN PEKING

A foundation stone of Communist Chinese foreign policy, probably far more important from the long view than the rivalry with the Soviet Union, has been hatred of the United States of America. Through support of non-Communist regimes in Asia, the United States has been the principal obstacle to Peking's ambitions to dominate the surrounding area. On a broader front, the American influence and example stand in the way of the Marxist ideal of a Communist world.

Communist China is going all out to teach its people to hate and despise the United States, and Nishimura reported a notable example of this at an exhibition held in the Military Revolution Museum in Peking. The display, designed to drive home the "invincibility" of the People's Liberation Army, featured a lampoon entitled "Ten Things That Scare the U.S. Troops." A large sign said in effect that the lanky American soldiers are afraid of hand grenades, bomb-throwers, hand-to-hand combat, commando attacks, night assaults, etc., etc. There was a mocking picture of "Yellow Yanks" whom the Liberation Army had encountered in the Korean War.

The Communist Chinese Government seizes every opportunity to disseminate the belief that the Liberation Army is sure to win battles against the U.S. forces because the Americans are nothing but craven cowards, Nishimura said. Caricatures of Americans form the theme of many motion pictures and traditional plays. A man dressed as Uncle Sam is booed and jeered in May Day celebrations and other festivals.

According to the Peking Government's propaganda, American imperialists are Public Enemy No. 1 to the people of the entire world, and irreconcilable foes of the people of China. The Government cites many examples of injustices allegedly done to China by the United States. These accusations include the plundering of Chinese towns by American troops at the time of the Boxer Uprising in 1900, the "massacre" of Chinese citizens that the Kuomintang Party was said to have perpetrated at the instigation of the United States during the Chinese civil war, looting of national cultural assets and "espionage operations conducted against China in the name of religion."

The Communists started the "Hate America" campaign, the Japanese reporter said, to change the image of the United States as a friendly nation, which had been deeply embedded in the minds of the Chinese people. The pro-American feeling of the Chinese in the pre-Communist days stemmed largely from the fact that the United States, unlike Japan and European countries engaged in the exploitation of China, had adopted the relatively moderate policy of the

"Open Door" and "equal opportunities for all countries" in the China trade.

Another factor was that the Americans had befriended the Chinese through ecclesiastical, educational, and philanthropic activities and by furnishing them with medical staffs and supplies. The military aid that the United States extended to the Nationalist Government had also burnished the American image in the eyes of many Chinese. The current attacks, designed to tarnish that image, were typified by Chao An-po, chief secretary of the China-Japan Friendship Association, who presumably reflected official opinion in an interview with the *Yomiuri* team. He described President Lyndon Johnson as a "tool of monopoly capital," adding that the President was unable to act freely because of pressure applied by the American armed forces, which Chao said were extending their power and becoming deeply rooted in the social structure of the United States.

Chao went on to say that all American Presidents since World War II fell into the same category as Johnson, and that John Kennedy was no exception. "In spite of this, Khrushchev—the revisionist—wept in sorrow when he stood in front of the deceased President's photograph at the World Peace Congress in Warsaw on November 28, 1963," the Chinese said, adding, "This is a shame."

Chao described the United States as "a country that is economically advanced but most backward in the sphere of politics," adding that the opposite was true with Communist China.

He declared, however, that Communist China was ready to make a compromise in its relations with the United States, although there was no intention of departing from principles. When a reporter asked what he thought of the American people, Chao said quickly, "They are a great people. This is evident from the fact that the Americans gained independence by overthrowing British colonialists."

Nishimura found that Communist Chinese officials, while condemning the United States as an irreconcilable foe, did entertain the possibility that relations might some day reach a friendly basis. The view apparently rested on the assumption that the American masses were awaiting an opportunity to rise and overthrow an oppressive government. The officials to whom Nishimura talked in Peking were not hopeful that the expected uprising in the United States would be realized quickly or easily.

"We respect the American people, but we have no illusions about them," one Communist Chinese spokesman told the Japanese correspondent. "Even if they should rise in action, the American Government would repress them by force of arms." But the "Hate America" campaign of the Peking regime had gone so far that Nishimura felt that public sentiment could not easily be reversed.

It would be asking too much if the authorities in Peking expected the masses to become friendly to the United States once the regime adopts a pro-American policy.

FROM EASTERN EUROPE

A less extreme view of the outlook for improved relations between the United States and Communist China was reported from Poland by Yasumasa Oshima, a 49-year-old professor of philosophy at Tokyo Education University, who was assigned as the Yomiuri Task Force's observer of attitudes toward China in Eastern Europe.

Certainly, there are many touchy issues between Communist China and the United States, he wrote, but he pointed to the fact that diplomats of the two countries have been holding secret negotiations in Warsaw every two or three months. However, there are no such behind-the-scenes negotiations going on between Communist China and the Soviet Union, and the relations between the two Communist countries are becoming worse daily, his Polish informant said.

LIBERATOR OF OPPRESSED PEOPLES

Chairman Mao, who has taken upon himself the task of liberating all oppressed peoples in the world, has no intention of reaching a compromise with the United States in regard to the Vietnam problem, the Task Force decided. He contends that there has never been a case of an aggressor bowing out of his own will, and that the only way to end the Vietnam war is to drive the United States out of South Vietnam by force.

From Communist Chinese sources, Nishimura summed up Peking's outlook on Vietnam in four points:

1. We respect the North Vietnamese people engaged in the war.

2. North Vietnam is not isolated, but has the support of the peoples of the world.

3. All peace moves by the United States are hoaxes. The United Nations has no right to deal with the Vietnam problem.

4. China is prepared to give every kind of support to North Vietnam.

What Communist China fears most, the Japanese newsman said, is the possibility that North Vietnam and the Vietcong might run of breath and, aided by the Soviet Union, begin to seek peace with the United States. If this happened, Mao's policy of conducting an anti-American drive together with peoples of other countries would become meaningless, the prospects for the liberation of Asian and African countries would dim, the United States and the Soviet Union would continue to rule the world, and China would become isolated.

However, Communist China's policies toward North Vietnam and the Vietcong are more moderate than they may appear, Nishimura suggested. He thought that Communist China was refraining from forcing anything onto North Vietnam and the Vietcong. Hanoi and the National Liberation Front in South Vietnam are cooperating with Peking, not because they want aid from China or are being intimidated, but because they have common views and policies with the Red Chinese in regard to the aggressive policy of the United States.

With such a relationship, it is hard to find discrepancies in the policies of Communist China and North Vietnam and to use them as a means of alienating the two countries. But this, Nishimura indicated, is precisely what the Chinese believe the Soviet Union is trying to do.

"We are doing everything possible to help North Vietnam —spiritually and physically, that is," he quotes a Communist Chinese official as having said in an interview. "I think that the United States knows this, too," the official continued. "We are acting at the will of the Vietnamese people. They can defeat the United States by themselves. China is leaving the Vietnam problem to the Vietnamese. China has the duty to help Vietnam, but it has no right to make any decisions in connection with the Vietnam problem."

Communist China apparently aims to drive U.S. troops out of Vietnam by keeping the Vietcong and North Vietnam fighting, and by gaining the support of public opinion in various countries, Nishimura went on. "In dealing with the Vietnam problem, Communist China is acting on Mao's principle that 'all reactionaries are paper tigers. . . .'"

Nishimura also felt that Peking's foreign policies are not inflexible. In support of this, he cited a remark by a well-informed Chinese in Peking to the effect that Communist China has no intention of trying to regain Sinkiang and Manchuria from the Soviet Union, despite highly publicized territorial claims to these areas.

The Peking official expressed irritation, however, when Nishimura mentioned Japanese cooperation with the Soviet Union in the development of Siberia. "Japan is apparently trying to form an anti-China 'Holy Alliance' with the Soviet Union," he remarked.

"It is up to the Japanese people themselves to carry out a revolution in their country," the Chinese added. "If the Japanese do not wish to carry it out, the revolution cannot be achieved, no matter how hard we try to induce them to arise in action."

Nishimura learned that the affection held for Communist China by numerous national leaders in newly freed former colonial countries of Asia and Africa is not reciprocated in Peking.

"Leaders of Asian and African countries are not fit to give proper guidance to their peoples, which is a prerequisite to the achievement of a revolution," he was told. "Once they have won independence, some leaders begin to imitate the bourgeoisie. They wear gold rings and carry canes, and lord it over their peoples, acting like emperors. They cannot achieve real revolution like this."

The belief is prevalent in Communist China, Nishimura said, that Peking has a mission to implant Marxism-Leninism and Maoism in the minds of Asian and African peoples so that they will maintain their independence without making a compromise with bourgeois elements.

The Japanese journalist returned to Japan with a conviction that the leaders of the Cultural Revolution expect the movement to exert a powerful influence on international affairs through spreading of the Maoist principles abroad.

"No one can prevent the Cultural Revolution from wielding great effects on the world," he was assured by Maoist zealots, who asserted that it was nothing else than the Cultural Revolution that was crushing United States in Vietnam.

258

Chapter XI

ASSESSING THE FUTURE

A NATION OF CHANGE

Tadashi Kawata, a 41-year-old professor of international economy at the University of Tokyo, traveled through Communist China separately from the Task Force and on his return to Japan contributed an undiluted impression to the paper that emphasized the vast changes resulting from a surge of national fervor.

There is such a thing as national aspiration, and it is probably more evident in Communist China than in any other country in the world, he said. Faced with a difficult international situation and complex domestic problems resulting from the Cultural Revolution, he found the Chinese people going all-out to attain a goal that they have set for themselves.

He spoke of the warm, intense faces of the Chinese who were criticizing themselves—and each other—in an effort to establish a socialistic society through the remaking of thought, and he remembered how the entire Chinese countryside resounded with the ear-splitting chorus of eulogy for Chairman Mao and the Cultural Revolution.

China today, he said, is filled with the fever of a new racial state embracing 700,000,000 people who are determined to attain the goal that they have set for themselves, no matter how long it may take. He asked one Chinese, "When will the Cultural Revolution end?" and was told, "We will achieve the revolution even if it takes a hundred years or ten thousand years!"

On another occasion, Professor Kawata asked how much the total acreage of cultivated land in China has increased since the Communists came to power. The answer was: "It has increased by 250 percent during the past several thousand years."

The Japanese professor found, however, that his academic colleagues in Communist China were almost scornful of exactitude. He had little success with factual questions when he participated in a round-table conversation at the Chinese Academy of Science with members of the faculty from the Department of Mao Tse-tung Thought, Philosophy, and Social Sciences.

He was surprised by the indifference toward facts and figures; when he asked what was the per capita national income of China, one young economist said proudly, "I would not know, because the per capita income is not even published in newspapers." Time and again, he was perplexed by answers like this, since he knew that Mao Tse-tung once said, "Always keep figures in your mind. You must always pay attention to the aspect of quantity involved in conditions or problems."

It seemed to the Japanese economist that a basic change in the Chinese character had taken place since he had been in the country during World War II, as a Japanese Army private on an island near Tsingtao for about four months. During that time, he said he often heard Chinese say, "It cannot be helped. I must give up." But nowadays, he reported, they say, "Once we have undertaken a task, we will accomplish it even if it takes a long time."

The Chinese have changed, and China has become a

different nation, in his view. What remains unchanged is the vast expanse of plains, gigantic mountains, and mighty rivers. Yet, he remembers, the Chinese are quick to say, "When people change, the landscape will change also. And when the landscape changes, production will increase. When people change their thought, they will be able to struggle against heaven and earth to remake the landscape."

He knew what that meant when he stood on a substantial, rounded embankment built along the Yellow River and saw fine rice fields and orchards laid out on a plain that had frequently been flooded with muddy water from the river.

During his inspection trips to Chinese farms, Kawata carefully compared his findings with what he had seen in India and the Philippines, and he could see that China has surpassed those two countries by a large margin in the development of agriculture. People nowadays often refer to undeveloped nations as "developing" countries, but not until he visited Chinese farms did the Japanese scholar feel that the expression was appropriate.

Everywhere he went, he too saw groups of Red Guards and revolutionary rebels staging demonstrations, singing in chorus, and marching along the roads. He met them on airplanes, in buses, and on the streets.

He visited several People's Communes, factories and workers' living quarters, a number of universities and research institutes, and numerous theaters and cinema houses. At each of these places, the "remaking of thought" and class struggle against "unarmed enemies"—the surviving bourgeoisie—existed as a powerful undercurrent running beneath the surface of the people's activities.

But it must also be noted, he went on, that each district had its own distinct characteristics. There were considerable regional differences, not only in the climate, food, and speech, but also in the spheres of politics, economics, and culture. Therefore, he summed up, he found it extremely difficult to describe conditions in China in detail or to predict future developments.

EVIDENCE OF DISSENT

Takagi agreed that nothing is more difficult than to come to a conclusion on the situation in Communist China, which is always changing, but the following story, he thought, would serve as a start in forming a conclusion:

The incident occurred at 2 A.M. on October 10, 1966. Tsai Yung-hsiang, a member of the Third Regiment of the People's Liberation Army, was on guard at the southern end of the Grand Bridge spanning the Tsientang River. He was an 18-year-old recruit was had joined the army in February of that year. Like many teen-agers in China today, he was a devout believer in Mao's thoughts—if he had not been, he could not have hoped to join the People's Liberation Army.

Tsai was humming a poem that he had written himself:

"Stars twinkle in the sky.
I think of Peking as I am standing on the Grand Bridge.
How I wish to go to the Gate of Heavenly Peace!
Chairman Mao is our savior."

The 764th train, carrying only Red Guards from Nanchang, was scheduled to cross the bridge at 2:34 A.M. Tsai looked attentively in the direction from which the train was to come. The headlight of the locomotive approached him, and then the beam picked out the outlines of a huge log lying across the track. Tsai opened his mouth to utter a cry, but no sound came from his mouth as he ran toward the log. He rolled the log off the tracks, and the train roared safely past. But behind it lay the body of the 18-year-old soldier, Tsai Yung-hsiang.

Tsai's name was added to the endless list of heroes of the Liberation Army: men like Wang Chich, who delivered a number of soldiers from imminent danger; Ou Yang-hai, who had also prevented a train accident; Liu Yang-chun, who saved a child from a bolting horse; and so on.

But Tsai Yung-hsiang's deed raised another point for the Japanese newsman. The presence of the log on the track could have meant only that there are elements in China still active in attempting to overthrow the current regime. The incident suggests not simply that the culprit was a reactionary element, but that anti-Communist agents who hate the Peking Government are active in mainland China. In the eyes of the opposing camp, Takagi noted those having the courage to engage in such anti-Communist subversive activities when every one of the 700,000,000 people is said to be armed with Mao's thoughts and millions of "people's soldiers" defend the country must be heroes indeed.

Are such agents Nationalist Chinese? he asked. Or is this the work of the "rightist revisionist elements" who are being attacked in the Cultural Revolution? If such instances as the attempted derailment of the train were the work of the rightist faction within the Chinese Communist Party, it would be a grave matter he suggested.

Communist China is very much on guard against Nationalist Chinese agents infiltrating the mainland. When the country was hit by disasters in 1959 and 1961, several hundred American-trained Nationalist Chinese "ranger" troops sneaked into the continent via the South China coast in small groups from boats. Referring to the outbreak of the Cultural Revolution, the Chief of the Nationalist Chinese General Staff on Taiwan declared on September 3, 1966, that "This is a good time to launch an over-all anti-Communist revolution."

Takagi surmised that Taiwan, which has been restrained by the United States from launching a military counteroffensive against the mainland, must be feeling the urge to capitalize on the Cultural Revolution by intensifying its subversive campaign inside Communist China.

Considering as well the terroristic acts by anti-Mao groups that have been reported in various parts of China, it can be inferred that disruptive activities do exist.

Foreign travelers who readily conclude that Mao's political setup is unshakable have made only a superficial observation of events in Communist China, he implied.

AFTER MAO, WHAT?

The next great individual power in Communist China, Nishimura said, hazarding a prediction, will be Chou En-lai.

A cursory glance at Chou's record, the experienced China correspondent said, shows that the Premier is a man of action and not a theoretician. Chou is credited with many achievements in running Communist China's governmental machinery and working as the right-hand man of Chairman Mao. There is no question whatsoever about his ability as a politician. He is said to have persuaded Chiang Kai-shek to make peace with the Communist Party for a joint fight against the Japanese forces. As Prime Minister, he has run a huge bureaucratic machinery consisting of the central Government agencies, two special cities, and 28 provinces and autonomous regions, manipulating more than 50,000,000 bureaucrats all over the country with great skill.

No other Communist Chinese leader has been involved so deeply in the work of the Administration. Mao makes important decisions and directs the operation of his Party, but he does not attend to administrative affairs. The efficient management of the governmental machinery by Chou has been an important factor in the success of the Cultural Revolution, enabling the central Government to issue orders to local agencies and collect information concerning condi-

264

tions in the provinces even when the operations of the Communist Party were paralyzed in the early period of the political upheaval. The nation would have been thrown into turmoil if Peking had been unable to keep effective contact with local administrations.

Nishimura took issue with a popular conception that the urbane Premier is an opportunist—as Japanese say, a *daruma*, the doll that instantly rights itself when knocked over.

The impression that Chou has been able to hold the premiership for such a long time because he has a knack for getting out of a tight spot is a myth that has arisen from the fact that he is an amiable man who mixes well with other people, Nishimura declared.

In fact, he continued, Chou is a dedicated Communist with a strong moral backbone. He is trusted not only by Mao, but by the people as well. On the other hand, Lin Piao—described as Mao's "closest comrade in arms"—is unpopular with the public.

When Mao dies, Nishimura suggested, Chou will probably be appointed as head of state, while Lin—who could not stay in power if Chou were not working hand-in-glove with him—would become chairman of the Chinese Communist Party.

A POWER STRUGGLE OF THE MIND

Sifting their impressions after their return to Japan, the *Yomiuri* correspondents hesitated to make predictions as to the outcome of the struggle in China, which they were convinced would continue for a very long time, yet they kept coming back to the phenomenon of Mao worship, and the emphasis on thought reform.

Nishimura contended that it would be a misjudgment to interpret the Cultural Revolution as merely a tactic by Mao to expel the power clique from controlling positions in the

Party and the Government, although his struggle to over-come dissident elements was an important phase of the movement.

"There is now a need to take a loftier view in studying the Cultural Revolution," he said. "This is because Mao is not an ordinary person who can be judged by the Western standards of rationalization. He is an exceptional man, with exceptional pride and dreams. . . . Therefore, unless we understand his dreams, pride, confidence, and ambitions, it will be difficult indeed to understand his goal in the Cultural Revolution."

Nishimura recorded a calm analysis of the Cultural Revolution confided to him in the privacy of his Peking hotel room by an important official of the Chinese Communist Party who also happened to be an old friend. For obvious reasons, the correspondent left the informant nameless in setting down the dialogue, which the Communist functionary began by saying:

"I believe you have heard the phrase, 'The Cultural Revolution touches the human soul,' again and again during your stay in China. This phrase is not what you might call a typical Chinese exaggeration. We are now engaged in a struggle to crush the power clique. The next stage in the struggle would be in wresting away the authority held by these people. You might think that this would be a difficult task, but with the strong support of 700 million people it would not be hard work. The hardest part comes in the next stage, the power struggle within our own minds."

"A power struggle of the mind?" Nishimura echoed, puzzled.

"Yes. The Cultural Revolution is a movement to rid our minds of the ego and replace it with public spirit. But be-cause of human weakness, it is very difficult to cleanse our minds of private desires such as the yearning for an easy life or personal advancement. We must, however, get rid of

266

personal desires. Unless we do this, our minds will be occupied by revisionistic thoughts. It is useless to repeat the movement to wrest power from the authority clique if our minds are not cleansed. Because of this spiritual aspect of the struggle, we may say that the revolution touches the soul."

The rhetoric was too much for the pragmatic Japanese journalist. "I don't understand you," Nishimura said bluntly. "The things you have said are not down to earth."

The Communist official shrugged. "Perhaps you are right," he conceded.

"What he probably meant to say," Nishimura explained to his Japanese readers, "was that as it was difficult even for the Chinese to 'stage a power struggle in one's mind,' it would be even more difficult for a liberal thinker to comprehend the spiritual struggle."

Summing up, *Yomiuri*'s chief reporter commented that in order to enter the age of Communism, according to the Chinese view, it is necessary to carry out a revolution not only of politics and the economy, but also of culture, and all this, he thought, will take many years. As the present administrative structure imitates that of the Soviet Union, he predicted that there will be drastic changes from the present system. And in the army, he added, the Communist Party may take over political direction more strongly than before.

Mineo Nakajima, while deeply impressed by evidence of material progress in Communist China, came home feeling dissatisfied with the visible prospect for a successful conclusion of the Maoist experiment.

"If the Cultural Revolution results in the success of the present policy line, it is conceivable that a society which cannot be imagined under our concepts will be formed. But there is excessiveness in the present Communist China. It is all right to advocate spiritualism, but this must be backed by an abundant increase in production. If the Maoist faction

267

prevails, perhaps they will bow to the inevitability of accepting at least a modest amount of rationality."

At the end of a round-table discussion staged by *Yomiuri* to publicize the newspaper's coverage of Communist China, Takagi was asked to sum up the conclusion. He replied simply, "I cannot draw a conclusion by any means."

INDEX

274